"*Philosophy of Poker* allow............... of one of poker's greatest thinkers. Y................ ......y brand new tools to add to your poker arsenal."

> —Sorel Mizzi a.k.a. "Imper1um" & "Zangbezan24", *high-stakes poker pro and 2010 BLUFF Player of the Year*

"Wow. Haseeb has written an amazing and ground-breaking book. There's truly nothing else like it. An absolute requirement for anyone serious about poker."

> —David Williams, *Team PokerStars pro, 2010 WPT World Champion and 2nd Place Winner of 2004 WSOP Main Event*

"This book is in a class of its own. I'd honestly prefer if it wasn't released. Required reading for anyone who wants to take their understanding of poker to the next level, beginner or professional."

> —Asad Goodarzy a.k.a. "Glittering-prizes", *high-stakes poker pro and BlueFirePoker Instructor*

"This book is a must-read for everyone who is interested in poker and wants to remain on top of their game, especially for gaining a mental edge over their competitors."

> —Johannes Strasseman, *high-stakes poker pro and founder of cardcoaches.com*

"Great poker players are seldom great writers. Amongst the literature, Haseeb's book is uniquely attentive to the linguistic aspects of poker, to the subtexts of the game, and also to its beauty. No book I have previously encountered takes the same approach, and it is this which makes the writing of interest to poker players of any caliber, and other game players alike."

—Peter Leggatt, *critic and essayist for the Financial Times*

"Haseeb's book will help poker players of all levels improve their theoretical understanding of poker and the mental game. Haseeb is brutally honest about the deliberate practice and intelligence it takes to win in today's game, and yet I still found myself inspired upon finishing it."

—Jennifer Shahade, *author, journalist for PokerStars*

"Learning to become better at poker is a continuous endeavor, one that never ends or can be fully mastered. There is more and more good content to choose from in today's poker world, but I highly encourage serious students of the game to take a look at this great book."

—Fredrik Keitel a.k.a. "Fisheye1984", *high-stakes poker pro and founder of clans.de*

How to Be a Poker Player:
The Philosophy of Poker

By Haseeb Qureshi

ISBN: 978-0-9913067-4-9

This book is also available in all major e-book formats. For more information and links to retailers, please visit http://www.haseebq.com/book

This book is compiled from articles originally written for http://www.haseebq.com/blog, along with original content.
Cover photography by Haseeb Qureshi
Design and typesetting by Haseeb Qureshi
Author photograph by RB

ACKNOWLEDGEMENTS

First, I'd like to give special thanks to Rachel, Peter, and Michal for their continual input in helping me refine and rework this book. Without their critiques and tireless editing, this book would not have been possible.

And then, there's my family. Since leaving the poker world they have been by my side, and have allowed me to be by theirs. They have been a lodestone for me as I've worked on this book.

I also have to give many thanks to my friends when I was a poker player. As much as I want to take credit for the ideas in this book, they are the gestation of countless arguments, hare-brained theorizing, and late-night discussions. Everyone I have ever gotten into an argument with about poker theory—and there are too many to name—I must thank you.

Most of all, I must give my thanks to all of the supporters who've followed me over the years and who have kept up with my blog. Without your love and encouragement, I probably would never have been able to put this book together, much less my life. I therefore dedicate this to you all, and hope that you will get as much value from it as you have given to me.

Haseeb

Table of Contents

8 THE LIMITS OF POKER THEORY 230

9 THE POKER COMMUNITY 244

10 THE LIFE OF A POKER PLAYER 255

INTRODUCTION

You're reading this book because you want to improve your poker game.

I know all too well how that goes. When I began poker, I was constantly searching for the tricks the pros were using to win, convinced they had to be hidden away somewhere. I tore through books like this one, expecting to uncover clever ways to play draws, sneaky bluffs that no one knew about, or maybe the secret to handling aggressive players or 3-bet pots. Deep down, I hoped that some hand, theory, or principle would suddenly illuminate everything I couldn't see.

But that moment of revelation never came. And with time and experience, I learned that this wasn't for lack of trying. If there is a secret in poker, it is this: the way is as hard, rigorous, and disenchanting as the way has ever been.

I've met and taught hundreds of poker players during my time as a professional, and I have never met one whose game was transformed to a high level by merely reading a book. That's just not the way that poker works. You can seek out books claiming to teach you such things, but I suspect that, after working through them, you will find yourself right where you started.

The aim of this book, then, is not to make you better at poker. Instead, it is to make you a better poker player.

What do I mean?

Someone once told me, "Nobody teaches us how to be poker players." We are taught strategy, how to read hands, how to size bets, but being a poker player requires more than that. Poker is an isolating and confusing profession. The moment you sit down at a poker table, you are submerged in a profoundly backward and contradictory culture.

I asked myself one fundamental question when I decided to write this book: if I could go back eight years, to when I was just beginning my exploration into poker, what would I tell my 16-year-old self? What have I learned that he needs to know? What are the most valuable ideas that would equip him for the long and maddening journey ahead?

If you want to better understand what it means to be a poker player, this book is for you.

You may not be ready to absorb all of the ideas and perspectives presented here. That's okay. I wasn't either the first time I heard them, and I heard them many times from many different people before they were ingrained in me. Chances are it will take someone else, maybe a year or two down the road, perhaps a friend, a mentor, a stranger telling you the same thing before it convinces you. And who knows—some of these ideas may be wrong for you. That's okay. It's part of the process. But let this book be a step in your journey, and even if it does not change your beliefs or your perspective on the world or on poker, trust that it will help, whether or not you agree with it. Trust that it has a place in your process.

I want to remind you that your life as a poker player is a journey. Treating it as anything less is a disservice to yourself. Everything that I write, I write because I want you to thrive and grow from this journey.

That said, you don't need to be a professional to understand the contents of this book. It is written to be useful to all ranges of players, from high-stakes professionals to those just curious about the game.

What is poker to you? Is it an interest? A hobby? A passion? Is it your calling? Think carefully about this. This is where it all begins.

THE PHILOSOPHY OF POKER

A gambler is nothing but a man who makes his living out of hope.

WILLIAM BOLITHO

Let's start with a simple question. *What is poker?*

You could say that poker is a card game, played between multiple players, involving cards and chips and positions and so on.

But we can delve deeper than that. How would you describe the *abstract* structure of poker? For example, say you had to describe poker to a Martian. You'd have to explain this card game to somebody who doesn't know what cards are, or what a table is—and after all, those things are only symbols.

A naïve understanding of poker is going to be fixated on the surface of the game: the numbers on the cards, the suits, the felt table, the round chips. But those things are incidental to poker. A game can be identical to poker that uses pebbles, or even markings written down on paper, so long as it has sufficient rules. What's important is not the cards. We want to explore the relationships *beneath* the cards.

Modeling Poker

Poker players are especially fond of describing poker as though it were like chess. There are a few more common metaphors, such as a gunfight or a battleground, but I've found a chess match to be the most popular.

What does it mean to think of poker as a chess match?

Describing poker this way suggests that poker is mechanistic. It suggests that despite all the apparent randomness and luck involved, deep down it behaves deterministically—a game of pure skill.

To take the randomness out of poker is to take the mysticism out of it. Poker is commonly assumed to be the game of gamblers, risk-takers, the steel-hearted and intuitively-minded. But when we call poker a chess match, we turn those presumptions around. Instead, poker is meant to be analyzed, theorized about, dissected into its smallest possible chunks and then reassembled like a machine. It becomes the domain of rationalists, mathematicians, and cold strategists.

Poker players are taught to think this way. EV is the lens through which they're supposed to see the world. They're taught that everything can be optimized, exploited, and broken down into frequencies.

It's reassuring to think that, isn't it? That beneath all the chaos, the whizzing cards and splashing chips, under all the downswings and bad beats, the tilt and the frustrations, that all the way down in the boiling heart of the thing, there is an equation or two that describes it all. Is that not the idea? That if you had but the time and mathematical prowess, you could plug in some equation or execute some algorithm that would "solve" it all for you?

Of course, we all know that there are ways in which poker can be described by math. But let's think deeply about this. Why is this the way we are inclined to see poker at the deepest level? Do you really believe that's how things work? Is learning poker the uncovering of a pristine, logical machine?

Is poker a chess match?

Poker as Chess Match

Perhaps you believe that, distilled to its essence, poker is merely a mathematical system. You would not be alone in thinking this way. Most serious students of poker have come to believe this, although not one of them has probably ever been told this outright. It is one of those ideas that is embedded in how we talk about poker; it is unconsciously absorbed, like an element in the air. You might not know how or from where, but somehow it's found its way into your mind, and it makes perfect sense. Poker is a discrete system. A chess match. A set of equations and matrices acting themselves out, over and over again.

But the reality is that poker is *not* a chess match, nor a gunfight, nor a machine, nor a battleground. In fact, poker is none of the things that you imagine it to be.

Poker defies your sense of it. Throughout your lifetime as a poker player, poker will take many different forms for you. You will formulate it consciously or unconsciously; you will imagine new shapes, metaphors, axioms, and laws of mechanics. Things will seem to work a different way; you will find new rules and laws and equations. You will be absolutely certain that poker is one thing, and the next day you will claim it is another. It keeps changing and changing. Yet, underneath it all, poker itself is always the same.

Some of you will insist—but I know poker has always been the same!

14

Ah, but how wrong you are! We are all in this predicament, and I will explain to you why.

The Elephant's Tail

Every poker player has in their mind a poker **schema**. A schema is simply *the way you think things work*. When you are in a hand faced with a decision, or when you are trying to understand why a play went right or wrong, you consult the network of assumptions and intuitions you have about how poker functions. Perhaps they're about why checkraising certain boards is bad, about what hands are too weak to valuebet, and so on—all that, but a great deal more than that. Your schema includes *all* the notions you have about poker, how matches evolve, what it looks like to lose or win, what variance feels like. It includes all of the language and concepts you use to describe and analyze poker

But this schema is not static. Every time you learn something new about the game, your schema is altered slightly. Sometimes it's added to, sometimes it's tweaked in a certain spot. And of course, your schema is not always changed correctly. You might learn a lesson where there is none, or where there is a lesson, you might learn the wrong one. Your schema is constantly changing and shifting, introducing and fixing errors. This is inevitable in a game that involves random and imperfect feedback. There is a chaos that underlies your schema too.

So is poker a chess match? Well, you are not wholly wrong to imagine poker that way. *Beneath* all the chaos, poker is a chess match. It is logical and obeys fixed mathematical rules. *But we don't have access to that.* We don't know the chess match, and we probably never will. The only thing we have access to is how we experience poker, which is always mediated through our evolving schema. For us, the schema *is* poker.

There is an ancient story from India that serves well here. It was said that there was a king who purchased an elephant, a rare and exotic animal, from a faraway land. He summoned five blind men who'd never heard of an elephant, and he asked each man to describe the creature to him. The first man squeezed the tail, and said, "An elephant is like a rope." The second man wrapped his arms around its leg and said, "An elephant is like a pillar." The third man grabbed the trunk and said, "An elephant is like a tree branch," and so on, each man coming up with his description from his limited perspective.

This is how schemas work. Our limited experiences and perceptions congeal into a mental model of the subject. Of course, an elephant is none of the things the men described, and it is even more than the sum of all their perceptions.

In this way, we are blind men groping at the limbs of poker. We graze against it again and again, even over hundreds of thousands of hands, but our schema is all we can make of it. It's the only access we'll ever have. The utter truth is inaccessible to us; all we know is what presents itself, what we have had the luck of running our fingers over, and the picture that we've stitched together from our experiences.

What I mean more concretely is this—every time you try to formulate a match, or try to analyze a situation, you will be wrong. You might win, make the right adjustment, even the right read, but you'll still be slightly wrong. Wrong about what—that will depend—but the fact will remain that reality will be shaped differently from your schema. It has been and always will be. Since the day you started playing poker, you had some schema of how the game worked, and every day you've played poker, without fail, your schema has changed. And it will change again. This is true even for the strongest players in the world.

As a poker player, you doubtless want to think of yourself as a student of logic and mathematics. You imagine rationality to be the mortar with which you build your castle of poker. You may be correct that poker is governed by mathematics and logic. But *you yourself* are not.

Poker is played by humans. It is experienced and learned by humans. Humans are not rational machines. The operations of their brains are not a chess match.

And yet, I am not saying that mathematics and logic will get you nowhere, and I don't mean to suggest that you abandon them!

Build your castle. You have to, even if the only materials you have are the sand and mud beneath you. That's the path you've chosen, after all. Go on constructing your poker game. But know that your castle must collapse again and again. Know that your strongest and most steadfast reasoning will eventually fall. It is your fate; at best, you are a creature that only approximates rationality, and that's as far as your brain can go. But so it is; the building must go on.

Do you agree to it? Do you want to be a poker player? Then this is your path, the only one. You will be wrong, always wrong. But you must keep being wrong and keep whittling away at that wrongness.

A Copernican Turn

It is from this point that we begin. The turn is essential. Once you understand it, you can begin to face the philosophy of poker.

And what does this turn tell us?

Here is its most important fruit: that we are fallible. You might say to yourself: of course I am fallible!

But I am referring to something more dire. I mean more than some watered-down platitude like "everybody makes mistakes," by which we mean errors in calculation, execution, emotion, etc. Those things exist, but if that's all you are looking for, you will miss the vastness of your predicament.

What I want to teach you instead is *mistrust*. Yes, mistrust. An uncommon virtue, but one you must learn as a poker player. Not merely to mistrust your teachers, or received wisdom. That sort of mistrust is good, but it's not enough. What you must learn is to mistrust yourself. Mistrust your brain. Mistrust your logic, your math, your confidence, and even your own story. Cast doubt over it all; imbue everything with a shadow longer than the thing itself. This is how a great poker player must think.

Self-doubt is the most important ability for a student of this game—but not in the sense of being timid or flimsy. Those traits have no place in a poker player. What you must have is a confident self-doubt, a powerful mistrust of the parts of yourself that ought to be mistrusted.

You might ask: well, what parts are those?

We will explore that question gradually throughout this book—but first, we require a framework in which to understand it. First, we must establish (or re-establish) the fundamentals of poker theory. You cannot build a castle until you build a foundation, after all. In beginning our exploration into the nature of poker, we will start by posing the question, "How does one construct a poker game from the ground up?"

2

THE STRUCTURE OF A POKER GAME

Cards are war, in disguise of a sport.

CHARLES LAMB

I began by implying that the reality of poker is inaccessible to us and that we are inescapably bounded by our humanness. But it is not futile to try to understand those limitations. On the contrary, we have *no other choice* but to try to understand them as best we can, using whatever resources are available to us.

We will begin, then, by exploring models of poker as a system. This is the way you are used to thinking about poker— poker as an external thing, out there in the world. But as this book progresses, we will move past that and turn inward, to eventually explore the interface between the human mind and poker. Both are essential to our understanding of poker. But we must start from the outside and gradually work our way in.

Since you are reading this book, I am going to assume a thorough acquaintance with elementary poker theory. The concepts I will discuss supervene on more basic ones, such as value, ranges, reverse implied odds, balance, game flow, game theory, and so on. If you do not have a grounding in these concepts, I urge you to acquaint yourself with them before trying to tackle this chapter. You might also want to consult the glossary as you read. If you are not a professional poker player or otherwise don't feel ready to sink your teeth into discrete poker concepts, then I encourage you to skip to **Chapter 5** and continue your reading from there.

If you are in the early stages of learning poker, don't worry if some of these ideas are confusing or intimidating. As we explore poker theory, these first few chapters may get pretty complicated. Just move through at your own pace, and don't be afraid to skip a passage and come back to it later.

Now, let's get started.

Holism and Reductionism

To become a great poker player, you must first learn to think like one. But ideas are useless if you don't have the requisite experience and knowledge to talk about them. So the first step is to equip yourself with the language, concepts, and perspectives through which advanced players view the game of poker.

To become a high-level poker player, you must make a structural shift in your perspective. You must start to look at poker **holistically**, rather than **reductionistically**. In other words, you must look at a poker game *on the whole*, rather than looking at it piece-by-piece.

The foremost example of this is in how you analyze hands. This is the most important first step in developing your poker perception. There are three stages in the evolution of a player's perception of hands:

♦ Stage One: Hand against Hand

The first stage is the most basic. You choose a single hand that you "read," or, essentially, *guess* that he has and decide what your hand should do against it. So if you have top pair, you guess whether or not he has a hand better than top pair, and you play accordingly. Generally, this is how beginners think about poker.

♦ Stage Two: Hand against Range

The second, more advanced level is thinking about how your hand is doing against his *entire range* in a certain spot. So you might think of how your top pair is faring against his sets, his overpairs, his top pair lower kickers, and his missed straight draws, each weighted according to their probability. The number crunching is usually only approximate, but you come up with an overall equity against his hands, and you use that to make your decision. This level of perception requires you to perceive *his* range.

♦ Stage Three: Range against Range

The third and most complex level of range perception is to think of how *your range* is faring against *his range*. This requires you not only to be able to generalize his range, but also to be able to visualize how you would be playing all of the other hands you could have in a given spot.

How do we get from the first stage to the third? Initially, a large part of the gap is a lack of familiarity with the equities involved. How would a beginner evaluate how well top pair is doing against a range of 80% OESD with overcards and 20% sets? That's something you must simply learn through time and exposure. But actually, learning the equities is the easier part. What's more difficult is managing your mental resources so you can play individual hands effectively, while still keeping higher-level poker dynamics in mind.

When you are beginning as a poker player, you likely aren't able to think in terms of more than a single hand at a time—whatever is directly in front of you is complex enough to keep your mind fully occupied. But as you gain more experience, your brain starts to handle single hands unconsciously.

Once your brain is automatically processing the trivial hands, you no longer have to consciously puzzle out things like board texture or betting patterns for most hands. Your brain will tell you automatically to call, fold, or raise, freeing up your conscious mind to deal with higher level ideas, such as evaluating the interplay between ranges, exploitation, or game flow.

Many people believe that holding such high-level ideas in your mind while playing requires a great intellect or some special genius. This could not be further from the truth. If there's one thing I want to do in this book, it is to dispel any idea in your head that there's something "special" about high level players.

The primary difference between those who can think on this level and those who cannot is the *amount of experience* they have. Once you've played a million hands of poker, your instincts will be so honed that you will probably struggle *not* to start thinking about higher-level things. Consciously focusing on single, ordinary hands will feel like a waste of your conscious attention.

Experience, then, is the first step. Gain experience—lots of it. And once you accrue enough, you will free up the mental space to think about holistic ideas while playing.

Of course, this doesn't necessarily mean that experience will make you think soundly. Experience will free up the resources of your mind, but without the proper perspective and theory guiding you, that won't necessarily do you any good.

So we must go looking for that perspective. Let's take stock of your resources—both mental and strategic.

Poker as Shipbuilding

I implied in the previous chapter that you should distrust metaphors, since all metaphors ultimately fail to capture the complexity of poker. Despite that, I am going to be employing many metaphors to elucidate various aspects of poker to you. These metaphors will each be useful, but only in describing that aspect of poker. Like in the story of the elephant, each metaphor may only capture one limb of the beast, but nevertheless, they will be useful within that specific domain.

The first metaphor is one that will help you to think about poker structurally. It will make you think about poker as being "out there"—for now, to simplify its interface with our minds.

Imagine that your poker game is a ship, and you, the poker player, are the shipbuilder.

Your ship is not an extension of you. It is not something internal, which exists in your mind. We want to imagine instead that a poker game is an external object—your object, certainly, the product of your craft and hard work, but nevertheless something that exists "out there," ready to be analyzed, taken apart, and put back together. As a shipbuilder, you have a lot of choices to make on how to craft your ship.

What kind of poker game do you want to build?

You look out into the sea of poker and see hundreds, thousands of ships, all constructed differently, with seemingly varied ideas and intentions behind their construction. Naturally, you only want to choose the best ships to emulate. So you watch videos of great players, sweat high stakes games, read well-written articles—and you try to fashion your ship in their likenesses.

But there is a fatal fallacy embedded in this process: no matter how many ships you look at, be it hundreds or thousands, even ships of the finest quality, no amount of studying such ships is going to make you able to build one for yourself. Because *looking* at ships is a very different process from actually *building* them. Even if you see a hundred ships which have solved the problem of how to construct a ship, how to keep it upright, how to balance the hull and the mast—you will still have to figure out *through building* how to solve these problems. You must learn how to build a ship not just in your mind, but in your *hands—put plank against plank, hammer against nail.*

This is all to say, in building your poker game, you are going to have to solve problems that other people have already solved. You must do more than merely emulate the surface of other people's games. You have to figure out *why* their games are structured the way they are before you can truly build a game comparable to theirs. There is no shortcut to the art of shipbuilding. As frustrating as it may sound, you must re-enact the evolution of ships through your own hands.

Using Your Stack of Wood

The moment you step into the world of shipbuilding, you are handed a stack of wood. You are told, "Here's your stack. It might not seem like a lot, but it's the same amount the best in the world get. Using just these supplies, you have to build the best ship you can. Good luck."

You might interject—but that's silly! As a poker player, you don't have the assets that the best players in the world have. They have speed, intuition, or reading abilities that you don't.

But remember, in this metaphor, you are not your ship. The ship is *external* to you; you are merely the builder. Follow the metaphor here: we all get the same stack of wood—the set of all hands. We all get dealt the same hands, with the exact same frequency, and over a long enough period of time, both we and the best players in the world will get pocket aces and kings and T9s the very same number of times. The only difference is what we *do* with those hands—that is, how we use those hands to build our poker game.

Your most limited resources are good hands. In the long run, everybody gets the exact same good hands with the exact same frequency. The decision is chiefly yours how you want to distribute those good hands over your flops, turns, rivers, among your flatcalls and raises and slowplays, between your small bets and overbets, and so on. This is how you construct the structure of your game.

The true action of poker takes place in exploitation. **Exploitation** is taking advantage of weaknesses in your opponents' ships. But you cannot exploit someone without becoming exploitable yourself. It's like firing a cannon—to fire a cannon from your ship, you must create a hole in your ship to fire from. Of course, that hole can be more easily fired into. By attacking, you open yourself to counterattack. This is the nature of attack and defense in all things.

We must each decide how to allocate our hands in order to create the defensive structure of our games. This is the fundament of our ship, which we want to be robust, fortified in every direction, such that no simple strategy can hurt us (or, more likely, that the average strategy won't hurt us). Once we establish a powerful base, we start opening ourselves up—creating openings from which we can attack, choosing those openings based on the ship we're up against, and consequently opening up different weaknesses.

Once you enter into a poker match, you are faced with a decision on how best to utilize your good hands. Do you use them to strengthen your defenses, or are you going to use them offensively? The best players are able to optimally use their hands to both attack their opponents' ships and defend their own. But ultimately, with each hand you must always either do one or the other.

Putting it into Practice

How does this perspective demand that we think, and where does it come into play in a real poker match? For simplicity, let's imagine you're in a heads up game.

You're in a spot, say, on the flop or turn. Your particular hand doesn't matter—remember, we're thinking in terms of range against range here.

The central question becomes this: how do we orchestrate our range so that we're best exploiting his range?

The question is easier to pronounce than it is to follow to the end. It forces us to consider a constellation of subsequent questions. First, what weaknesses in our opponent's game can we exploit? Where is he allocating his good hands? Where are his good hands missing? Inherently, this question requires you to integrate all of the information you have about your opponent, allowing you to narrow down his hand range through process of elimination. It also calls on your psychological profile of your opponent, as well as betting patterns you've noticed in how he plays his good hands.

Remember, the art of building a ship is the art of allocating good hands. We want to be tracking his good hands as closely as we can, paying the utmost attention to them as they move through the skeleton of his game, like magnets tracing through a field of iron shavings. His good hands will show us where his game is strong and fortified. Wherever he is extending himself *away* from that skeleton, we know he is weak.

For example, if he is using all of his good hands on the flop by checkraising them and playing them fast, and he hasn't in this hand, then you know here on the turn you should be battering him, because his skeleton is inherently weak here. You want to construct your ranges so that you're attacking him where he's weak, and routing your own hands away from his flop checkraising range. It's a simple example of course, but it gives you the idea of a holistic view of the exploitation.

If you're an advanced player, there's a good chance that you find many of these conclusions so far pretty intuitive. But understanding these building blocks explicitly, using precise language, will allow us to soon build bigger, more complex ideas.

Centrality

Now we'll look at a more advanced concept.

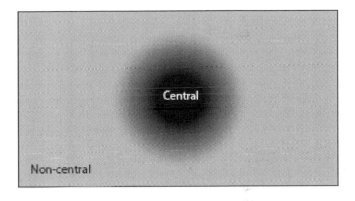

Imagine the rectangle above is a map of poker. This rectangle represents the field of possibilities, and every point on this rectangle represents one possible sequence for a poker hand.

The dark spot in the middle represents what happens in 99% of all poker hands. Yet, you will notice that it doesn't cover 99% of the rectangle. This is because the dark spot represents *not* 99% of all the possibilities, but 99% of possibilities *weighted by frequency*. If we were to enumerate *all possible hands* that can be played in poker, the range would be astronomically large. But enumerating 99% of the most common possibilities produces a much smaller range.

This is partly because so many hands end on early streets and are therefore less complex. It's also because most hands are not very exceptional and essentially play themselves—by either c-betting, or flopping a hand so good or so bad that the decisions are simple.

So we can think of this as a probabilistic map—the places of highest frequency are darker, and the lowest frequency is lighter. For the farthest parts of the map, which represent very strange or uncommon situations, there is only a slight grey tint, which indicates that those hands rarely happen. For the most part, most poker situations fall within the 99% circle.

This illustrates a concept which I call **centrality**. Centrality is, basically, a measure of how common a certain spot is. In terms of this diagram, it is how close a spot is to the center of the probabilistic map. A spot that is highly central would be something like 3-betting light preflop—it is a decision that is made a great many times a session, which makes it very central. A spot that is very non-central would be something like 3-bet bluff-shoving the river to represent a rivered runner runner straight. It's a situation that probably doesn't even arise once every two thousand hands.

What are the important differences between central and non-central spots?

For one, any spot that is highly central is going to be *easier* than one that is non-central. If the spot is central, then it is one that most players have been exposed to so many times that they'll understand the dynamics of that spot fairly well. Therefore, most players play well in spots that are highly central. On the other hand, in spots that are non-central, people are more likely to make mistakes, since they inherently don't have as much experience in rarer spots.

A corollary of centrality is this: people will only be good at what they need to be good at. You can think of this as a kind of natural selection within poker—an evolutionary principle. It means simply that if your opponent has never had to be good at doing a certain thing, then he won't be. People only develop the skills they need and, generally speaking, not much more.

Any spot that is highly central is a spot where there's less room for you to exploit your opponent, because your opponent is naturally going to have a more robust strategy. He has, just like you, faced this spot so many times that he's needed a good strategy in order to survive until now (again, the evolutionary principle).

For example, six years ago, 3-betting light was an enormously powerful strategy, because it was a very non-central; few people had experience against it and knew how to deal with it. Poker players literally did not need to be able to deal with light 3-bettors, and so they weren't good at it. But by now, six years later, 3-betting light is so common as to be trivial, and everybody has dealt with it so much that they've arrived at near-optimal strategies.

The truth is, preflop game is fairly simple. Since it limits poker to only the first street, which is inherently the simplest, it leaves the least room for complexity, and therefore the least room for maneuvering, mistakes, and exploitation. Thus, you are not very likely to be making much money if you are limiting poker to the preflop game, because it's highly central and everybody is pretty good at it by now.

Two major implications follow from this. First, if your poker match stays within the circle of centrality (that is, it remains highly central), you will diminish your chances to exploit your opponent, since you are inviting him into a space where he's very comfortable, and naturally has a robust strategy. Second, by leading him intentionally out of the circle of centrality into a terrain with which he's unfamiliar, you allow the possibility for bigger mistakes. This is why players who have very unconventional styles, even ones which sometimes seem distinctly suboptimal, are sometimes dramatically winning players. Part of the reason why they might continue to be successful is because they jostle their opponents out of their circle of centrality, while still remaining in their own.

The Stevesbets Effect

I used to be baffled by a guy named Stevesbets, a poker player who I believed was fundamentally very weak. In fact, although I consistently beat him, he was making quite a bit of money from other regulars. It wasn't until I realized how centrality worked that I figured out why he was so successful against many players.

I found a helpful analogy in the guerilla warfare of the American Revolutionary War. In that war, Americans were pitting weaker soldiers and armaments against the better-trained British. But because the Americans were fighting on terrain that they knew and their opponents didn't, they created many more opportunities for their opponents to make mistakes that they themselves wouldn't make. This effect was amplified by the fact that the bulk of the Americans' experience was in fighting against those who weren't experienced on their terrain, so they were good at predicting *what kind* of mistakes their opponents would usually make.

Sometimes, you are playing against someone who has a very peculiar strategy, and you immediately assume he is a fish. But after some time, you might realize that he's fairly intelligent postflop, and you may even have trouble beating him.

If that player is like Stevesbets, it's safe to assume that most of his experience is in battling regulars like you, who struggle to adapt to his style. This allows him to have an immediate upper-hand against many less adaptable opponents.

These phenomena are essentially the same.

To beat somebody with a very unconventional or non-central style of play, there are two main strategies. The first is to explore *his* circle of centrality and acquaint yourself with the terrain, even if you make some missteps along the way. Once you learn the landscape of his style, the hope is that your inherently more powerful structure will defeat his inferior one. But you can only get to that point if you have the patience and foresight to understand that terrain, and can do it quickly.

You may notice, however, that this strategy is somewhat passive. It simply acquiesces to the space our opponent chooses and then tries to settle into that space. We will call that the **reactive** strategy. Most "grinders" tend to play this way (and many of them do it poorly, which is likely why strategies like Stevesbets' can be profitable).

The second strategy is the **proactive** one, which actively moves around and tries to search for *new* non-central spaces in which to challenge your opponents. Poker players who prefer this mode tend to be more aggressive, risky, and creative players; when you are playing against someone who is fundamentally worse, this is often the more high-reward strategy, as you are likely to adapt better in a mutually non-central space than they are.

It is important to remember, however, that centrality is relative. What is central to one player may not be central to another. Centrality is defined by probabilistic frequency, so if two players have vastly different styles, then chances are, what is frequent in one player's game will be infrequent in another's. For example, if one player minraises preflop and always tries to play small pot poker, and another player is used to 3xing and doing lots of overbetting postflop, it is likely that each of them will be pushing the other into many non-central spaces.

Centrality is also contingent on complexity and other player-dependent factors. For example, in a 6-max game, cold 4-betting when an aggressive button 3-bets may be a relatively central play. It is not uncommon, so we can assume that people can deal with it and will respond relatively well. But if instead you cold 4-bet when an unpredictable fishy player 3-bets, *that* may be a non-central play, and it's something that other players will likely be unsure exactly how to interpret (which often means they'll tend toward lower-risk responses). Complexity and rarity tend towards non-centrality.

Centrality and Difficulty

The second aspect of centrality is a psychological one. I claimed before that spots within the circle of centrality are easy. But what exactly does it mean for a spot to be "easy"?

There are a lot of complex ways to articulate this, but for now we will say that "easy" hands are ones that don't require a lot of psychological processing in order to make a decision. That is to say, they are mostly automatic and unconscious.

A highly central spot is easy because your opponent will be processing it mostly unconsciously. This implies that *he won't be paying much attention to highly central spots*. He knows he's solving them efficiently, so he'll be focusing his conscious attention elsewhere. Non-central spots on the other hand will have the opposite effect. Once your opponent runs into a non-central spot, he'll be shaken back into conscious awareness. His autopilot will turn off and he'll retake his place at the cockpit.

This has an important implication for us in the psychological game. Knowing where your opponent is paying conscious attention is vital. If you can tell where your opponent is paying attention and where he's not (strategic and speed-reads also come in handy here), you can better predict his reactions. In central spots, we can assume your opponent is going to be cognitively autopiloting, and your read on his general style and character will be applicable. I.e., if he's somebody who usually does too much of x or tends to do y, you can fully expect this behavior to present in a central spot. But once a non-central spot arises, your opponent is going to change psychologically.

If you think about it in another way, his autopilot is essentially a pre-calculated program. It's a set of algorithms that have been formulated by his past conditioning, his post-session tinkering and video-watching, and so on. Whenever it applies, he trusts it. But once he reaches a new spot where he has to focus his attention, he's going to re-invent a solution to the new spot, using his poker theory and reasoning. But this *only* happens when he has focused his conscious attention on this new hand. This means that your opponent is likely to deviate from his prefabricated strategy in a non-central spot, and is instead going to be acting on a new analysis, based on his psychology and his integration of nearby data about the match at hand.

Central and non-central spots are *processed differently*, and understanding this will allow you to predict what would otherwise appear to be psychological anomalies.

Let me illustrate with an example. Let's imagine you're playing a match against a strong opponent, but who is somewhat of a calling station and doesn't like to fold. So far you've decided to adjust to him by only showing down good hands in big pots. We can say that, generally speaking, in central spots he will probably retain his style of being a calling station, because that's his automatic game. He has mentally chosen that strategy as the optimal one to use against you. But once you move into a non-central space, suddenly he will be jostled awake. You might make a big bet to the river, and you can predict that, at that moment, he will be *forced* to re-think the hand. If you are attentive, you will notice all of the nearby information that he'll be integrating—that you've only shown down good hands and have a solid image—and you might be able to predict that he will think to himself, "Oh, this guy always has it," and make a big fold. His moment-to-moment psychology will deviate from the prefabricated strategy he chose to employ.

That fold might appear to be uncharacteristic and unpredictable to someone who doesn't understand this concept, but good players are able to predict this sort of thing with some accuracy. They may not use these words (or even be able to articulate the process behind it), but this is what they are doing. By being aware of the difference between the automatic and subconscious decision-making in central spots, as well as the deliberate thought that goes into non-central spots, you'll be able to predict otherwise unpredictable moves. That is the power of centrality.

As a final caveat, it's important to keep in mind that centrality is, at best, a principle to keep in mind. The adjustment game hinges on a lot more than centrality, and a strategy that only consists of trying to push people into non-central spaces would likely border on maniacal. Rather, centrality is simply a way of understanding some of the dynamics that underlie adjustments, aggression, and comfort, which are all important elements of the adjustment game.

A Balancing Act

With centrality, we have breached the landscape of holistic poker theory. This landscape is populated by many familiar big ideas: balance, exploitation, game theory, and so on. But to really examine and manipulate these concepts, we have to understand their roots. One of the biggest concepts that intermediate players often misunderstand is balance, so we will begin there.

Let's pose the question: what is **balance**?

We might start by saying that, basically, it's the idea that you need to balance your bets with both bluffs with value hands. That's not a bad start, but balance gets much more subtle.

The truth is that balance is a fuzzy concept, which people often use to fill holes in their poker thinking. If you ask somebody, "Why are you checking back a set here?" or, "Why are you betting middle pair?" or, "Why are you bluffing this river?" many times the confused mid-stakes player will answer that it's for "balance." But if you press him on a definition, he won't be able to tell you exactly what that means. The word is thrown around liberally and rarely interrogated, but for our purposes it is essential that we dissect it.

Balance boils down to two basic ideas, depending on the way it's used. The first idea is that, in order for a range to be balanced, it must contain both value hands and bluffs. The second idea is that, in order for a range to be balanced, it must contain both nutty and medium strength hands. If you have too much of one and not enough of the other, you are imbalanced in that spot.

Let's look carefully at this definition. What exactly does it mean to say that a range must contain both value hands and bluffs? How many of them? Is one bluff per 100 hands enough? It's here that the concept of balance gets tied in with the notion of **unexploitable** play. Unexploitability is a concept from game theory, which simply means that our strategy cannot be exploited by any other—that is, it can never lose to any other strategy. For example, if we take the game rock-paper-scissors, the unexploitable strategy (also called **GTO**, game theory optimal) is to randomly play each move exactly 33% of the time. This makes it so that no matter what your opponent plays, he will on average be breaking even against you.

Many poker players end up equating balance with unexploitable play. They think, in order to be balanced, their range must be completely unexploitable, or what we might call "perfectly balanced." This would mean something along the lines of intentionally creating a range such that when you pot the river when the draw misses, you're bluffing 33% of the time and valuebetting 66% of the time (which would make your opponent's EV for calling a bluff-catcher exactly 0).

Posed this way, balance sounds grand and attractive, and makes us think that it's going to solve our problems. But there are two great fallacies in most people's understanding of balance. The first fallacy is the assumption that balance is all-or-nothing. That is, that you're either "balanced" or "not balanced." The second fallacy is thinking that balance is inherently valuable when, in reality, it isn't.

Imperfect Balance

Let us begin with the first: balance is not all-or-nothing. Your ranges don't need to contain an unexploitable proportion of value hands and bluffs in them, nor do they need an unexploitable amount of nutty hands in them. This is due to **imperfect information**. In a real poker game, your opponents are going to get information about the actual hands that comprise your range very, very slowly. Think about it—your opponent only sees one hand per showdown, and most hands are never shown down in poker. Furthermore, it takes some time for him to see a hand that shows him exactly what's going on with any specific part of your range—it may be hundreds of hands until he sees another hand of a relevant situation. Because information is gleaned so slowly for highly specific ranges, a lot of your ranges will remain totally hidden for some time, which means you can essentially *do whatever you want* until your opponent catches on and adjusts correctly.

But there is more to it than that. Not only is information in poker imperfect, but people also *respond to it imperfectly*. For example, even if your opponent starts catching onto you in a bluffing spot, you don't need to show that you have "enough" nutty hands in any given range to get him to respect you again. Often, it is enough to show that you have some, even if it's a small amount. If your opponent suddenly sees you show down the nuts in an uncommon spot where you'd been bluffy before, he's not going to attack that part of your range anymore because he's likely to assume that you've enacted a large-scale adjustment. This sort of overgeneralizing from salient observations is very common. Instead of thinking, "Okay, I've only seen the nuts once and 8 bluffs, which makes his range 89% bluffs," he is likely instead to think that you've completely changed your strategy. After that, he will probably need to see a significant number of hands to be convinced that *you don't have enough nutty hands* in that range to be unexploitable. This is due not only to the fuzziness of information and how slowly he'll be acquiring it, but also because salient observations tend to stand out more psychologically than slowly accrued data.

Often in trying to balance their ranges, players will commit the **fallacy of omniscience**. This is a fatal cognitive error. The fallacy of omniscience is when you assume your opponent knows everything that you know, or sees everything that you see. This is one of the biggest mistakes that a poker player can make, and often causes players to forego making very profitable bluffs.

For example, say we're in a spot where we're considering 3-bet bluffing somebody on the river to represent a runner-runner straight—a highly non-central spot. You might be thinking over this bluff, and realize that you would never have a straight here because you would have played it differently earlier in the hand. And so you think to yourself: it's irrational here to bluff because this isn't how you would actually play a straight. This is potentially a fallacy of omniscience, because you're assuming that your opponent knows everything that you know about your own game. The fact is, *even if he has seen all of those things*, he may not assume that you *always* play your backdoor straights that way. He might not have even had the chance to analyze those facts about your game yet. He may not have even noticed the relevant data, even if it was in front of him. Or, he may have even seen it, but forgotten it. There are many stages of the transmittance of information in between what you know and what he knows. You must *always* consider both gaps and corruptions in those channels of information, otherwise you may end up foregoing very valuable bluffs.

There are important and obvious exceptions to this rule, where truly unexploitable or "perfect" balance is important. This would be in spots where information acquisition is relatively quick and fluid. For example, in any highly central spot, such as in preflop 3-betting games, you won't be able to get away with 3-betting purely junk hands. Your opponents will accurately note your tendencies and respond to them very rapidly. But the less central the spot becomes, the more information becomes scarce and becomes difficult to respond to, and the more other psychological elements can protect you from being spotted and exploited.

But there's still one important question that remains un-answered. Why does balance actually matter?

The Value of Balance

The word "balance" is a recent arrival in the vocabulary of the average poker player. It wasn't long ago that balance simply wasn't talked about. With its arrival into poker language, a certain presumption found its way into many people's thinking—the presumption that balance is inherently valuable. I.e., that it's better to be balanced than imbalanced.

There is an obvious connection between being imbalanced and being exploitable. But being exploitable is not the same thing as being exploited. Remember, in order to attack, you must create a hole in your defense. In order to be maximally exploiting somebody, your strategy must be exploitable as well.

For example, say your opponent is bluffing very rarely in a certain spot. In order to exploit his strategy, you choose to never hero-call, since he almost always has it. This occurs to you as the natural adjustment—but in terms of game theory, you are becoming exploitable in order to exploit him. If you are now folding 100% of your bluff-catchers, then you are inherently making it possible for him to exploit you by simply bluffing 100% of the time. This sort of thing doesn't happen in a match, which is why you're okay with doing it. But realize—there's nothing *inherently bad* about being exploitable. You must be exploitable in order to be playing well and adjusting to your opponent.

You are probably well acquainted with the term **optimal**, but optimality has a very specific meaning in terms of game theory. To be optimal means to be maximally exploiting your opponent (in other words, maximizing your own EV). Playing optimally necessarily means *not* playing unexploitably, since you cannot exploit someone without being exploitable yourself. Therefore, in a vacuum, to play unexploitably against a human opponent is to choose a suboptimal strategy.

Now, you might wonder: if it is literally never optimal to be playing unexploitably and perfectly balanced, why do people say you should be balanced? Why is balance so important if it's never optimal?

The reason why balance is important is because poker is not played in a vacuum. Poker is played *over time*. Instead of looking at poker **synchronically**, as one moment frozen in time, we want to look at poker **diachronically**, as it changes over a period of time. For a single hand, if our opponent is betting the river with a perfectly balanced range such that our EV for each hero-call is 0, it's fine to never hero-call him, or to hero-call him 100% of the time. His frequencies should make our synchronic response irrelevant. However, this doesn't take into account the change of the match over time. Once we start hero-calling our opponent 100% of the time, our opponent is likely to see that, and react to that information by changing his unexploitable strategy into an exploitative one, where he stops bluffing altogether. This would make our diachronic EV dramatically negative, and his positive. If you think about it, his unexploitability—his balance—has created a stronghold from which he can choose how and when to attack, how and when to let down the drawbridge of exploitability, whenever he gains enough information.

This means that balance and unexploitability is a powerful *defensive* strategy. It is a way of safely biding your time until you can find an optimal strategy.

Unexploitability is also a valuable defensive strategy because humans have limited attention. One must be wary of a common cognitive fallacy—that of assuming that in the future, you will react the same way to information as you would right now. Realistically, one must always factor in error, emotion, the possibility of simply not noticing the requisite information, etc. Ironically, when looking at other people, you will often factor into your assumptions the chance that they miss or incorrectly evaluate information, but you rarely consider this about yourself.

The fact is, over a poker match, you are faced with countless frequencies and patterns in your interactions with one opponent. You are faced with his preflop raising ranges, his 3-betting frequency, his flop c-betting percentage, the different ranges of hands with which he c-bets and checks back, the frequency with which he checks monster hands, the ranges that accord to different flop betsizes, and the list goes on. In reality, although all of these things are there in front of you, you *don't* perceive all of them. Your attention is limited. There are only certain things that you can actually focus on and play the adjustment game around, and the rest essentially just gets thrown away. And even among the things you've chosen to focus on, you don't react perfectly all the time.

Recall the ship metaphor: it would be silly to open up holes all around your ship. Even if you had a cannon for each of them, you can only focus on so many at once. You are, after all, the only crew member on this ship, so you must plan for that! Keep your ship fortified where your attention cannot reach, and in the places that your attention is active and continual, that's where you want to be playing exploitably and opening yourself up to attack. Because your own attention is limited, it is a valuable defensive strategy to try to play unexploitably.

The Theorem of Balance

I've given you reasons why balance is good, yet I've also claimed that balance isn't always good. So when is balance worth pursuing? If balance is desirable, then it must contribute EV to our game. So let's try to pinpoint exactly where that EV comes from.

Imagine a spot where you're the preflop raiser, and you flop three of a kind. You decide to check the turn because you want to balance your bet/check/bet line, instead of bet/bet/betting. You decide to use this hand to balance. Let's assume that balancing here is a +EV decision—where does the EV of your balancing actually come from?

You might guess: "if you're against an opponent who floats a lot and likes to checkraise rivers in spots like this when you're going for thin value, then you can induce a lot of bluffs here."

But be careful—that's not balance, that's inducing a bluff. While it's true that many spots where you might rearrange your ranges for balancing may induce bluffs, and may even be as a consequence the optimal play, balance doesn't play a role in that. So let's imagine that we worked out this opponent's tendencies, and calculated that bet/bet/bet would be slightly more +EV on average than bet/check/bet in this single hand. Mathematically, if balancing is superior, it must give us some other EV *external* to this hand. Where is that EV supposed to come from?

The answer is that the EV for balancing is realized not synchronically, but *diachronically*. That is, it's not realized over one hand, but it's realized over an *entire match*. Think about it. If taking a bet/check/bet line here allows you in the future to be able to bet for value a thinner range on the river, since your bet/check/bet line is balanced by having three of a kind, then your opponent is going to checkraise-bluff you less. Not only does it let you valuebet thinly more effectively, but it allows you to bluff effectively with the bet/check/bet line.

Notice, then, that capturing this EV is contingent on the situation arising again before the match ends. Because the EV of balancing is realized diachronically, balancing *only has value over the course of a longer match*. If you are playing somebody for 10 hands, balancing is going to be worthless unless it's synchronically optimal.

There's a second factor as well. If your opponent isn't aware of the fact that you're balancing, then your balance isn't netting you any EV. That is, if your opponent isn't observant or aware enough to notice that you've included three of a kind in your bet/check/bet line, then you're not going to get any EV in future hands from it. Against somebody who is essentially unaware of what is going on, you are better off playing each hand optimally in a vacuum. Thus, balance is only valuable in and of itself against people who are aware enough to perceive and respond to your balance, and who you'll be playing long enough for it to matter.

There are certain times when balance isn't very valuable, and certain times when it is more valuable. It falls along a spectrum; balancing isn't always preferable to not balancing.

So to sum all this up, we can state the final theorem of balance:

The Theorem of Balance: one should balance *if and only if* the external EV of balancing on average over the entire session (diachronic) is greater than the EV you'd gain by playing the single hand optimally (synchronic).

Balance in Bet Sizing

Balance, however, isn't limited to distributing hands among different actions (as in between betting and checking). There is also balance in bet sizing.

If you consider balancing bet sizing to be a completely separate arena from range balancing, you're likely to find the task overwhelmingly daunting. But it's simpler than it might seem at first.

Balancing bet sizing simply means that each individual bet size needs to be balanced independently—that is, you have to treat each bet size as its own range. If you only have one bet size in a certain spot, then this is an easy task, but there are many spots in which you'll have more than one "go-to" or predetermined bet size. None of us is ever going to use *every possible* bet size in any spot; usually, you will have two or three predetermined bet sizes, and rarely any more than that. If you simply imagine a bet size as simply being a *different range* from another bet size, then we can extend the line of argument about range balancing to come at a theory of bet size balancing.

Consider this example. Imagine that you 3-bet your opponent preflop and he calls, the board runs out K♠Q♠5♦3♦7♥ and you barrel every street. You may have three different bet sizes on the river: ¾ pot, which is your standard size and includes top pair; an overbet of 1¼ pot, which includes nutty hands for value like two-pairs and sets; and a smaller bet of ½ pot that includes only weak kings and AQ for value. Other than those value hands, those ranges would be populated solely with bluffs, and each with a different proportion relative to the whole. So how do we distribute our bluffs?

We could decide to achieve perfect balance in each range by doing some simple math with the pot sizes, and orchestrate a mix of bluffs and value that would be unexploitable for betting size. But is that really what we want to do?

First, let's remember the fundamental theorem of balance. You should use a hand to balance a bet size *if and only if* the EV of the effect that hand has on your bet sizing averaged over the session is *greater* than the EV you gain by sizing that hand optimally in a vacuum.

Keep in mind, in order for bet size balancing to be useful, you must ascertain what your opponent is paying attention to. If he is simply ignorant, inattentive, holding onto presumptions (or not gathering any information by folding every time), then there is little need to balance, because your balance won't be affecting his future behavior. There are obvious examples, such as when you're playing a super-fish, but there are also more subtle ones. There are some good opponents who will never call 1/3 pot sized bets on certain rivers because they assume you're always going for thin value, and some opponents who will never call overbets on certain run-outs because they think no one ever bluffs on them. Because your opponent is getting almost no access to that information, and because he's likely to cling onto his presumptions about how people play those spots without paying attention to your actual style, you are often free to play maximally exploitatively in those spots. But in spots that are highly visible and central (and in matches of sufficient length), balancing bet sizes becomes more important.

There is yet another level of complexity to choosing bet sizes. Balancing between one bet size and another is a simple enough decision. But how do you decide *how much* to actually make your preset bet sizes? This is another question of holistic poker theory.

Consider another example. We're 100bb deep, we 3-bet our opponent preflop, he calls, and flop comes out A♠2♦3♥; the pot is 20bbs. For simplicity, let's say that in this case we're only going to choose one bet size for our entire range. We could choose 5bbs, 10bbs, or 15bbs. How do we make that decision?

We make this decision by asking this question: what does this sizing allow us to do with our *entire* range? Remember, at any given time on this board we might have KK or AQo or 79dd, and in each case we will naturally want choose the best bet size for that specific hand. But in order to balance effectively, we must think holistically. Instead of thinking about the best bet size for our hand, we must think: what is the best bet size for my *average* hand? In other words, how much work does the bet do over all the hands I'll have here, rather than just the hand I have here now?

In this specific case, the answer is usually going to be close to 5bbs, since it's a WA/WB (way-ahead/way-behind) type board, whereas on a much drawier board on which your opponent is more likely to have significant equity, you would bet bigger and less often with your range. But, as always, this depends on a constellation of things—most importantly, how foldy your opponent is to different bet sizes, which is something you should always be probing. If you can manage to find a bet size that your opponent is convinced no one ever bluffs with, then you've found yourself a golden hen.

And that leads us to our last big idea.

The Art of Bluffing

Bluffing is something that every poker player thinks they know how to do. But there are many subtleties to bluffing that escape most players.

The first important concept is **bluffing equity**, which is the equity you get from being able to bluff on a later street. If you imagine somebody who's dealt two napkins—two cards that can never connect with the board—that person can still win pots, and possibly even beat some really bad opponents. All of that person's equity is coming from his bluffing equity, or his ability to win pots with bluffs.

Bluffing equity is important to consider, because sometimes bluffing equity is a valuable equity consideration for staying in a pot rather than folding out early. Many poker players never think about this, but a negative EV decision on an earlier street may become positive EV from profitable bluffing situations that may appear later in a hand. It's analogous to the concept of implied odds. According to implied odds, a negative EV decision on this street may become profitable by the likelihood of making money on the next street. Bluffing equity is the same. You may continue in a hand that's slightly negative EV because a good bluffing opportunity may appear on the next street. Of course, people are much less comfortable using this justification for a play, because they feel really sure about the positive EV of being able to hit a straight or three of a kind, but the positive EV of a bluffing spot doesn't *feel* as solid to them. They're more afraid of having to rely on it. But EV from value hands and EV from bluffs are the same— EV is EV.

There is some validity to this trepidation, however, because in order to use bluffing equity as a justification for a play, you have to be sure that the bluff is going to actually be +EV. Therefore, you have to hand-read really well and know how your opponent thinks. If you're confident in your reads, then your true bluffing EV is going to be close to your projected bluffing EV. If you're not confident in your reads, then your actual bluffing EV might not be close at all to what you projected.

For a confident player, it might be a good idea to rely on bluffing equity, but a less confident player should be more careful using bluffing equity as a justification for immediately   -EV plays.

Ironically, people rarely consider this when it comes to implied odds. People will chase sets and draws, under the presumption that if they hit, their opponent will pay them off. Many players never acknowledge that their opponents rarely pay them off when they actually hit, often because their own bet sizing or nittiness is tipping their opponents off. In all likelihood, this is a leftover behavior that many players learn from playing low stakes (which involves lots of setmining and draw chasing, with full expectation of getting paid off by fish).

This is what I call a **vestigial habit**. Vestigial habits can be a big problem if they don't get extinguished once you move up to tougher games. Given how poorly the brain intuitively responds to probabilities (your brain is very bad at perceiving odds of ¼ or smaller), many vestigial habits like this are unlikely to go away simply through unconscious conditioning—your brain simply will not adapt to the difference between getting paid off 20% of the time and getting paid off 10% of the time in tougher games. This means you must always try to be cognizant of making faulty, outdated assumptions about how often you get paid off in any given spot.

Just as implied odds gone awry can turn into reverse implied odds, bluffing equity can become **reverse bluffing equity**. Say that we're staying in a hand with a nut blocker, planning to bet hard if the flush draw hits, because we believe he'd never play a draw of his own the way he has. If he actually decided to play his own flush draw differently than we expected, we are setting ourselves up to lose even more money if a flush card hits. Using bluffing equity against someone who's slowplaying or has structured his range differently than you expected can lead to your bluffing equity to backfire on you. Thus, the less confident you are in your reads, the less you should be veering from immediately profitable plays.

Aside from bluffing and reverse bluffing equity, there is another important principle of bluffing that is not very well understood by most people. Consider this question: when you want to bluff someone, what kind of hand do you want to represent?

Most people will intuitively answer "a strong hand." But this is absolutely wrong.

If you think about it, your opponent doesn't actually care whether or not your hand is strong. What he cares about is whether or not his hand can beat yours. That is to say, you need to represent a hand that's *better than his*. So if he has a weak hand, you don't need to represent a strong hand. You just need to represent a hand slightly stronger than his, even if it's merely mediocre.

This is a common fallacy that poker players make when thinking about how to bluff. They concentrate their bluffs in places where they can represent flushes and straights, sets and overpairs and hands of that nature. But inherently, all of those hands have a very low absolute frequency. You don't get flushes and sets very often. So why try so hard to represent them?

Instead, you should be representing more hands like top pair low kicker, or second pair betting thinly, or a medium pocket pair. You should be using more bluffing lines like check/check/bet, or check/bet/bet, or bet/check/bet, which inherently represent these weaker types of hands. These hands get dealt with a lot higher frequency, and so you can bluff to represent them much more often. You don't tend to win as *big* of pots by bluffing in this way, but the pots you are going to win will add up dramatically in the long run. Winning one extra 10bb pot per 100 hands amounts to a dramatic increase in winrate.

You can take this principle of bluffing to a more advanced level, which hinges more on psychology. Let's assume that your opponent is fairly intelligent, and is actively thinking about your ranges. You're in a spot where all of your hands will have at least *some* showdown value. There's nothing in your range that will always definitely lose the pot. Generally, your opponents will assume that you are going to choose the path of least risk (which is usually a good assumption). So since they know you can probably just check through and at least occasionally win without risking anything, they will assume you're not going to turn those hands into bluffs. They will thus put your bluffing frequency as very low. Therefore, *this is a spot where you should be bluffing.*

As a general principle: in spots where your opponent thinks you shouldn't have any need to bluff, you should bluff. Of course, this is only valid when your opponent is thinking about things like this, and the spot is salient or non-central enough for him to be consciously thinking about it. If he's not thinking about your psychology, or if he's simply oblivious, then this principle goes out the window.

As you can see, there are many subtle aspects to thinking about bluffing, much more than simply representing a big hand once in a while. There is a tremendous artistry involved in being a good bluffer, which will take you a career to fully master.

I've shown you these different perspectives on how to arrange your poker game on the holistic level, but we must next return to the reductionistic level, which is, after all, where all the real action happens. We may think about poker holistically away from the game or when we're conceiving of match dynamics, but when it comes down to it, poker is made up of individual hands. It's played through checks and bets, making decisions, and constructing ranges, one after another. So now that we've set the foundation for large-scale poker strategy, we can look at the more atomic elements of poker thinking.

3

THE ART OF RANDOMNESS

In a bet there is a fool and a thief.

ENGLISH PROVERB

There are two primary aspects to poker decision-making: strategy and psychology. But what's the difference between them? Intuitively, it seems obvious, but putting it into words is tricky. Really think about it. How would you define the difference?

A simple way of getting at it would be to say: "strategy is having good fundamentals, while psychology is about getting into people's heads." This is a good start, but we can do better.

It's true that psychology is about getting into people's heads, but the reason why we want to get into their heads is *to predict their gameplay*. Strategy allows us to exploit decisions, but psychology is what lets us predict them in the first place. You cannot exploit someone if you don't know what they're going to do—but simply knowing what they're going to do doesn't mean you're going to be able to maximally exploit it.

In short, strategy works from a static place. It's algorithmic. You input your opponent's strategy, and it spits out the proper counter-strategy. Psychology, on the other hand, is more fluid. It allows you to predict and pre-empt those strategies and how they change, based on a stream of observations. Neither strategy nor psychology is sufficient without the other.

Psychology and Bluffing

We can narrow down the role of psychology in poker even further. In the previous chapter, we discussed orchestrating your bluffing and valuebetting ranges. You might presume that bluffing and valuebetting frequencies are essentially the same sort of thing, and that to manipulate them you just raise one and lower the other from your control panel. In reality, it's a lot more complicated.

If you think about it, to say that your bluffing frequency is 0% is another way of saying that you never choose to bluff when given the opportunity. Almost always in a given spot, you'll have *some* hands you can bluff with. So to say your bluffing frequency is 0% is to say that you *forego* making bluffs. But on the other hand, to say that your valuebetting frequency is 0% is to say that you don't *have* any value hands in that spot. When you have a value hand, you don't "make a choice" whether or not to valuebet; you always valuebet when you have a set or top pair (thin value bets excluded).

Let's assume you want to alter your balance in a certain spot. Changing your bluffing frequency can be done immediately, because bluffing frequency is pretty much a matter of choice. It is **local**. You simply "decide" that you want to bluff more in this spot, and then you do it; there are no other external factors you need to consider. On the other hand, if you want to valuebet more in a certain spot, you cannot simply "decide" to valuebet more. Remember, your stack of wood, your supply of good hands, is finite and limited. If you don't have any here with you, you'll have to take wood from elsewhere and re-allocate it here. Therefore, raising your value-betting frequency is not local; it is **systemic**, because you have to make changes to other parts of your game in order to use the resources you need. You have to remove the hands from somewhere else to bring them here.

We can use this insight to frame the difference between psychology and strategy. Strategy is about making systemic, large-scale changes to our game to exploit our opponents. But psychology is more about internal, localized decisions. Furthermore, psychology usually centers on bluffing, because bluffing is where actual moment-to-moment choices are made. Valuebetting, on the other hand, tends to be more a matter of large-scale strategy and range construction.

Of course, this is a simplification. Technically speaking, there are some times that your range is so strong in a certain spot that you need to start including bluffs, and times when you'll decide to make thin valuebets, and so on. But despite its simplicity, this is a useful way of thinking, and it will give us a place to begin.

What the Hell is Game Flow?

It's impossible to talk about poker without invoking psychological concepts. And yet, it seems most of the language that we use to talk about psychology is incredibly imprecise. If you query random players about why they do what they do, you'll often hear people talking about reads, their guts, timing, game flow. But if you probe them to explain these concepts, they're usually unable to do so. And how can you blame them? Much of what happens on the psychological battlefield is more intuitive than rational. But that doesn't mean that psychology is impervious to rational analysis. It simply means that it's difficult, and we're going to have to use language and concepts more precise than those we're used to.

Psychology will take us many chapters to fully unpack, but we can start with the most slippery of all psychological terms: **game flow**.

Game flow is notoriously difficult to define. Just the word "flow" suggests a sort of gooey elusiveness. Yet anyone who's put in a lot of hands at a poker table seems to know intuitively what it means.

The first way to get at this term is to look at how it's actually used.

When someone says "the game flow wasn't going my way," this really refers to the *momentum* of the match. We will fully discuss momentum later in this chapter. I'll avoid this use of "game flow," since there's a more exact word for this concept.

When someone says, on the other hand, "you should either bet or check here depending on game flow," this is the more typical use, and the one more recalcitrant against definition.

"Bet or check depending on game flow." What phrase can we substitute in here for "game flow"? We might say "the flow of the match," but that doesn't help at all. We could try "what you think he's going to do," but this seems vague. Game flow is more specific than that.

How do you define game flow?

Let's try a little experiment. Historically, poker notation has been designed to notate hands synchronically. That is, we've come up with a language to denote how a single hand was played, notating every action on every street. This has evolved into the modern hand history. But we don't have any accepted notation on how to notate hands *diachronically*. The only way that we can show someone an *entire session* is by cutting and pasting every single hand history played over that period of time. That's far too verbose to be useful. So why don't we invent a new language, and see if we can do better?

First, let's come up with a symbol for each major hand. We'll define a hand where someone valuebet as V, a hand where they bluffed as B, where they folded as F, and where they called as C. So if there's a sequence of hands where, on the river (or any other constant pivotal point), on the first hand our opponent valuebet, then on the second hand he bluffed, then he valuebet again, then he check/folded, and then he called, we'd denote that as: $V \cdot B \cdot V \cdot F \cdot C$. That is, value, bluff, value, fold, call.

You might notice that this notation discards a lot. We don't say how big the pots are, or how similar they are, or even who the raiser was. So we'll have to stipulate that we will only use this notation to analyze *similar* hands—i.e., pots that are around the same size, with the same person betting, in relatively similar situations. For the purposes of this example, let's imagine that we're analyzing preflop 4-bets in a heads up match by our opponent. In other words, we're using this notation once we 3-bet this player, and he chooses either to 4-bet for value, 4-bet as a bluff, to call our 3-bet, or to fold. So let's imagine the sequence of 20 hands that looks like this (which is transcribed from an actual match):

$$F \cdot F \cdot C \cdot F \cdot V \cdot F \cdot B \cdot V \cdot F \cdot C \cdot F \cdot F \cdot F \cdot B \cdot F \cdot F \cdot F \cdot V \cdot F \cdot C$$

Read over this sequence. The first thing you might notice over this sample is that this person 4-bets quite a bit (adding up the *V*s and *B*s, you get 5/20 or 25%), but this is only a small stretch of hands. Nevertheless, seeing all of these post-3-bet hands notated this way allows us to make valuable observations.

First, recall that we don't really "choose" to valuebet. We simply valuebet when we're dealt a good hand. The same can be said for calling hands to 3-bets. Although there is *a little* variation in players' 3-bet calling ranges, most players are calling pretty much the same range, with a little variation along the tails of that range. Along those lines, a call doesn't really tend to influence the game flow of the 4-betting game, because people are almost always calling a relatively pre-defined range, and tend not to play with that range too much. Our opponent simply calls when he's dealt a certain hand that thinks he's supposed to call with, he doesn't really "choose" to call. A call is also transparent—an opponent usually knows exactly what you're doing and what your range looks like when you call (you might try to mix this up by flatcalling AA sometimes, but this is so infrequent that it doesn't really affect the point).

So given all this, we can say that a call is a non-decision event in the game flow. It's a systemic choice he's making about his calling range, rather than a momentary decision. Thus, we may as well eliminate the calls from the sequence, which will get us closer to the psychologically relevant action. By paring out the calls, the sequence then becomes:

$$F \cdot F \cdot F \cdot V \cdot F \cdot B \cdot V \cdot F \cdot F \cdot F \cdot F \cdot B \cdot F \cdot F \cdot F \cdot V \cdot F$$

The same argument we made about how our opponent doesn't "choose" to call can be extended to 4-betting for value. Although there is a little variation in player's 4-betting value ranges, most players are 4-betting largely the same range for value (some players will 4-bet/call off AJ, 77+ in a heads up match if there's a very aggressive 4-betting dynamic, but these are only on the tail ends of 4-betting ranges, and are not a dramatic difference from the average).

Thus, in a sense, this player has no control over his *V*s either. If this same sequence of cards were dealt to any of us, our *V*s would likely appear in the same spots in the sequence.

However, this doesn't mean that we can eliminate the *V*s, because in fact his *V*s are indistinguishable to us from his *B*s (his bluffs). Therefore, they are significant events. From our perspective both events look identical—they are both simply 4-bets, and we cannot know which one is which without a shove or a showdown. His *V*s therefore influence the psychological game, even though he has no control over them, because every *V* and every *B*, to us, is evidence of him having more *B*s. In other words, every 4-bet that we see is evidence that he's 4-bet bluffing more often. Even if he 4-bets ten hands in a row with value hands, we are only likely to see one or two of those to showdown, and we will probably assume that the ones we didn't see were bluffs.

54

Let's see what the sequence looks like when we emphasize the *B*s and *V*s—the 4-bets.

$$\text{F·F·F·} V \text{·F·} B \cdot V \text{·F·F·F·F·} B \text{·F·F·F·} V \text{·F}$$

By highlighting it this way, the *F*s become like the spaces around the 4-bets. With this, we can analyze the dynamics of this sequence.

Look at his pattern of *F*s here. First he makes three continuous folds, then he has a value hand. Then he folds one hand, then he makes a bluff. He gets dealt a value hand immediately afterward. After that, knowing that we just saw a condensed sequence of bets, he decides to cool it, and he make four folds. Then one bluff, then three more folds, then a value hand comes by again, and after that a fold.

So it looks like this player is usually choosing to fold three hands or so between his bluffs. After the sequence of $V \cdot F \cdot B \cdot V$, he folds for an extra-long sequence of four hands, probably to compensate for the fact that his opponent assumes he's getting out of line, and he wants to restore his image. At the end of the sequence there is one last valuebet, followed by a bluff. If I were a betting man, I'd bet that following this pattern, the player in this example folded the next two or three hands after this.

So what was the point of this exercise?

Basically, we've just analyzed the game flow of this twenty-hand sequence. That's right. This is what game flow is.

Using this perspective, we can now define the term more concretely: game flow is the *pattern* of decisions made over time, and how that pattern influences subsequent decisions. (We might be inclined to call it the pattern of bluffs and valuebets, but it's not necessarily restricted to those.)

There are two main elements that constitute the patterns of game flow: **simulated randomness** and **emotional dynamics**. Before we go over each in depth, I want you to consider this central thesis in the background:

Game flow is a *human* phenomenon. That is, if two computers played each other (and both computers knew the other was a computer), then game flow would not exist.

Faking Randomness

How good do you think you are at being random?

According to the bulk of scientific studies, you are pretty bad at it. All of us are. For example, let's say that you took a bunch of people into a room, and asked them to simulate random coinflips. You don't give them any coins, but tell them to imagine that they're flipping a fair coin 20 times, and to write down the imagined results. What do you think they do?

Well, they end up pretty close to 10 heads and 10 tails, usually within one flip. This might be reassuring to you, but it shouldn't be. This is the first problem. People will almost never end up with 7 heads and 13 tails, or 6 heads and 14 tails—if you take a graph of all of the simulated coinflip runs, their bell curve will be unnaturally narrow. No one will be at the edges—whereas in true coinflips, there would be many uneven runs.

The second problem is that their listed clusters tend to be too small. That is, if **h** is heads and **t** is tails, people would tend to write something like **hhhtthttthtttthhhthth**. Observe this sequence. The longest cluster here is three letters. That might seem fine and random-looking to you, but what that means is that, predictably, the chance of the pattern discontinuing after three consecutive repeated letters is close to 100%. Obviously, it should be 50%.

Here is an actual randomly generated sequence: ththttththhtttttththt. As you can see, this particular string has 7 heads and 13 tails, with one cluster 5 letters long. Of course, this sequence is nowhere near the median. But the point is that human beings almost never generate this type of string.

Another example of this phenomenon is arranging dots in space. If I ask you to imagine what a random grid of 100 points looks like, you're probably going to imagine something like this:

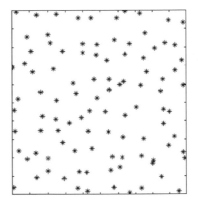

Again, this is actually not random at all. A *truly* randomly generated grid of 100 dots looks more like this:

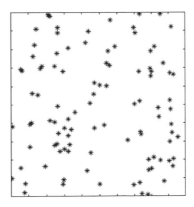

Notice the differences. The randomly generated grid clumps together into various clusters and constellations; it doesn't look quite as spaced out and roomy as the faux-random grid.

What can we conclude from this? People have a poor idea of what randomness "looks like." Their image of randomness tends to be pristine and orderly compared to the real thing.

Faked randomness is unnaturally periodic and uniform. True randomness, on the other hand, has clusters and looks less pretty. This is essential to game flow. After all, a large part of what we're doing in game flow is *attempting to simulate randomness*.

Let's look at the sequence from before:

$$\text{F·F·F·v·F·B·v·F·F·F·F·B·F·F·F·v·F}$$

This time I've emphasized the folds and bluffs. Recall that we don't "choose" when to valuebet, we simply valuebet when we have good hands. By that logic, the bolded plays are *the plays we're in control of.* It is through this pattern of folding and bluffing that we attempt to simulate randomness in the 4-betting game.

Now, why and when exactly do we want to simulate randomness? From a metagame perspective, we have two choices at any given time. The first is to appear random and honest, and the second is to appear non-random and intentional. By non-random and intentional, I mean giving your opponent the feeling that you're picking and choosing *when* to attack, rather than just getting randomly dealt hands.

These two choices can each be advantageous, depending on the situation. In the 4-betting game, for example, if you are 4-betting as a bluff and you look pretty honest and random, your

58

opponent is going to give you credit and your bluff will usually succeed. If, on the other hand, you're 4-betting for value and you look pretty nonrandom and intentional, then you're likely to get some action on your hand. We know this intuitively, because when we get big pocket pairs three times in a row—a pattern that looks very nonrandom—we tend to get paid off on the second or third. This is why.

Unfortunately, getting dealt good hands is outside of your control. You cannot decide to orchestrate your game flow patterns so that you're allocating good hands where he won't believe them.

Thus, the only truly random events in the 4-betting game are getting dealt value hands. Everything else is simulated randomness. And the goal of that simulated randomness is to get your opponent to think you're valuebetting when you're actually bluffing—in other words, to overrepresent the Vs in your sequence.

Game Flow and Wordplay

Distilled to its essence, game flow is a language. The phrases in this language are the patterns of folds and bets that two players make with one another. As in any language, they are not communicating directly—their phrases only have meaning by way of their signification. In this case, they signify the patterns of simulated randomness.

Recall the grids of dots we looked at before. People tend to have an inordinately tidy notion of what randomness looks like, and poker players are no exceptions. Furthermore, when poker players are faced with randomness, they face it *experientially*. Even if they are intellectually aware of the biases in generated randomness, they don't get to face randomness in poker as a discrete string of letters to analyze, like the Ts and Hs we were dissecting.

We know what our opponent expects randomness to look like—orderly and uniform. In that case, it doesn't matter that we know *true randomness* tends to cluster and look more irregular. Our goal is, in fact, *not* to be truly random, but to make him *think* that we're random, which means we must accord to his preconceived notions of randomness.

In creating our game flow strings, we ought to make them look regular, and to distribute them as evenly and orderly as possible (with enough variations to look random-ish—not simply a repeating pattern of a bet after every third fold). We want to simulate an obvious, periodic, pseudorandom game flow.

That would be an easy conclusion if we stopped there. In fact, I'm betting you probably already do that part intuitively, although you may not necessarily realize it. But it is from this point that leveling game and complexities of game flow begin.

This simple way of depicting randomness is the first level of the randomness-simulating game. Because almost everybody tries to construct their game flow in this way, it has become the norm. Your opponents will automatically assume that this is what you're doing, too. If you're any good at all, your opponent will assume that you know this is how randomness-simulating is "supposed" to be done. It's the basic rules of the language.

What we can do next, then, is depart from this basic level and start to engage in wordplay.

Remember that our valuebets, the *V*s, which are truly random, will sometimes unavoidably cluster after *B*s. This is simply a matter of happenstance. A first-level randomness-simulator will almost always immediately cool off after such a cluster of bets, signaling to his opponent, "Don't let this reflect on my image! My hands just randomly clustered; it wasn't my fault!"

The second-leveler decides to start playing with this language. He knows that his opponent has been conditioned by

60

other poker players to see clusters as unintentional—something that a poker player will almost apologize for, and avoid with his bluffs. In this way, clusters have effectively taken on a meaning of harmlessness. And because he perceives that, a second leveler realizes that he can sneak in clusters as a weapon in his game flow arsenal.

Instead of always trying to simulate spacious orderliness, he utilizes clusters. He bluffs twice in a row. Three times in a row. He'll $B \cdot B \cdot F \cdot B$. Not too often of course—he cannot afford for his opponent to be completely sure how he is playing with this language. The second leveler wants his opponent to believe that he is a first leveler on a good run. In this way, he develops second-order game flow phrases. For example, if we define phrase 1 as $B \cdot F \cdot F \cdot F$, his basic spaciously random phrase, and phrase 2 as $B \cdot B \cdot F \cdot B$, the second-order game flow might look like:

$$1 \cdot 1 \cdot 2 \cdot 1 \cdot 1 \cdot 2 \cdot 1 \cdot 2 \cdot 1 \cdot 1$$

See what he's doing? By employing the same notion of spaciousness on a larger level, but taking advantage of the perceived first-level innocence of clusters, he can increase his bluffing capacity within shorter individual strings.

In order to attain mastery of game flow, one must learn how to play with clusters. Great players are aware on some level of their mutual capability to play with these clustered strings, and it becomes the battleground for serious mind games. In the end, it is only through play and experimentation that you discover how your opponent reacts to these clusters, how willing he is to believe them, and what threshold he has before he is compelled to action. Ideally, you want to skirt the very edge of this threshold. You want to bluff and bluff up until the very edge of his patience but no further, for that is the line of maximal exploitation.

I have obviously simplified this example. Generally speaking, you won't choose 4-bet bluffing hands solely on the basis of game flow. You'll usually choose hands that have some card-cancelling effects (i.e., ace-rag) or some playability in case your opponent calls. This further randomizes your 4-bets, provided that you never 4-bet unless your hand falls within this acceptable range. Certainly, this dampens the game flow. But it still exists, even if it is less granular than in other more obvious game flow sequences.

Escaping Game Flow

In the end, game flow is the stream through which everything in poker flows. It is omnipresent and inescapable. Every hand that is ever played between two humans will be processed through these patterns.

Consider the large-scale structural approach to poker we discussed in the previous chapter. There, we discussed sweeping ideas like balance, constructing frequencies and ranges, and so on. Perhaps when it comes to being dealt value hands, since it's completely random when they occur, the only thing we can do is construct the range. But when it comes to bluffing, we see how many decisions there are to make, how many games within games, how inexhaustible the complexities of any given moment. It is one thing to say we want to bluff 66%, a grand holistic number, but the art of bluffing from hand to hand is atomic, reductionistic, one puzzle after another.

Do these perspectives contradict one another? Which one is the right way of looking at the game?

Say that you wanted your bluffing frequency in spots like X to be exactly 50%. On first glance, if you bluffed in spot X 50 times out of 100 over a match, you might say that you have accomplished your desired 50% frequency. But if you never bluffed for X_1, X_2, X_3,...,X_{50}, and then always bluffed for X_{51}, X_{52}, X_{53},..., X_{100}, you would naturally call this instead a bluffing frequency of 0% for 50 hands and then 100% for the next 50 hands.

Let's extend that same argument to a more realistic sequence. Perhaps you think you're being balanced over a 10 hand stretch, but your pattern of bluffs is $F \cdot B \cdot F \cdot B \cdot F \cdot B \cdot F \cdot B \cdot F \cdot B$. You might call this a balanced sequence where your bluffing frequency is 50%. But we could also say that for each individual spot in the sequence, your bluffing frequency is either 0% or 100% depending on whether the instance is odd or even. You see, even if we make the pattern more complex and not perfectly repeating: $B \cdot F \cdot B \cdot F \cdot B \cdot B \cdot F \cdot F \cdot B \cdot F$, you can extend the very same argument, albeit with lower accuracy (instead of 100%, it might become 80% on every even number).

You can see where this argument is going. Perhaps it's possible that in our humanness, in our limited ability to generate randomness, we will never be able to truly randomly re-create any large-scale statistical frequencies. Perhaps over an entire match, when we attempt to bluff 33%, we're predictably (perhaps we don't know the algorithm that predicts it and perhaps our current opponent doesn't either, but predictably nevertheless) bluffing much higher or lower than 33% in a given spot, and never at any given time are we close to the distributions we're aiming for. Perhaps we are foolish to even plan on something like that to begin with.

It's not an unjustified fear. But let's say that we install a random number generator on our computer, into which we could enter a frequency (e.g., 50%), and it would output either B or F perfectly randomly. We'd forego trying to simulate randomness—we'd use *real* randomness. Imagine the consequences.

It's tantalizing, isn't it? If we did this, we could throw off the burden of our humanness. We would become one step closer to machines, and escape the stream of game flow. Would that not be a molting out of our human shells? Would that not be a victory over our primitive minds?

In fact, I know people who have attempted to play poker this way. Such programs are actually trivial to make. And yet, you look around, and just about nobody uses them. Why? Why didn't this catch on?

In a way, doing something like this—randomizing your game flow—is like trying to be perfectly balanced. It doesn't attempt to exploit your opponents, but instead, absconds from the exploitative game altogether. The field of battle becomes smaller. Whatever potential mistakes your opponent could be induced into making in game flow are now dismissed when you randomize in this way. If in every spot *X* you always bluff exactly 50% of the time completely randomly, then it doesn't matter how your opponent *patterns* his guesses over time, the only thing that matters is his overall proportion of guesses. The stream of game flow dries up.

It is true by necessity that if you are not perfectly randomizing your game flow, then *someone is always going to be better than the other at the randomness game*. Either you will make your opponent guess wrong better-than-chance, or your opponent will be able to guess right better-than-chance. It's always one or the other, in every match. If we were to choose when to use the randomizing program, the optimal strategy would be to only use it in cases where we believed our opponent was *better than us* at the randomizing game. In any case where he isn't, we should choose instead to play within the stream of game flow, to dissect his language into its individual syllables, to stare our opponent down and try to outwit him.

The reason why people haven't started using randomizing programs (other than that they tend to overestimate their own skill) is because reading and creating game flow are essential skills that can only be honed through repeated practice and stress. Using a program of that nature to escape game flow only retards your growth as a poker player. Against a fish, you will simply be throwing away another opportunity to optimize against him. And the players who are better than you are the very players against whom you want to be honing and practicing your game flow, in order to get to the point that you can overtake them. It is only through challenge—and failure—that any of us have the opportunity to truly evolve as players.

Tilt and Emotional Dynamics

In our reductionism so far, we have been overly simplistic. We have assumed we can dissect a poker match into discretely related hands, and analyze that sequence in isolation. But we all know that in reality, a poker match is not that cut and dry. In reality, most bluffing spots affect one another, even if the spots are dissimilar. It's clearly relevant to a 4-bet whether or not somebody just lost a huge all-in the previous hand.

This is due to the **emotional dynamics**—the way that emotions and the perceptions of emotions affect gameplay. The perceptions of emotions are almost as important as emotions themselves.

For example, let's say that you just got married today, so you can't get angry after losing—you're just too elated. You lose a big pot. The fact that you don't feel any anger doesn't mean you don't have to make any adjustments—you have to respond to the fact that your opponent *expects* you to be angry. The fact that you're "supposed" to feel anger implies that the next hand, your opponent will expect you to get out of line, and so you must make an effort to do the opposite. Emotional dynamics are just as much about perceptions and stereotypes as they are about reality.

As human beings, we are acutely sensitive to the ebb and flow of emotions. Long before we were assigning preflop raising standards and checkraising tendencies, we were saying "this guy must be pissed off," or "that guy must be scared." It is the most apparent way of making sense of what's going on at a poker table, and even at the highest levels of the game, it is essential to deciphering poker dynamics.

We cannot talk about emotions without first addressing tilt. But tilt is itself an enormous topic in poker, so I will be addressing only the smaller part of it in this chapter—the tilt of other players. **Tilt** can be defined as allowing one's emotions to negatively affect one's gameplay. Generally speaking, you will see tilt triggered by five major causes: a lost pot, a failed play, getting insulted or disrespected, an atrophied mental state (e.g., tired, hungry, hung over), or being affected by concurrent life events (e.g., having a bad day, losing a job, etc.). This much is obvious if you have any experience at a poker table. But there are a few important aspects of how tilt arises that we need to explore.

The way tilt arises can be likened to boiling a pot of water. There is a threshold of emotional turbulence that a player can handle and maintain his composure, just as a pot of water can take a certain amount of heat before it starts bubbling. Once it gets near the boiling temperature, it begins to visibly react—and once you push it far above that boiling temperature, it reacts more and more violently. This is essentially how tilt works. Any opponent will be able to take a certain amount of beating, until he hits his tilt threshold and starts to react. The further you push him past this threshold, the more and more he will react. But not all opponents will tilt in the same way.

There are many different ways of tilting, but there are two main species of tilt that you should be looking out for: **hot tilt** and **cold tilt**. Hot tilt is the more familiar one. It is generally tilting out of anger (whether from entitlement, frustration, victimization, or whatever). The player will be desperately trying to get even, and so he will play more aggressively, making more wild calls and crazy plays. The emblematic play of a hot tilter is a preflop open shove. Of course, once you start playing serious stakes, you're almost never going to see an open shove (especially not these days), but it captures the spirit behind hot tilt. Every bad play of hot tilt is essentially just a preflop shove with less money behind it.

The second kind of tilt is cold tilt. Cold tilt is more passive—it is generally a tilt of resignation. A cold tilter will start playing more passively, making less plays at pots, folding more to big bets, and acting as though he's incapable of fighting for pots. You'll find a player going on cold tilt when he is running poorly, you've got strong momentum on him, and he can't seem to muster anything together, but you haven't yet outright destroyed him in the match. It's a sort of learned helplessness. He'll feel like all of his moves are getting squashed, but he won't feel like you're completely beating him down, so he's not convinced yet that he should quit. His aggression will be mollified, his fancy moves will be locked away, and you'll be playing against only the skeleton of his game. Where hot tilt tries to overpower and strong-arm his opponent to get even, cold tilt is essentially hoping for a good run of cards to get him even.

Not all players tilt the same, and you should be reacting to each of these two types of tilters differently. Against someone who's going through a stretch of cold tilt, aggression is key. Once your opponent has put down all of his weapons, you should pull out your entire arsenal and snatch away every dollar he doesn't fight for. Against someone on hot tilt on the other hand, it is often enough to just play solidly and adapt to his wider postflop ranges by calling down more; incorporate some heavier aggression to attack his weaker overextended ranges, but don't move too far outside your normal tightness. Simply playing reasonably will inherently exploit a hot tilter fairly well—just be sure you're not giving up too many pots simply because of his aggression.

Tilt: The Customer Is Always Right

Say we know our opponent is on hot tilt, and he wants to play a high-variance game. What do we do against him now? Do we just keep playing our normal game and let him eat his own screw-ups, or should we try to start minraising and make him play in a low-variance environment?

First, you must consider an important question. Why is your opponent tilting? If you can identify the emotion underlying his tilt, then you can take advantage of the situation. Realize that even in tilt, *your opponent is not acting irrationally.* On the contrary, he is still acting in accordance with his values, but his values have now shifted. The value of playing soundly and taking the most +EV line has been superseded by the value of trying to increase variance, or maximize his winnings, or vent his anger, or whatever he's trying to do. You need to ask yourself—what does my opponent value right now? And once you figure out what that is, *you need to give it to him.*

What does this mean?

It's the most common thing in the world. You play against somebody who's tilting, he's starting to really spew, and soon after, he quits you. You probably don't even notice or think this is a big deal, but it is. It's a huge opportunity lost. When your opponent is tilting, you want to *keep him tilting.* And in order to do that, you must understand how and why he's tilting, and how to keep him in that headspace.

Say, for example, that you can tell your opponent wants to maximize variance—he's on hot tilt, he's 3-betting 50%, and he seems to be potting or check-folding on flops. So your opponent's incentive is *maximizing variance.* An adjustment a lot of people will make to this will be to start minraising, since if he keeps 3-betting the minraises, it'll create much deeper SPRs (stack-to-pot ratios) postflop, and they figure that will give them the advantage. This is a horrendous mistake, because the tilting opponent will leave pretty fast if you start doing this. But because you usually don't know *for sure* that he left because of your minraising and not that he was going to leave anyway, most people will just dismiss this event and not recognize it as a mistake.

A wise player knows to *give the tilter what he wants.* The moment that you are playing against a tilter, he has established a symbiotic relationship with you. You are now exchanging value. You are giving him what he wants (variance, a chance to get even, a way to vent) and he is giving you what you want—EV. In the end, he doesn't have to tilt against *you.* He can go off to some other table for someone else to tilt against, or he can go play roulette, or punch his wall, or whatever. If that's what your opponent wants, then it's your job to *be all those things for him*—be his roulette table, his wall to punch, his whatever. Be what he needs, and he will keep playing you.

So what does that mean in practice? It means if your opponent wants to maximize variance by 3-betting you 50%, then let the variance increase. Tighten up your opens, play bigger pots, and increase your playing speed. Rather than minraising 95% on the button, 3x 75% instead, widen your 4-betting range, and try to play faster to make the game speed up. This will make him feel like the game is moving and that he can get all the variance he wants in a shorter amount of time, and with the game sped up, your increased folding frequency is not as likely to frustrate him. Chances are, your opponent will stay with you if you keep this up, and you can rest assured that, if he leaves, you did all you could to keep him.

Remember, if your opponent chooses a suboptimal strategy, there is generally more than one way for you to exploit it. You want to weigh each of your options based first on how much they feed his tilt, and second on how much value they net you. You don't want to just submit to the *most* tilt-feeding strategy, of course, since it's not likely to be optimal. It would be silly to 5x every button just because your opponent seems to want variance. But the bottom line is that if a tilter wants something, you give it to him. Your customer is always right.

Is Momentum Real?

Momentum is another one of those intuitive words that we all use but that eludes definition. How can we define momentum, exactly?

We've already come to the conclusion that game flow is a uniquely human phenomenon—is momentum the same way? Is momentum simply "imagined into existence," a psychological construct, or is it a real thing, rooted in the cards themselves? Would a computer playing poker experience momentum?

This is a question my students used to pose, and I think it warrants investigation. To begin, let's look at a real instance of momentum.

Suppose we are down two buyins, facing a river third barrel on a board with a missed draw, and we tank for a long time and then fold. Our opponent thinks and doesn't show. We're now down three buyins and, as one would expect, we feel like we're at a disadvantage. We feel that he has the momentum.

Where does the momentum actually come from in this example? Certainly, a big part of it comes from our emotional reaction. Even the best, most level-headed poker players would have at least a small emotional response here.

But let's try a thought experiment. Imagine that we *don't* have an emotional reaction to this hand. Totally cut out the emotional element. Say an estranged uncle of yours just bequeathed to you ten million dollars, so you don't really care about being down three buyins; you've just become a multi-millionaire. The money just doesn't matter to you. Really imagine this!

He shoves, you tank-fold, and he doesn't show. Now what? Is the negative momentum still there? Do you still feel it?

I'm guessing you do. Even if you don't feel anything physiologically negative or painful, *you still feel like you're playing from behind.* You feel the momentum.

If that's true, then momentum must be more than just the emotion. You could make the argument that, as with emotional dynamics, your opponent's *expectations* affect the match just as much as the emotions themselves. So if your opponent expects you to feel behind, you have to react to that expectation—maybe *that's* what momentum is really about.

Although this is true, this doesn't satisfy the problem either. His expecting you to feel emotions is due to imperfect information—your opponent is making assumptions about you because he doesn't know you. But let's say you're playing someone who *knows* that you've just come into ten million dollars, and so he knows three buyins isn't going to affect you emotionally. Is the momentum still there? Close your eyes and imagine it. He knows how much money you just made. He shoves, you tank fold. Are you playing from behind?

Yup, still playing from behind. So what creates momentum then?

Some people suggest that momentum is an example of the gambler's fallacy (the tendency to see illusory patterns in random events), but this, too, is not quite enough. The true answer is more interesting.

If you think about it, when you tank-fold a river on a missed draw and don't get to see what he has, what has taken place is more than an emotional spike. You have also created an **informational asymmetry**. In other words, your opponent has now acquired more information than you have. From the fact that you tank-folded, *he knows* that you were considering a hero-call but decided to fold instead. From this, he can reconstruct your mindset and strategy. *But you don't know whether he was bluffing.* While you have gained little information, your opponent has gained a great deal. This is informational asymmetry, and it's a significant part of the reason why when you have negative momentum, even with the emotions removed, you continue to play from behind.

There are, however, certain negative momentum situations that don't necessarily have informational asymmetry. One such example is a big hero call. Say you bluff on a board where the draw misses, and your opponent snapcalls your river shove with bottom pair. He learned the information that you are shoving that river with air, but you also got the information that he's calling with anything and clearly doesn't believe you. So although you lost a buyin here, you can actually make a useful adjustment by tightening up and not bluffing anymore in these spots.

This is an instance of psychologically induced momentum. But again, in real matches, negative momentum will still persist, partially from emotional reactions (who wouldn't feel their gut recoil a little to get their bluff shove snapcalled by bottom pair?).

But it also persists in part due to the fear that your opponent has a better and more accurate read on you than you do on him. I don't know anyone who wouldn't be psyched out by that.

Momentum is real, in more senses than one, so you should never feel bad about quitting a match when your momentum is negative. By simply getting away from the match and starting a new one, you can begin with a blank slate and informational parity. There are always more fish in the sea and more matches to play, so quit liberally when the momentum is against you.

Image and First Impressions

We've looked now at the art of randomness and emotional dynamics, which leaves the final and largest element of psychology—image. **Image** is the picture of a player's behavior that other people see. It is the basis upon which poker players are judged at the table. Put this way, image is a rather large and complex phenomenon, isn't it? So what can we usefully say about how it works?

The preeminent rule of thumb that dictates image is **the strength of first impressions**. The strength of first impressions is a cognitive bias that is widespread and universal. Because of this bias, *our initially constructed models tend to resist being altered by later information.*

For example, if in the first couple of hands after you sit down, you 3-bet twice (perhaps the second time for value), your opponent will immediately form a model of you as an over-aggressive 3-bettor kind of player. Even if, after twenty hands, your frequency becomes depressed enough to appear normal, it will take much longer for him to expunge the attributes that he initially ascribed to you. Furthermore, if he does eventually change his model, he will be quick to return to the initial one if he sees you ever do a run of 3-bets again.

You should take advantage of this bias by always being sensitive to what your initial plays are, and how they are likely to appear to your opponent. Rather than thinking about your *actual* frequencies (whether you're really a tight or a loose 3-bettor), learn to focus instead on what he has seen you do in his limited experience. In other words, resist the fallacy of omniscience. He doesn't know what you know about your game.

The second rule of thumb for image is **the projection bias**. The projection bias refers to a subconscious presumption that other people think like we do. By extension, this means that they perceive poker like we do, and thus will act as we do in most situations.

This is essential to understand: on average, poker players will expect others to think and act the way that they do. This implies that, all things equal, *conservative players will expect other people to play more conservative, and loose players will expect other players to play looser.*

Generally speaking, if you're playing against a nit, he probably assumes you're nittier than you really are, and if you're playing against a maniac, he probably expects you to be more maniacal than you really are. This is not to say that they think you will do *exactly* what they would do. Rather, their perception of your behavior will consistently be swayed in their own direction. Acknowledging this bias will serve you well in reconstructing other player's perceptions, and expectations.

So we have some rudimentary insights into how image works, but to delve further into our analysis of psychology, we must begin to turn inward, and make a deep and substantial analysis of the art of opponent modeling. Only by learning how we construct models of our opponents and predict their behavior will we be able to effectively adjust against them.

4

OPPONENT MODELING AND THE ADJUSTMENT GAME

No matter how much you may want to think of Hold'em as a card game played by people, in many respects it is even more valid to think of it as a game about people that happens to be played with cards.

PHIL HELLMUTH

In poker, it is not our opponents against whom we make our decisions.

There is a sense in which we make our decisions against our opponents as they are—the same sense in which poker is a chess match. In a profound way, our opponent is inaccessible to us. We only have access to the shadow he throws against us—the schema we can construct of him. When we play poker, we make plays and adjustments not against our opponents, but against our *mental models* of them.

The process of creating predictive mental models of players is **opponent modeling**.

The models that we develop in a poker match are fluid and constantly changing. But as we improve as poker players, one of the chief ways we develop is by learning to construct better and more accurate models of our opponents.

I am going to lead you through a step-by-step examination of every aspect of developing a mental model of your opponent, as well as the common pitfalls that might hinder you along the way. But we must begin our exploration from the ground floor: an actual poker match.

Developing a Standard Model

You sit down at a table. There's your opponent. You've never seen him before. Here's your first hand. The action's on you.

We've all been in this situation thousands of times. But we often fail to notice how special this first hand is. The first hand is the only point in the match where you know absolutely nothing about your opponent. And yet, you have to make plays against him. So what do you do?

Well, you obviously act on something. You don't throw your arms up in the air and surrender to ignorance, and you don't throw a dart on the wall and guess wildly what kind of a player he'll be. What you act upon is your **standard model**. The standard model is the mental model you've created of the *average* poker player.

In observing all of the poker players you've ever played, you slowly accrue and shape your standard model, conditioning it bit by bit, incorporating all the things you see people do, all the ways they seem to think, until you have in your mind a pretty firm idea of what the average player looks like. Of course, the more experience you gain and the more observant you are of your opponents, the more accurate this standard model is going to be.

In a way, the moment you sit down at a new table with someone you don't know, what you face across from you is not your opponent as he truly is. What you are looking at is your standard model of an opponent. It is this standard model against which you are reacting, upon which you ascribe intentions, and whose hand you are trying to read.

Say you see someone 3-bet the first hand in a match, and you fold. What can you infer about this opponent?

If you were looking solely at his HUD stats, you'd see that his 3-bet frequency was 100%. So are you going to play him assuming that he's 3-betting 100% of hands? It's not an inherently irrational conclusion. It seems silly to us of course, but *why* is it silly?

The reason it's silly is because we know that *no one* 3-bets 100%. 100% 3-bettors do not exist within the population of poker players. Note then, we are not merely using his actions to inform our model of him, otherwise it *would* be correct to assume he's 3-betting 100%. Instead, interpret his actions in light of how we know frequencies to be *distributed over the entire population*. In other words, we are already thinking about the wider population of poker players, and using that as a basis to build our model of our opponent.

In statistics, this is known as **Bayesian updating**. Using the average 3-betting frequency, the standard deviation (how wide the distribution of 3-betting frequencies is in the population), and the piece of evidence we're presented with (one 3-bet), we could use Bayesian updating to compute his average 3-betting frequency given the evidence of one 3-bet. To throw out a number, chances are it'd be something about 1% or 2% higher than the average based on this one event.

This might all seem like a trivial problem—how to play against someone on the first hand. But this is the origin of how all reads on our opponents work. From the first hand of every match, we create another instance of our standard model, like a readymade figure of clay. Then, with every subsequent decision that we observe in our opponent, we begin to sculpt this figure, departing from this standard model bit by bit—never abandoning it, but transforming it slowly. Over enough time and information, this model starts to develop its own distinct personality. We start to see the shape of its eyes, its jaw, and all the various irregularities of detail that make a real person.

It is clearly important then to have an accurate standard model, since the more accurate your standard model is, the better you are able to initially predict your opponent's play on average. This is the first skill in opponent modeling. Before you can model any particular opponent, you must have a clear idea of what the average opponent looks like. World class players are highly knowledgeable of *common* leaks, *common* weaknesses, which they will infer onto players they don't know, and then attack them. This is a huge part of any player's winrate. In order to develop this standard model, you must play a lot of players and pay close attention to what they do. Over time, you will begin to recognize common patterns, faults, and presumptions of the average opponent, which will inform your standard model.

I mentioned the projection bias in the previous chapter, which is the tendency to impute one's own perceptions and tendencies on other people. You are no exception to this bias. Every standard model that you produce will be biased to be more like yourself. Where you don't clearly and distinctly see otherwise, you will tend to think that people make the same sorts of mistakes that you do, think about spots the same way you do, process game flow the same way that you do, and so on. Every standard model that you produce will be, in some way, in your own image. In spots that are highly non-central, this bias is amplified, since in non-central and rare spots you don't have a wealth of empirical data to counteract this bias. The only real way to fight this bias is to be hyper-aware of it, and to remain open to the idea that your opponents don't always see poker the way that you do.

I said before that your standard model is continually sculpted, but never completely abandoned. But you could also view yourself as having multiple standard models. After using your initial standard model for some hands, and noticing that your opponent is fairly aggressive or fairly passive, you might swap out your standard model of the *average* player for your standard model of the *aggressive* player, or passive player, and so on, continually swapping models as your read becomes more and more nuanced, until you finally have a truly individual model of your opponent. Each of these readymade models would still be subject to projection biases. But the important point is that deconstructing and analyzing your opponent always begins from a standard model you've assigned for him, which is derived from your experience of the average player.

Constructing Psychological Profiles

To make a significant departure from your standard model and deconstruct your opponent, you must develop a robust theory of mind. You must learn to put yourself in your opponent's shoes, and figure out how he sees the world. The first level of deconstructing your opponent begins with a **psychological profile**, a generalization about your opponent's psychological tendencies. This is not so much about particular plays, but about overall patterns in his thinking and attitude.

For example, let's say that your opponent, who you've been playing for a while, is raising the river in some spot where he can only represent a runner-runner straight. Say that we've never gotten into a comparable spot with this opponent before, so we don't have any hard data on what he'd do in this situation. Because of that, are we forced to resort to our standard model?

Not at all—as poker players, we are able to extend psychological inferences into spots we've never seen before. There are very simplistic profiles that more basic players use, like "he's aggressive" or "he's a nit," but we want to develop a robust and nuanced psychological profile.

There are four main dimensions a thorough psychological profile will generally span:

1. *Risk-taking behavior*

2. *Attitude toward complexity*

3. *Image/momentum sensitivity*

4. *Attachment to investment*

Risk-taking behavior is your opponent's willingness to make plays that may fail. It can be inferred most immediately from your opponent's likelihood to make risky bluffs. There are some bluffs which are universal, such as 4-bet bluffing preflop, or 3-barreling in obvious spots where your range is weak. Those spots don't necessarily reflect on this dimension. To discern this dimension, focus instead on spots where a bluff is not mandatory and would be high-risk. If your opponent is consistently choosing to take risky bluff spots, or if he is consistently averse to them, then you can place him accordingly on this dimension, and generalize this behavior to other kinds of risk-taking.

This also extends to making risky, heroic, or creative plays in general. Players who are high on this dimension tend to make more "heroic" plays, riskier bluffs, FPSy plays, and at times, will care more about making "sick" plays than optimizing EV.

Tilting also affects risk-taking behavior significantly. A player on hot tilt will tend to have increased risk-taking behavior, whereas a player on cold tilt will tend to have depressed risk-taking behavior. Also, players who are playing above their rolls will tend to have lower risk-taking behavior, which is why you are able to generally lean on and steal lots of pots from them, unless they are also concurrently on hot tilt.

The second dimension, **attitude toward complexity**, is how your opponent perceives and plays with **complex lines** in his game.

By complex line, I mean a line that implies either a trap, or a hand that is not at the top of one's range. There are two main types of complex lines. The first is one where, for the hand you're representing to make sense, you would've had to do something tricky at some point in the hand, such as checking back in a weird place or betting smaller than expected. The second type of complex line is when you take an intentionally weaker line to rep a medium or low strength hand, as we discussed briefly in Chapter 2.

Attitude toward complexity is a measure of how your opponent perceives those complex lines. Most medium-level players tend to over-believe complex lines, precisely because they don't appear like straightforward bluffing lines and are rarely utilized at lower stakes. In the highest level games, interspersing lines of various complexity is much more common, and the dynamics of line complexity becomes dense, mature, and nuanced. At lower stakes, however, you will find that opponents tend to either over-believe or under-believe lines of high complexity—a psychological tendency which can be generalized throughout their game.

Over-believing or under-believing lines of high complexity also tends to be correlated with beliefs about other people's intelligence. Under-believers tend to view people as generally intelligent, while over-believers view people as generally not very intelligent. The former is likely the kind of player who is going to level himself frequently, convincing himself that people are doing all sorts of things that they aren't. As a result, you should be especially wary of trying to run complicated bluffs on these players.

Image and momentum sensitivity is, just as it sounds, how reactive a person is to their image and to the momentum of the match. For example, somebody who is highly sensitive to image will tighten up significantly after losing a big pot (since he thinks you will infer that he's likely to start tilting and trying to get even). Somebody who is less sensitive to image and momentum will be more likely to continue to play aggressively after losing a big pot, either because he's unaware or not paying attention to his image, or because he thinks that you respect him enough that he does not need to react straightforwardly to a bad image.

Finally, **attachment to investment** is a measure of how much he gets attached to investments he's already made. Somebody who has a high attachment toward investment is going to engage in loss-chasing behavior, will have trouble folding strong hands when the board changes, is often going to pre-decide whether he's going to bluff in spots, and is less reactive to disqualifying information. This person will often get stuck on the belief that "they deserve" a pot, and will end up making questionable plays to try to claim it. This is a dimension on which emotionally stronger players will be low, and bad and tilty players will be high.

Players who are playing above their rolls will tend to have high attachment to investment, even though they have low risk-taking behavior. That is, even though they will be overly cautious among the spots they choose, when thcy do choose a spot, they will overcommit to pots they invest in, due to how valuable each individual pot becomes to them. This means that, generally, once an under-rolled player shows significant investment in a pot, you should bc more cautious to bluff.

By observing each of these psychological dimensions in your opponent, you can make strong inferences to a spot that you have never seen before.

For example, say you know your opponent is risk-prone, over-believes complexity, is insensitive to image, and is highly attached to investments. Right after losing a big pot, you see him shove a river trying to represent a runner runner straight. What inferences can you make?

First, he's willing to try risky plays. Second, he likely doesn't think you're terribly intelligent. Third, he's not likely to tighten up or react appropriately after losing a big pot. Finally, he gets attached to pots and doesn't give them up easily. Even though this shove might be an abnormal bluffing spot for your standard model, the inferences from our psychological profile suggest to us that this is a spot where we can reasonably make a call against this opponent.

Levels of Leveling

Before we can go any further in our analysis of mental models, there is an important concept that we have to explore: **leveling**.

There is probably no word in the poker vocabulary that is more misused, misappropriated, and misunderstood than leveling. People use leveling to justify all sorts of horrendous plays, and to explain away all sorts of complex phenomena. In poker culture, it has evolved into a colloquialism for "tricking someone." The word has become so vague that in order to make sense of leveling, we must define its limitations very clearly.

Leveling is misunderstood due in part to the linguistic implications of the word. When we talk about "levels," especially as someone being on a "higher level", our metaphorical language is distinctly vertical. You might imagine someone on a lower level as being on the ground, someone on a higher level as being in the sky, and even higher than that, a level above the clouds, and so on and on, like the rising layers of the atmosphere. It's not explicitly stated this way, but this is the metaphorical implication from way the word is used. We imagine great poker players as playing on such fantastically "high levels" that it would be impossible for us to fathom what was going on between them so high up.

But what is a level exactly? Let's be obvious here. When we choose one "level," what we're really choosing is one action, or strategy. When our opponent tries to counter our strategy, the level "above that" is what counters their counterstrategy. The level "above that" is the strategy that counters their counterstrategy against our counterstrategy. And above that?

Actually, there is nothing above that.

Let's take an example. Say a drawy board runs out flat, like 4♥9♥7♣ 2♣ 2♦. There were tons of draws on this board, but they've now missed. Let's say our opponent has the initiative and has been betting every street, and he's shown us that he's fairly risk-prone and investment-attached. Then level 1 is for us to call our bluffcatchers, since we expect him to bet here. If our opponent guesses that we're likely to conclude that, he might counter what he expects our adjustment to be, and not bluff at all. But if we preempt *this* by consequently calling none of our bluffcatchers, then we've just hit on level 2. Now, say that he has tremendous foresight, and expects us to make this high-level counter, so he switches back to the original strategy to counter this change. That's his level 3. Our level 3 would be to revert back to calling all of our bluffcatchers as well.

Notice, level 3 and level 1 are actually identical strategies. But what's the difference?

The difference is in terms of adaptability. Players who play on level 1 will rarely deviate from their level, or play the leveling game at all. Level 1 play is also typified by the fact that it is the play that most bad players make and requires the least amount of awareness. Level 2 play is defined as a counterstrategy to the level 1 play, which makes it the first level adjustment (i.e., the level 2 play exploits a standard naïve opponent), but using a level 2 play doesn't necessarily imply a flexibility of switching between levels. A level 2 player might only stay on level 2, consistently trying to exploit level 1 players.

So when we say a play is level 3, really what we mean is that it's a *self-aware* level 1, or an adaptable level 1. It is someone resorting to the level 1 play, but with the flexibility and knowledge to be able to switch between different levels as the adjustment game requires. And above that?

It makes no sense to talk about a level above level 3. This is a silly idea, and it betrays the fact that many people don't understand how adjustment games work. As you can see, theoretically there are only two levels, but we choose arbitrarily to define a first level as the level for people who cannot participate in the leveling game. To say that somebody is making a "level 5" play is meaningless. You see, as level 3 is simply a repetition of a level 1 strategy, level 4 would be a repetition of level 2 strategy, level 5 would be another level 1, and so on.

What really happens at level 3 is a free-flow of gameplay through the level 1and level 2 adjustment. A "level 1 player" might never or rarely adjust, and a level 2 player might be said to exploit a level 1 player, and perhaps make a few jerky adjustments, but a level 3 player is fluid, aware, and masterful of how to detect and transition in and out of levels as necessary. In a high-level match, what you will see is interplay between level 1 and level 2.

Above all, it is important to know that the leveling game ends. It does not rise into the air, ascending into infinitely higher and higher levels. It is limited, conquerable—a small arena, when you see it clearly. There is nothing special about a high level player such that you are unable to play the leveling game with him "on his level." Once you attain a basic degree of adaptability, the arena will be open to you, the very same as it is to the strongest of players.

In essence, the leveling game is a guessing game, like rock-paper-scissors. One guesses what level one's opponent will choose, and makes the proper adjustment to that guess. Thus, it is very similar to game flow. If we define skill in game flow as being able to read and predict an opponent's pattern of intentional plays, then analogously, skill in leveling is the ability to predict which pattern of counterstrategies your opponent will choose over a match.

Mistakes of Valuation and Mistakes of Psychology

Despite the pervasiveness of leveling, we don't talk about getting leveled in every spot where we make a losing play. What makes a spot a leveling spot?

Generally speaking, there are two kinds of mistakes in poker: **mistakes of valuation** and **mistakes of psychology**. Valuation is your ability to evaluate the optimal play from a static situation. Mistakes of valuation are therefore choosing suboptimal strategies despite already having all the information. Mistakes of psychology, on the other hand, are mistakes of incorrectly predicting information that is not already available.

A mistake of valuation is generally a failure of your poker theory. If you've made such a mistake, you have not accurately evaluated the ranges, combinatorials, odds, or whatever in making your decision—but all of the necessary information is there. A mistake of psychology is one in which you need to infer more information to make a decision against your opponent, but the inference you've made is poor. This is generally characteristic of a leveling spot.

So if you end up 4-bet/calling off ATo against somebody who's not shoving very wide (and you know his range), that would be a mistake of valuation. But if you call a river overbet on a dry board when your hand is obvious but you think he expects you to fold, and it turns out he has the nuts—we would call this a mistake of psychology, or getting leveled.

So what does it mean when we say things like that an FPSy player "leveled himself"? We can now state more clearly what this means. To level yourself is to mistake valuational spot for a psychological spot, or to mistake a leveling situation for a non-leveling situation. When we say "someone leveled himself," we mean that the right play was obvious, but the player somehow convinced himself to do the opposite (usually, a more psychologically complicated play). The correct way to view and solve the situation was using valuational analysis and frequencies ("his bluffing frequency is high in this spot, so I'll call"), but the player incorrectly tried to splice the hand into a leveling problem, and thus made an overreaching inference.

You could frame the difference this way: a leveling spot is not merely psychological, but also binary. It makes little sense to say his frequency leveled you, or that his overall strategy leveled you. When we talk about leveling, we are taking a *reductionistic* view of poker. We frame the hand as atomic and momentary, and his decision as either X or Y. This is an idea we'll explore more later in this chapter.

For now, let us take leveling for what it is, and use it to probe the next stage of opponent modeling: strategic perception.

The Elements of Strategic Perception

We've developed a psychological profile of our opponent, and we've looked at how leveling works. But to really be able to predict an opponent's behavior, we need to see the game through his eyes. This requires more than merely appreciating large-scale patterns or biases. We need to reconstitute his perception as well—all of the idiosyncrasies of the way he sees the world. This is the next step of opponent modeling, modeling our opponent's **strategic perception**.

Strategic perception is the sum total of how your opponent evaluates various boards, situations, and so on for their strategic potential. Where does your opponent think are good spots to bluff? To valuebet? To checkraise, slowplay? This is different from a psychological profile, which uses wide generalizations. We want instead to use very precise empirical methods to reconstitute our opponent's strategic perceptions. This is where observation skills become of chief importance. We must ensure that no valuable information about our opponents is thrown away unwittingly.

There are two main elements of strategic perception: game flow perception and board texture perception.

Game flow perception is a player's perception of various game flow variations. I.e., how does your opponent tend to interpret two bluffs in a row? How does he think *you'll* interpret two bluffs in a row? After you make a big bluff, does he tend to perceive the next big pot as less likely to be bluff? This boils down in large part to your opponent's standard model of poker players, and also to his own projection bias—if he tends to perceive those game flow variations a certain way, he will usually expect others to do so as well.

Board texture perception is how a player perceives board textures, and the relative weight of each new card to that board. For example, how bad does your opponent think c-betting air is on J♠9♠5♦? Or J♠8♠2♦? Or A♠J♠9♦? How good of a barreling turn card on Q♠8♣4♦ is K♦? Ace? Ten? Four?

Of course, there must be an objective value to each of these boards for the viability for bluffs or semibluffs. By doing some intense combinatorial analysis, you could rank each of these in terms of how good they are to bluff in a vacuum. But that may be beside the point. Everybody learns poker through a different path, and nobody's poker perception is ever perfectly calibrated with mathematics or objective reality. Some people put more or less weight on certain cards, some people are more likely to think they have more fold equity on certain sorts of turns than others, etc. This is a reflection of how poker has idiosyncratically conditioned them.

In order to reconstruct your opponent's board texture perception, you must pay close attention to which sorts of flops, turns, and rivers he likes to attack, and how perceptive he is (or how much faith he has) in various bluffing and semibluffing situations.

Weaker players tend to have naive board texture perception. They tend to be unaware of implied semibluffing, or bluffing opportunities in repping hands that they don't have. They tend to overvalue boards of the highcard-flat-flat nature, such as A♠5♣8♦ or K♦5♠5♣ . They will very rarely consider the possibility of repping turned flush draws or straight draws, or their hand's ability to turn semibluffing opportunities.

When evaluating your opponent's strategic perception, you must also consider the second level—how he perceives your perception. To be attuned to this, you should pay attention to what hands have been shown down, what sort of turns you've attacked thus far, and which ones you've given up on. Your opponent will almost always have a more precise image of you than you have of yourself, but a self-aware player will always have at least some awareness of what sort of boards he's been attacking and what sort of boards he's been going easy on.

As a match progresses and history builds up, it's essential that you engage in these adjustment games—on cards where your image is that you are unlikely to bluff, you must raise your bluffing frequency, and on cards where you have shown frequent bluffs or semibluffs, you must slow down and lower your bluffing frequency. A large chunk of your winrate against a decent opponent will come from these adjustments.

And what about the third level? The third level would be how your opponent thinks about how you perceive *his* strategic perception. That's a mouthful, but it simply means that he's going to be adjusting based on his own image. So for you to think on the third level is to track your opponent's adjustments to his own board texture tendencies. You should be thinking about what boards you've called down on, where he's failed in bluffing you out of pots and is most likely to adjust down, and where you've folded in a lot of spots and thus where he is most likely to adjust upward.

These adjustments must be evaluated with respect to the **equilibrium of semibluffs**. This is the *standard* frequency of semibluffs against which these adjustments are occurring. The standard frequency is likely to not be very exploitable initially. But as psychology, game flow, and individual observations make players start to stray from the equilibrium of semibluffs, their frequencies become more exploitative (and exploitable).

The difficulty in poker is in positively identifying these deviations and delineating them from the chaos of poker—in other words, being able to spot them through the sandstorm of randomness. Your opponent will sometimes get a lot of hands on certain board textures, and though you might assume he's adjusting upward, instead he could just be lucky and getting a lot of hands. Being able to identify the difference between signal and noise is a difficult art, and it's probably one of the least teachable aspects of poker. Indeed, overadjusting or underadjusting in response to random fluctuations is probably the most common mistake that great players will make. But on the whole, a big part of being able to read a true adjustment goes back to the theory of mind. If you can see how mature and intelligent a player is, how perceptive his mind is in other spots throughout his game, and his overall psychological tendencies, this will give you an idea of how likely he is to actually perceive a spot as a point of gameplay and make an adjustment—or not adjust at all.

Tracing the Comfort Zone

There is one last, seldom analyzed concept in opponent modeling that I want to consider. It's most commonly known as your **comfort zone**.

Delineating a player's comfort zone, unlike analyzing his frequencies or psychological patterns, is more of an artistic task. To figure out a player's poker comfort zone is to figure out what a player *feels* about certain situations, or what they *like* within the field of poker. That is to say, there are certain bluffs that simply feel wrong to your opponent, and others that feel right. There are certain styles, strategies, or situations that your opponent enjoys and others he avoids. Reconstructing how your opponent feels about various bluffing and valuebetting situations is a very subtle, but important task.

As you explore the psychology of an opponent and start to really understand him, you are likely to see that there are certain bluffing situations that he consistently won't take, even if it seems that, with his understanding of poker, he should know they are good spots to bluff. This is a good indicator of comfort zone impeding a player's strategy.

Comfort zone is inversely correlated with centrality—the more non-central something is for a player, the farther it's likely to be from his comfort zone. But comfort zones tend to cause a player to resist certain ways of conceiving a hand. For example, some players will be mentally resistant to certain kinds of thin value bets, or bluffing with certain made hands, to trying to bluff their opponents off hands of a certain strength, or even to make a certain sequence of bluffs in a game flow sequence. Even if the situation calls for it, and they might even mentally be able to identify that it's a good play, a competent player with a weak comfort zone might forego making that optimal play. It is thus essential to look for specific types of bluffs that your opponent seems to resist making, or that give him pause. You can use those observations to derive the limits of your opponent's comfort zone.

The Taxonomy of Bluffs

Let's integrate some of the ideas about bluffing we've laid out in the last few chapters. We can say that there are three essential kinds of bluffs in poker: fundamental bluffs, game flow bluffs, and comfort zone bluffs.

A **fundamental bluff** is to bluff somewhere that your opponent doesn't have a lot of hands but you do. In such a spot, your opponent simply can't do much with his range, even if he knows you're bluffing sometimes. A **game flow bluff** is a bluff based on a read that, at this point in game flow, your opponent won't put you on a bluff. A **comfort zone bluff** is a bluff where your opponent's comfort zone will impede him from making a correct call. He might have the hands of sufficient strength to make the call, and game flow might even be working against you, but you have the read that the spot falls out of your opponent's zone of comfort, you can often run very effective bluffs.

Of course, in reality, bluffs aren't neatly divided between these three categories. Most bluffs will work on multiple levels, or may work well on two levels and not as well on the third. But these are merely the three primary ways in which bluffs derive their efficacy.

Incorporating all of our insights, we can come up with a two-part maxim of bluffing:

The maxim of bluffing: Bluffing is the science of knowing where to bluff, and the art of knowing when your opponent will fold.

The first part, the science of knowing where to bluff, is what we discussed in Chapter 2—attacking the structurally weaker parts of your opponent's game and making fundamentally strong bluffs. This part of bluffing is the tactician in you, who studies a blueprint and plans an assault.

The second part, art of knowing when your opponent will fold, is the psychological game—knowing his mental tendencies, his comfort zone, and his grasp of game flow. This allows you to time your bluff when he is likely to believe it and fold; i.e., game flow and comfort zone bluffs. This part of bluffing is the matador in you, the deadly artist, attuned to your senses and the rhythm of action, pulling back the cape at the precise moment. A masterful bluffer must be skilled in both the science and the art of bluffing.

Observational Skills

How do we acquire information at a poker table? This might seem like a simple question, but there's more to it than first appears. Not only is there the problem of gathering information, but we need to sift the noise out of what we receive. Once that noise is eliminated, we must then interpret that information and integrate it into our mental models. Although we do much of this automatically, it's no simple task.

The process begins with the gathering of information. Gathering information, however, means more than merely playing poker and letting stuff happen to you. Think of information gathering as the art of **selective attention**. Human beings are by nature imperfect; we will miss things. Our attention and perception are limited. Because of that, we must decide which elements of a poker match to focus on, and which to ignore. Selective attention, then, is the process of filtering what's *important* out of all the information in a poker match.

People often believe there's something "special" about high-level players that makes them able to gather information better. That their eyes are somehow more vigilant, more piercing. Perhaps they have some innate ability to spot tells, or pick up on subtle patterns better than the rest of us.

This is nonsense. If high level players can notice tendencies more accurately and interpret them better into usable models, it is for two reasons. First, they have had an enormous amount of experience in psychological model-building, which has sharpened their sensitivity and usage of mental models. Second, they have had so much experience that much of the surface-level phenomena of a poker game are relegated to their unconscious mind, leaving their conscious mind free to focus on the psychological game. In other words, it's not that expert poker players "are able to focus on more" but simply that they are already so experienced, they are able to spend their conscious focus on other problems. Their conscious attention is free to look for subtle tells, patterns, and valuable pieces of information, which a weaker player might never have time to notice.

But if you want to improve your observational skills, other than gain experience, what can you actually do? Although brute experience is the most important factor, there are a few other things you can do to actively improve.

The first way to develop your observational skills is to focus. This probably seems too obvious to be worth stating, but remember that being focused can be something you *do*, not simply something you *experience*. Certainly, sometimes you will be focused without having to think about it. But you should not be satisfied with letting your focus as a poker player be decided merely by your internal weather. By reminding yourself to focus on your opponent, where your conscious mind might be either in autopilot or thinking about something else, you can call yourself back to the match at hand. Focus! Say it to yourself, and remember that focusing can be an active and conscious process.

When you are observing your opponent, pay attention to every spot, and try to consciously articulate what that spot tells you about his play. Look at specifics and try to see how they fit into the overall pattern of his tendencies. Again, this does not happen automatically, except very weakly. Force yourself to actively and thoroughly process all of the information you're receiving—about his psychology, betting patterns, etc. Notice it, interpret it, and update your mental model of your opponent.

One of the best ways to do this is by talking through it (either aloud, or in your head). For example, if you see someone checking back lots of draws on the turn, tell yourself "he is checking back lots of draws on this turn, which means he's fairly risk-averse, he's not semi-bluffing much, and his range is strongly weighted toward value. I should be willing to put him on draws by the river." Obviously, you're not always going to have a great deal of inferences to make from any one hand. But it's important to remind yourself of your evidence for your reads, rather than merely repeating them to yourself continually. The more conscious and evidence-based your reads are, the more you'll able to overcome natural cognitive biases. Not only that, but going over your inferences consciously and explicitly will imprint them more powerfully into your mind, making it more likely that you will notice, remember, and act in accordance with these observations.

When playing online, you should always use note-taking to supplement your observations. The art of note-taking is highly subjective, and different things work for different people. It really doesn't matter so much *how* you note-take. What is important is that you take notes often, consistently, and that you use your notes effectively.

Ideally, your notes should mostly be doing one of these four things:

1) Noting a significant event in your history, such as "he called down XYZ board with bottom pair"

2) Note a psychological read, such as "likes to bluff twice in a row" or "very risk-averse"

3) Note a bet-sizing read, such as "overbets his flushes on river"

4) A note to yourself on how you want to adjust against him, such as "when you get a flush, bet small because he likes to raise small bets"

Remember, the value of your notes is not just in pulling them up and reading them when you feel lost or have forgotten your reads. A large part of why note-taking is so valuable is because it strengthens your mental impressions in the first place and makes them easier to remember. The process of continually taking notes will make you remember your reads better, even if

94

you never open the notes again. That's not to say you shouldn't use your notes—you absolutely should. But the mere habit of note-taking will make your conscious mind more attentive to your opponent as you're playing—so if you don't take notes, start now.

Despite all this, perhaps you've noticed that many great players seem to have amazing observational skills, but are often unable to articulate "how they know" what they read into their opponents. If you press them—how did you make that read?—they will shrug their shoulders, and say that they just knew. Again, there is nothing special about these players. They are not idiot-savants. They simply have relegated most of their observation skills to their unconscious, rather than their conscious mind. Their automatic brain has been trained into evaluating, synthesizing, and reconstructing their opponents.

I will have more to say on this in the next chapter, but as admirable as it is to have powerful subconscious skills, it's not something that you can count on acquiring. You have no direct control over your subconscious conception of your opponent. All you can do is pay attention to him, and use the conscious skills at your disposal to break down your opponent—through self-talk, actively exploring and reformulating his theory of mind, taking notes, and deliberately working through your sequence of inferences. If you do this often and consistently enough, slowly over time this process will become automated in your unconscious mind as well.

Make poker about your opponent. Subsume yourself in him. Breathe his air. Watch him, learn from him, prod and interrogate his strengths and weaknesses, his beliefs and fears. Only then will you be able to understand him, and, with a little luck, predict his actions. In the end, there is no greater feeling in poker than attaining true mastery over an opponent's mind.

A Primer on Stats

One of the biggest revolutions in the theory and understanding of poker has come from the introduction of HUDs and comprehensive statistics into online poker. Whether you think on the whole they are good or bad, they have changed the way that we conceptualize and interact with the game. If you are playing online, HUDs are indispensable tools. Let's take a look at stats and how to utilize them in playing the adjustment game.

HUDs and stats, of course, are not synonymous. Stats are discrete, mathematical representations of frequencies in poker; HUDs are merely the common way to display them. Although stats were never explicitly accessible in the days before HUDs existed, stats always *existed*. Without HUDs they were simply apprehended less accurately, subject to more sway by cognitive biases, and with greater lossiness or corruption due to inattention and failure of memory.

Moreover, our brains are not designed to process precise ratios, so somebody with a 7% and an 11% frequency might seem the same to your intuition, but they may mean markedly different things about somebody's range. When we don't have stats, the only way you can perceive anything like frequencies or opening ranges is through your intuitive impressions (and some information from showdowns). One of the reasons stats are so valuable is that they allow us to overcome our inexact cognitive machinery, and more accurately perceive our opponents. Most of us who use HUDs have been trained so that even if we even think somebody is really aggressive or loose, if his stats say he is not, then we trust the stats over our own intuition (since single, salient events tend to influence our intuition more than they should). Stats, then, are like a corrective lens on our poker perception.

In live poker, on the other hand, the only way to gather information is through intuition and observation. But again, even in live poker, stats exist; they are simply not explicitly accessible. It doesn't matter whether your conception of stats comes from a HUD or your intuition about how aggressive somebody's been at the table—adjustments based on stats are inherently effective due to the structure of poker.

First, a word on **adjustment schemas**. An adjustment schema is a codified system by which a player will exploit or react to certain stats. Different players use different adjustment schemas, and there is often more than one way to exploit a behavior.

I will be outlining for you a basic adjustment schema for some of the most vital stats in a ring game. Your adjustment schema need not necessarily follow this exactly, and it will likely be influenced by your particular style or preferences. But this basic schema is a good starting point.

Preflop Stats

First off, we want to conceptualize the adjustment game as beginning from preflop, and moving forward street by street. Preflop, there are a few main stats of importance— **VPIP** (voluntarily put money in the pot), **PFR** (preflop raise), **3-bet, fold to 3-bet**, and **4-bet**. Note, when I say somebody is "too loose" or "too tight," this should be interpreted with respect to the average player—your standard model. Slight deviations are irrelevant, so only make these adjustments when the deviations are significant.

♦ *If somebody is too loose preflop with VPIP and PFR*: in a shorthanded game, there are a few ways to exploit this. You can either 3-bet him frequently, call him more in position and put pressure on him postflop, or both. In heads up, an opponent with a high VPIP or PFR on the button is normal and not particularly exploitable, but if they have a high VPIP from out of position, then you can exploit this by simply betting a lot on flops and turns (chances are, there is little you need to do to exploit them if they're doing this, since they'll be hemorrhaging money to you by folding too many flops). If they are loose and attacking lots of flops, then it may be better for you to tighten up your open range a little bit, but you must always apply pressure on flops and turns. Ranges simply get wider and more aggressive, but being in position should make you come out ahead.

♦ *If somebody is too tight preflop with VPIP and PFR*: here, you should be winning automatically by having a good preflop raising range. Against somebody who's very tight, you're simply winning more blinds than he is, and that will add up in the long run. In the meanwhile, just play accordingly tight to his raises, fold more of the hands you'd call normally, and respect his flop bets more.

♦ *If somebody 3-bets too much*: in a shorthanded game, we can either 4-bet him more liberally, start calling him more often in position, or both.

Note, however, that 4-betting him more is an **inherent counter**, but calling him is a **potential counter**, meaning that if you call him in position, but you do not follow through on a proper exploitative strategy afterward, you will simply lose money. In order for a potential counter to be effective, you must enact later elements of the counter as well, which include floating bets in position, bluff-raising flops, and calling down more medium strength hands.

In heads up, the answer to an aggressive 3-bettor is essentially the same: 4-bet more and call more, but with the caveat that this adjustment game is much more important in heads up games, since 3-bet pots are a bigger proportion of the hands played heads up.

♦ *If somebody has too low of a 3-bet*: against this player, simply fold more to their 3-bets and give them more respect. Like in playing someone with a too tight VPIP/PFR, simply having a normal and healthy 3-betting frequency of your own will make you win in the long run.

♦ *If somebody has too high of a fold to 3-bet*: obviously, 3-bet this person often.

♦ *If somebody has too low of a fold to 3-bet*: when someone's folding to too few 3-bets, the best adjustment is usually contingent on how passive they are postflop. If they are very capable, floaty, and aggressive postflop, then it is often best simply to tighten up your 3-bets. But if they are more passive, then it is fine to continue to 3-bet a normal or even wider than normal range against this person, and simply take down lots of pots with flop and turn c-bets. Against weak or passive players who fold too little to 3-bets, taking down uncontested 3-bet pots with c-bets is one of the biggest edges you are going to have in a match.

♦ *If somebody 4-bets too much:* the adjustment to this player depends on whether he's actually widening his 4-bet/calling range, or if he's keeping his 4-bet/call range constant. Some players will simply 4-bet a higher frequency without widening their 4-bet/calling range to include weaker hands like AJ or medium pairs. If this is the case, then simply 5-betting wider is the ideal adjustment. If your opponent is widening his 4-bet/calling range, then calling more 4-bets and facing off postflop becomes a better play (5-betting is the inherent counter, and calling 4-bets is the potential counter). And of course, if somebody is 4-betting you a great deal then it's often a good idea to lower your 3-betting frequency.

♦ *If somebody 4-bets too little*: against this player, just 3-bet to your heart's content.

Postflop Stats

Next, let's look at primary postflop stats—**continuation bet, checkraise, fold to checkraise,** and **fold to bet** (OOP—out of position).

♦ *If somebody continuation bets too frequently:* against a frequent c-bettor, there are three primary adjustments. The first adjustment is to checkraise more often, the second adjustment is to call them with weaker hands (ace highs, low pairs, etc.), and the third adjustment is to float them more often. Obviously, floating is a potential counter, and must be done intelligently to be effective.

Note, contrary to what some players seem to believe, leading a wider range OOP is not a counter to a high c-betting frequency. An OOP leading range does not counter anything, other than somebody who is really bad at dealing with OOP leads (which is fine, but is irrelevant to their 3-betting frequency). Leading OOP simply circumvents the c-betting game by creating a different dynamic. While I have nothing against OOP leading, if you are OOP leading in response to frequent c-bettors, then you are mistaking a circumvention for an actual adjustment, and there is a good chance you will increase your EV by simply letting him c-bet, and then exploiting it.

♦ *If somebody continuation bets too infrequently:* this can be tricky. Against a good player, then there may not be a lot that you can explicitly do to exploit this, if he is well balanced and intelligent in how he arranges his handrange on the flop and turn. But against a weaker player, you can very easily exploit his passivity by simply winning far more pots than he will. Call wider preflop (since you get 4 cards for free more often), and lead out more turns. Respect this player's c-bets and checkraise him less. Against a weaker player of this type, I also strongly encourage lots of OOP leading—not because it exploits infrequent c-betting, but because such a passive strategy indicates a risk-averse psychological profile, and such a player is likely to respond poorly to OOP leads.

♦ *If somebody checkraises too frequently:* against a frequent checkraiser, you should lower your flop c-bet frequency. Check back more weak hands (both air and vulnerable low pair type hands), 3-bet his checkraises more often with both value and bluffs, and float some of his checkraises. As usual, floating is merely a potential counter, so you must play aggressively on the turn as well, or double float occasionally.

♦ *If somebody checkraises too infrequently:* this can be tricky, and often depends on other factors. If somebody is checkraising infrequently and calling your c-bets a lot, that means that he is floating you a lot out of position, and calling lots of high card hands. Against this, you can simply increase your turn and river barreling frequency. If he is checkraising infrequently but folding a normal or slightly less than normal amount, then it's likely that he's slowplaying strong hands that other players would be checkraising with, so be wary of this on later streets. If he's checkraising infrequently and folding often, then he's just burning money, so you don't need to do anything other than c-bet a lot.

♦ *If somebody folds to checkraises too frequently:* Checkraise him aggressively. This is one of the most straightforwardly profitable kinds of opponents to play against.

♦ *If somebody folds to checkraises too infrequently:* Checkraise this player with a tighter range that's weighted more toward value hands. When you do checkraise, barrel more turns and rivers, especially when draws hit, since he's going to be floating you more or simply arriving with weaker hands. Against a passive player who is going to fold flimsy hands under pressure easily, you may even elect to checkraise a standard frequency. If he's spewing money by folding lots of turns with bottom pairs or other garbage hands, this can also be quite a profitable strategy.

♦ *If somebody folds to bets OOP too frequently:* Lead a lot OOP with bluffs.

♦ *If somebody folds to bets OOP too infrequently:* Don't lead much OOP without a hand.

As hands move into the turn and river, they do get more complex, and more interconnections develop between different stages of a hand (i.e., how was he playing his draws before getting here? What sorts of hands was he using to bluff with on the flop? Where is he allocating most of his value hands?). You must holistically analyze his handranges, and figure out which hands your opponent can and can't have based on the structure of his game. But the principles of adjustment in postflop play will remain largely the same.

The Power of Momentous Aggression

So we've constructed a basic hierarchy of stats for interpreting the adjustment game. If you think about it, the adjustment game is just the shifting of frequencies, the dance of strategies waxing and waning in reaction to each another. But there is an aspect of poker that goes beyond the adjustment game.

Recall how, in our discussion of game flow, we said that a frequency can be understood as a single large-scale strategy, but it can also be atomized—subdivided into individual parts. We can look at a frequency and say it's 33%, but we can also look at a frequency and see it as a run of game flow strings.

The adjustment game works in the same way. There are some parts of the adjustment game that hinge solely on stats and large-scale strategy. That is, there are certain spots where we are making **range-based decisions**, decisions justified solely by large-scale or range-based reasoning.

For example, say that after c-betting, you pick up a nut flush draw on the turn. This is a spot where semibluffing the turn does not hinge on psychology. This bet is relegated to a purely stats-based, or range-based justification. You bet here because he'll fold enough, and you'll make enough nut hands on the river, and so on. Psychology never comes into it.

You will find that the vast majority of poker is composed of range-based decisions. Even sometimes a big call on the river, or a checkraise big bluff doesn't ever really congeal into a "psychological moment"—they are plays you merely make because you can mathematically justify them.

But what about the times when you can't? What about the times when your range-based abstractions fall short? When you truly don't know what's going to happen?

Recall what we said before about comfort zones. A player's comfort zone is the circle of plays that your opponent feels as being "good" or "solid." His comfort zone is comprised of the set of moves that he feels are readily available to him.

Part of your job as a poker player is to figure out the circle he has drawn, and then to step outside of it. After all, if certain plays are outside of your opponent's comfort zone, what that really means is that *he genuinely doesn't see them as options*. His schema of poker precludes him from doing those things. Figure out how your opponent's poker schema is limiting him. Then, when you push him somewhere where he's not willing to go, he will not follow you.

This leads us to the idea of **momentous aggression**. Momentous aggression is not merely being aggressive, or raising and betting a lot. It is not a matter of frequency. It is something more.

To make a range-based decision is to fight with your range, to construct an optimal frequency. It is a centralized, planned method of attack. But a momentous decision is a fixed, momentary event. It is deciding that your opponent has one hand, one state of mind, and trying to completely, in one hand, outplay him.

You could say that this momentous decision is thinking from hand-to-hand, but that's not quite it. To play a hand momentously is, in a philosophical sense, to face the moment as singular, rather than merely a cog in a larger match. It is to arrest the gears of the mind, to stop all the other action. When the spot you face is big enough, deep enough, and non-central enough, and the bet he's made is staring you in the face, it is no longer enough to say "I can choose a better spot," or "that's a fundamentally bad play, whatever he has." Deferrals and excuses ring empty. Your opponent has forced you to a decision that cannot be sidestepped. Of course, it might be a decision for all your chips, but it's even more than that. It's a situation where you must put the full resolve of your mind behind one decision.

Ordinary aggressive players may force you to play lots of large pots, but a great player will force you to make momentous decisions. This species of aggression is more ferocious than trying to win a lot of pots. Some aggressive players may be tenacious, but can be dispatched easily with some large-scale adjustments. Momentous aggression is different. Against a great player, you will feel as though you're not allowed to make a mistake. You cannot run or turn away. Every clash is a test. Every punch must be absorbed or countered.

What does he have?—What does he think I'm going to do?—The world telescopes into one ponderous moment, and the action is on you. Momentous aggression culminates in those big, time-frozen, everything-on-you-at-once moments. It is the pinnacle of psychological warfare.

In a sense, you cannot aim to *use* momentous aggression. You can only aim to make smart, powerful bluffs. But if done skillfully, enough smart and powerful bluffs will congeal into that feeling of momentousness. That is how one becomes a fearsome opponent—by making one good, thoughtful bluff at a time.

This concludes our analysis of opponent psychology. We've examined much of poker from the outside, but now it is time for us to turn inwards. Most of us have spent all our lives trying to understand other people. Just by playing poker, you will figure out what makes other people tick; figuring them out is just a matter of time and effort. But coming to understand yourself—this is something that most people never achieve in their lifetime. And it is self-understanding that we turn to next.

5

Cognition and Self-Awareness

Whether he likes it or not, a man's character is stripped at the poker table; if the other players read him better than he does, he has only himself to blame. Unless he is both able and prepared to see himself as others do, flaws and all, he will be a loser in cards, as in life.

Anthony Holden

In Plato's *Phaedrus*, Socrates recounts his allegory of the charioteer. According to Socrates, man's soul is seated at the head of a chariot, driven by two winged horses. The first is a white horse, "whose breed and character are noble"—it represents Reason, or Rationality. The second, a black horse, is the opposite, brash and temperamental. This horse represents Passion, or Emotion. The two horses are locked in an eternal struggle, each pulling the chariot in their own direction, while we as the charioteer are stuck refereeing between them.

It has long been believed that that reason and emotion are fundamentally opposed. In fact, this idea predates even Plato. But is it right? Is emotion the opposite of reason?

I'm going to show you that the common dichotomy between reason and emotion is the wrong one to make. Their relationship is more complex than one of diametric opposition.

In poker, at least, it's clear that reason is our goal. We want to obey the noble horse, to let it head our chariot. But what deters us from that path is not emotion, as Plato suggests, but rather irrationality.

Our struggle is not against emotion at all. I say instead, *poker is the battle against human irrationality.* You will see exactly what I mean by this over the next two chapters, as we explore the mind and constitution of a poker player.

But we cannot wage war against irrationality unless we understand our enemy. So we begin by delving into how our brains work and how our mental processes define our interactions with poker.

Neuroscience for Donkeys

We are going to start by looking at the basics of how the brain functions. Don't worry—it's not going to get overly technical. But it's really important that we understand how our brain interfaces with poker, so I'll give you the cursory framework of what you need to know.

The basic unit of the brain is the **neuron**. Each neuron is connected to other neurons through large networks, known as **neuronal networks**. These networks are formed by many individual neurons forging inter-connections, each of which can be either strengthened or weakened by how the neurons signal to each other. Two neurons can become strongly connected through frequent signaling, forming increasingly complex neuronal networks. Simply put, neurons that fire together, wire together.

This strengthening and weakening of neuronal connections emerges in high-level behavior as **conditioning**. In animal conditioning, we can actually see the footprint of neuronal networks very clearly . There are two main forms of conditioning:

classical conditioning, when two stimuli are mentally associated with another, creating an expectation or reflex (such as a dog salivating when the food bell rings), and **operant conditioning**, when the behavior's consequence, positive or negative, reinforces or inhibits that behavior (punishing a dog for chewing up your carpet, or rewarding him for kneeling). Conditioning is one of the basic ways in which animals—including humans—learn complex behaviors.

Not all neuronal networks or systems of behavior are created or learned from scratch, however. Some parts of our brain are highly **plastic** and therefore very changeable in structure; they will learn whatever you throw their way. Other parts of your brain are built with assigned functions, which exist in essentially pre-programmed **modules** of the brain. For example, the regulation of your internal organs, your sensory perception, and your survival instincts all come without having to be learned.

Now, let's zoom out and look at **cognition**—a fancy word for thinking. Cognition is great, but it comes out of the box with some bugs. We all sometimes have errors in our thinking. There are two main forms of cognitive errors we must be aware of: **learned errors**, and pre-cognitive or **inherent errors**. Learned errors are generally easy to fix, since they've been learned at some point, so they can be un-learned by the very same neuronal mechanisms of reinforcement and inhibition. Inherent errors, on the other hand, are trickier. Inherent errors are often embedded deep in the coding of our cognitive modules. It's like having glitchy hardware—we can't really fix it, since it's built into our machinery. These inherent (and largely universal) errors are also called **cognitive biases**. We'll explore them in great detail soon.

As we move forward and talk about learning, cognition, emotion, and strengthening and extinguishing habits, it is vitally important that you keep these building blocks of the brain in mind. Almost all of the vastness of human experience, intelligence, and creativity comes just from neurons firing, signaling each other, strengthening and inhibiting their mutual interconnections.

This is also where all of poker comes from. The game of poker, after all, is not simply a game played with 52 cards on a

108

board—it is a game played among humans. We are part of the game of poker as it is actually played. The game does not end with the cards. The game extends past the table, and continues into our brains. To understand poker, you must understand the way *we* operate, the way that we think, reason, bargain, and often, fail.

Of course, that's not to say that, as poker players, we can meaningfully reduce cognition to mere neurons firing (to say nothing of neuroscience itself). But nevertheless, these concepts will help you to make sense of the patterns and logic that underlie our cognitive functioning. Despite its richness and complexity, what is composed of neurons must be understood and treated in light of that composition.

A Divided Brain

A poker player must understand both their conscious mind and unconscious mind. The concept of the unconscious still carries unfortunate baggage from intellectual history; it is almost impossible to ignore the aftermath of Freud. Thanks to him, the term "unconscious" has become loaded with notions of repression, secret motivations, lust for family members, fear of castration, and a host of other pseudoscientific sensationalisms. Though modern psychology has largely repudiated Freud as scientifically dubious, the unconscious mind that he originally proposed is nevertheless very real and relevant, albeit in a different way than he imagined it.

Defining consciousness is notoriously difficult, but there's no need to get lost in the bogs of language and philosophy here. Let's simply say that the conscious mind is the part of your mind that you are *aware of,* and *over which you have direct control.* The unconscious mind, then, is the part of your mind of which you are, at most, tangentially aware, over which you have no direct control, and which governs your automatic processes, actions, and thoughts.

Most people are completely misguided in how they believe their minds work. Admittedly, that's probably fine; the details of cognition don't affect people very much in their day-to-day lives. But as a poker player, your brain is the final interface between yourself and the game, and your brain is also the central obstacle that will impede your progress. It is essential that you come to terms with its idiosyncrasies and its weaknesses.

The first essential truth about the brain is this: *the mind is not one continuous thing*. It is disparate, composed of many different parts, separated not just in space, but also in circuitry. Your conscious mind and its constructs comprise only one element out of many in your mental circuitboard.

There are a number of classical psychological experiments that demonstrate this disparateness of the brain.

Severing the corpus callosum, the bridge between the two hemispheres of the brain, was once the last-ditch treatment for intractable epilepsy (and is still performed in rare cases). When scientists observed their surviving subjects, they revealed very dramatic changes. For these "split-brain" patients, when an image was shown to their left eye only, the patient was unable to say what he or she was seeing. This is because the left eye's visual field is processed in the right hemisphere of the brain, but the speech-control center is located in the left hemisphere of the brain. Severing the corpus callosum cut off communication between the two sides of the brain, so the patient could recognize but could no longer *name* the object he or she was seeing. When asked to pick up and manipulate it, the patient was able to do so. The patient could *handle* the object perfectly, but could not say its name when it was located in the left visual field. Once the object moved to the patient's right visual field, which is controlled by the left hemisphere, the patient could then name it perfectly.

Another example is in blindsight. Blindsight is a rare neurological disorder that occurs in subjects who have had damage to their primary visual cortex. Subjects with blindsight believe that

110

they are blind. They claim to have no conscious experience of vision. However, when presented with an object in their visual field and told to *guess* its location or movement, even though they will insist that they have no awareness of the object, they will wind up making extremely accurate guesses. This is a striking finding. It suggests that the connection between their visual apparatus and their consciousness has been severed, but their unconscious brain is still processing and responding to visual information. Patients with blindsight can also competently manipulate and grab objects that they claim to be visually unaware of.

This is only the tip of the iceberg. Although much experimentation on functioning human brains is impossible (that is, unethical), we have learned a great deal about the architecture of the brain through incidental experiments—the accumulation of accidents and injuries that have befallen people. After enough time and observation, we have records of at least one patient at some point in medical literature who has had their brain damaged in every imaginably specific way. By seeing how somebody who has had only one or another segment of their brain damaged, and then seeing how that in turn affects their behavior, we have gained great insights into the functioning of the brain and its modularity (that is, how different parts control different highly specialized functions).

Telling examples of this are in aphasias—impairments in language processing. For example, Broca's aphasia is a condition in which a subject can understand the meanings of individual words, but is unable to form and comprehend sentences. This occurs from damage to a very specific module of the brain. And then there's Wernicke's aphasia, in which the subject can speak perfectly, but becomes unable to make sense of any written or spoken language from other people. These disorders demonstrate how highly specialized areas of the brain can be, even in something as seemingly complex as language.

The more we learn about the brain, the more we realize how fragmented it is. Evolutionary biology sheds even more light on this, showing how our brains developed out of reptilian and neo-mammalian brain architecture. The neo-cortex—the seat of consciousness, cognition, and "rationality"—is the newest addition to our brain structure. But much of our movement, behavior, and so on is already regulated by older, non-conscious structures of our brain. Consciousness is a late-comer. For pre-human mammals and proto-humans, chances are, consciousness was a byproduct that played a smaller role in their brain processes than it does for us Homo sapiens.

So what is consciousness? Consciousness is this newly arisen faculty in your mammalian brain. Centralized in your neo-cortex, it is continuously synthesizing your sense perceptions, your emotions, your memory and your cognition into one seamless experience. That's what consciousness is.

And certainly, consciousness proves to be an effective flashlight on the external world (and perhaps an abacus as well). But why should you assume it can play the same role on your internal world as well? Consider this question seriously. Why should you assume that consciousness is designed to perceive the vast unconscious circuitry of your brain?

In fact, what little of the rest of your brain your consciousness actually perceives, it filters through its own concepts and frameworks. Evolutionarily, there is little need for any more than that. While consciousness is chugging away, the rest of your brain is involved in all manner of complex neuronal activity, in the hurried business of keeping you alive and functioning.

Here is the second essential truth about the brain: the conscious mind does not have access to all parts of the brain. And this is not due to some failure on our own part—ignorance, lack of self-reflection, or anything of the sort. In reality, we are not aware of the rest of our brain *by virtue of the architecture of the brain itself.* It is not our fault; it simply is the way it is.

We feel like our conscious selves must be "who we are." Our conscious experiences are negotiated primarily through our neo-cortex, but in fact, our brain is comprised of many more elements than merely the conscious part. And thus, by extension, we are ourselves much more than our conscious minds.

The Conscious Fallacy

One of the greatest mistakes that a thinker can make is to commit **the conscious fallacy**. The conscious fallacy is the assumption that consciousness will be there in the future to catch you. The conscious fallacy begins by mistakenly equating yourself with your conscious mind. You then assume that after you form a conscious intention, when it comes time to execute that intention, since of course you are still yourself, you will resume the level of consciousness you had when you formed the intention. To commit the conscious fallacy is to misunderstand the nature of our mental life—in truth, most of our lives are navigated unconsciously.

Am I suggesting that we spend our lives in a walking daze, not consciously connected to the reality around us? Actually, this is not far from the truth.

Most people believe in some form of the mind-body divide. They believe that a person is a mind, or soul, inhabiting and controlling a body—the proverbial "ghost in the shell." If this were true, it would certainly suggest that you are continuously in control, and thus any mental failing would be attributable to your personal agency. But we know that it's not that simple. If you want to identify your self as your *conscious* self, then in reality, "you" are only one among numerous participants in your mental life.

In other words, to take full account of "yourself," you must consider the unconscious elements of your mind as part of that totality.

Have you ever told yourself you were going to do something in the future, and felt completely sure you were going to do it—yet when the moment came, you didn't follow through? An obvious example: say you tilt off a lot of money, and in the aftermath of your session, you tell yourself, "The next time that I'm down 4 buyins, I'm going to quit my session immediately. No exceptions." You feel completely sure, with all the resolve of your mind, that you will do this. After all, you are in control of yourself, and you *want* to do it. Why wouldn't you? But of course, when that moment next comes a week later, you keep playing past four buyins and tilt again.

This is the conscious fallacy. You presume that, because your conscious mind is dominating your mental life in that moment, it will also dominate at future points in time. In reality, there's no reason for that to be the case—especially so if you're tilting, which is when your limbic system (your unconscious emotional circuitry) is agitated.

So how do you overcome the conscious fallacy? The answer is simple. You must recognize that having full conscious command of your faculties is not the norm, but the *exception* in human life, and to *plan* for that.

This sort of thing happens not just in poker. It occurs in every facet of your life. Again and again, you expect things of yourself, believing deep down in some kind of continuous agency, some deep belief that "you" are really in control. But the truth, which you have hopefully learned by now, is that your conscious mind is not enough. Not that *your* conscious mind isn't strong enough; but more specifically, that the conscious mind *in and of itself* is not strong enough. It is not a matter of willpower, or "mind over matter." You are biologically, neuronally, electrochemically constrained. Your conscious mind is not running the show, no matter how much it's convinced that it is.

This sounds rather pessimistic, doesn't it? It kind of sounds like there's little we can do. How do we progress from such a fatalistic premise?

The Ghost of the Ghost

Perhaps you accept all this, but you're not satisfied with simply ceding your control. That's good. You shouldn't be satisfied. Do you want to improve at poker? Do you want to be the best? Then you must take hold of the mantle, in spite of these facts. Abandon, as much as you can, your sense of identity with your conscious mind. You are not just your conscious mind. You are *your entire mind*—your conscious mind is only your trusted emissary and negotiator. Your goal is to condition your unconscious mind through whatever means available, in order to cultivate your abilities as a poker player.

This training and conditioning is *led* by the conscious mind. After all, the conscious mind is the only part of yourself over which you have meaningful control. But ironically, although it is very good at helping you to change your immediate environment, *your conscious mind is not very good at altering your unconscious mind.*

Hopes, desires, and expectations are all lovely things to have, but your unconscious mind doesn't care about them, or might even be oblivious to them. The neuronal networks of your unconscious are going to sit there and keep doing their own thing, largely un-phased by your conscious goals.

We're in something of a catch-22. Our conscious mind wants us to change, but our conscious mind can't change us; it's only good at changing external things. This is the essence of the conscious fallacy; it is mistaking the conscious mind's ability to act on external objects as an ability to affect the unconscious mind.

So in a sense, we cannot affect ourselves directly, yet we still want to be our own masters. So what do we do? We circumvent the entire system.

Instead of expecting your conscious thoughts alone to change your unconscious mind, you must be circuitous. By co-opting your *environment*, which you *can* change, you can use the environment to train your unconscious mind in the direction of how you want to alter it. Thus, your conscious self-development, in poker just as with everything else, must be mediated through the environment. Create the *environment* that cultivates your growth, and you will grow. Merely trying to consciously strong-arm that growth yourself will usually result in failure.

The "ghost in the shell" metaphor is not a bad one. But like all ghosts, consciousness is not visible all the time—it only comes out at odd hours, when the conditions are just right. By creating an environment that reinforces our goals, we can create an emissary for our conscious intentions—a ghost of the ghost, which lives on when our conscious mind disappears, continuing to influence and mold the animal circuitry of our unconscious.

The first step, then, is to consciously change your environment to encourage your growth. The second step is to try to understand your entire mind-system—not merely your conscious mind (which is immediately accessible through introspection), but your unconscious mind as well. You must honestly and unflinchingly survey your unconscious habits, tendencies, fears, and all your deepest weaknesses as a poker player.

The Limits of Reason

You may have noticed the suspicion with which I use terms like "rationality" and "reason." It is an old cliché that human beings are exemplars of Rationality, the stewards of Reason. This idea can be traced back to the Enlightenment. By now, that optimism has become outdated. The accumulation of psychological research over the last 150 years has shown us just how far from "rational" human beings really are.

Let's look at this from an evolutionary-psychological perspective. Rather than assume, as philosophers in the 19th century did, that the human brain is the ideal implementation of rationality, let's instead think of the brain as having evolved to fulfill an evolutionary need. What we should expect from the brain is not necessarily rationality in and of itself, but *whatever would help us best survive.*

If the brain evolved to help us survive in the environments that primitive humans inhabited, then it should come as no surprise that the brain only became good at the things it needed to be good at. Why would primates in the jungles or savannah need to evolve brains that could accurately process things like probabilities?

We must take our brains for what they are and accept that, as tools for reasoning, they are *inherently* flawed. Our brains tend toward errors, and in poker, those errors can be our downfall. The only way to avoid them is to inform ourselves and try to overcome them through conscious oversight of our mental life.

When it comes to the limitations of cognition, there are two big ideas. The first is **bounded rationality**. Bounded rationality is the idea that human rationality is constrained by three factors: the *information* available to a person, the *processing limitations* of their brain, and the *amount of time* available to them in making a decision. Although we can imagine some ideal Rationality, which takes into account all the possible factors, weighs and processes them perfectly, and indifferently applies inferences to choose the best option—human beings don't do that. We cannot do that. "True" rationality is a fantasy, at least for us humans. The best we can do is a partial version of rationality, as approximated by our mental machinery and time constraints.

The second notion, one we've already encountered, is the **cognitive bias**. Cognitive biases are consistent patterns of cognitive errors that occur in human thinking. Again, cognitive biases are best interpreted as having evolved for some useful reason. For example, they may be beneficial to cultural or emotional well-being, or they may function as efficient heuristics, allowing us to make ordinary decisions much faster, perhaps in contexts where precision is not important.

There are many values which evolution seems to have privileged over rational integrity. Examples might be speed, efficiency, and of course, survival. Thus, our evolved brain often

117

prefers convenient delusions over reality. But we are poker players, and the values for which evolution selects and the values for which poker selects are different. Poker values indifference and cold rationality. There is no room for delusion in poker. The closer we get to reality, the better we become as poker players.

Cognitive Biases

There are several major cognitive biases of which every poker player should be vigilant. The first is the **anchoring bias**. The anchoring bias states that if a stimulus is presented to your brain, *even in an irrelevant context,* subsequent cognition will be "anchored" closer to that stimulus.

That's a bit abstract, so it calls for an example. Say we take two test groups and ask each to write down a number for some innocuous reason. Say, for example, it's the ID number for the experiment, so they each fill it out on their form. The first group writes down "1000", and the second group "10". Then we ask them each to guess how much the average guided tour of London costs. The first group, who wrote the larger number, will *consistently* guess a higher number than the second group, even though the initial bigger numbers were written in a completely irrelevant context. In other words, their later cognition was "anchored" closer to the number they had previously encountered. If you think about the networked structure of the brain, this makes sense—when neurons are activated, nearby neurons are more likely to be activated as well, and the neurons that correlate to larger numbers are more closely wired to one another than to those for smaller numbers. This bias indicates that the order and way in which your neurons are activated *profoundly* affect the way you think.

You might ask, what does this have to do with poker? A lot, actually—the anchoring effect manifests a lot in poker talk, as well as in gameplay and review. We'll discuss poker talk in chapter 7. As for the latter, let me provide just one obvious example. Say that you are playing a player who's tilting badly, making suicide bluffs, just throwing his stack into the most unorthodox spots where no one does, and you're calling him down easily. You stack him, he leaves, and some other aggressive regular joins, and let's say you get to a similar river spot as one in which the tilter made a ridiculous suicide bluff. Guess what the anchoring bias would predict?

Of course—and you can probably intuit this. You're more likely to call, even though what happened with a previous opponent is utterly irrelevant to how this opponent plays; for some reason you're just more able to *imagine* him bluffing here. It's simply easier to call. This is the anchoring bias in effect.

Another common instance of the anchoring bias is in reviewing a fresh poker session. When you look at a losing session immediately after you've played it, you're *very* likely to feel like you made the best play, and that all of your assumptions were right. Even though you lost, your story about the hand just seems like the "best fit." Yet, when you come back and look at the hand the next day, you realize just how unrealistic your assumptions were, and how your play was clearly suboptimal. This is another instance of anchoring bias—your perception is anchored to your previous perception, and it's harder for you to get an objective view until you move far away enough from the hand to leave that anchor behind.

There are many other ways to unintentionally anchor yourself—by analyzing a hand, talking about poker, imagining a hand, reviewing an old session, watching a video, or even engaging in something away from the poker table that makes you think about "aggression" or "passivity"—all of it has the potential to irrationally affect your subsequent decisions.

But of course, we can't sanitize our minds from everything. To a certain degree, we must learn to live with this bias, as we must with many of these biases. They are inherent to our mental architecture. But by being aware of them, especially in their particularly troublesome cases, we can try to consciously counteract them, and force ourselves into a more objective frame of mind.

We've already discussed the **projection bias** (refer to chapter 3, Image and First Impressions).

Another bias of note is the **innumeracy bias**. The innumeracy bias refers to two things: our inability to accurately process very large or very small numbers with our intuition, and our inability to accurately process probabilities. In poker, such errors can be fatal. The most problematic example of how the innumeracy bias deters us is in our intuitions about exploitation.

People tend to overvalue big pots. They also tend to assume that if they are winning or losing the big pots, that's what determines how much they're exploiting their opponents. The swings of big pots are very salient, of course. But first-rate players know that often times, big edges come from taking down lots of small and medium sized pots, which over the longer stretch, often equals more than what can be won in big pots. Your edges in small and medium pots are racked up through slow accrual, which your brain is *not* designed to intuitively perceive.

The brain is also very bad at grasping risk/reward situations which hinge on close margins. For example, in a spot where you're bluffing 3/5 pot on the river with a missed draw and he catches your bluff 60% of the time on the river, *your brain is likely to make you feel like this is a bad play*. This is because you are losing more than half of the time, which means more than half the time, your brain experiences negative conditioning. As it happens, your brain is not very good at "grading" these negative events—you don't feel appropriately better or worse depending on what odds you were given, or what margin of EV you were trying to capture. The brain is not designed to deal in terms of such numbers, but that is precisely what poker requires of us.

The reality is, of course, that for a 3/5 pot bet, you need 37.5% fold equity to break even, so if he's folding 40% of the time, you're netting EV. In order to be able to routinely capture such close margins of EV, you have to train your intuitive, unconscious mind to come more in line with your conscious understanding of odds and probabilities. If you force yourself into more situations where you're capturing a close margin of EV but losing more than half the time, your unconscious mind will gradually start to catch on. This is a lifelong struggle in poker—the challenge of being conditioned by odds and EV rather than by your intuition or fear, and it is one that we will come back to again and again in this book. (Note: the innumeracy bias becomes even more pronounced when it comes to something like having a 10% chance to win 15x your investment, but these sorts of issues are not as common in poker.)

A closely related cognitive bias is the **loss aversion bias**. Simply stated, the loss aversion bias causes people to overvalue avoiding losses, and undervalue making new gains. It causes people to be fundamentally irrational with regards to taking risks.

For example, if you're in a 300bb pot, and you have 200bb behind with which to bluff shove the river, and you think that he's folding 50% of the time, what do you think you'd do here? Turns out, even given these assumptions, the majority of people check back, because their mind is biasing them toward keeping what money they have. The 200bb they already have *feels* more valuable than the 300bb in the middle. Another way of saying this is that losing 200bb *hurts more* than winning the 300bb in the middle *feels good.*

The reality, of course, is that mathematically, every dollar should be equal to every other dollar (in most cases). A dollar gained should be equally as good as a dollar lost is bad.

This bias is one of the most difficult to overcome, because emotion plays a huge role in how we make internal decisions in poker. But to combat this bias, you must force your rational mental processes to influence your unconscious mind. If you tell yourself, "it's okay that I lost two buyins, because I had a good shot at three buyins and it was hugely +EV"—and *learn to accept this as a valid justification*, you will counteract the natural impulse of your mind to inhibit whatever behavior led to the loss. Stopping negative conditioning, and being able to tell yourself "it's okay that my huge bluff failed, I'd happily do it again and lose that money again" is the strongest defense against this kind of unwarranted loss-averse conditioning.

The **overconfidence bias** and the **superiority bias** are closely related. The overconfidence bias is having an overly strong degree of confidence in the accuracy of one's own judgments. One study demonstrated the overconfidence bias rather stunningly.

After handing out tests of commonly misspelled words to a group of subjects, they asked subjects what they thought the correct spelling was, and then asked how sure they were that their answers were correct. The subjects on average said they were 99% certain that their spelling was correct. They were wrong about 40% of the time. This bias manifests in poker as the tendency to be overly confident in your own reads, your own assignments of probabilities, and the robustness of your strategies. Again, this is something to be wary of, and another topic we will return to repeatedly.

The superiority bias is the human proclivity to overestimate your skill at things you excel at, and exaggerate your weakness at things you are bad at. As you can imagine, this is a quite widespread bias—the vast majority of people think of themselves as being "above average" at most things, while obviously only half can rightly claim that title. But notably, when it comes to skills at which people are poor, they tend to think they are terrible.

In poker, this can manifest in different ways, depending on a player's conditioning history. Most mid-high stakes players tend to have a vastly overinflated sense of their own skill. This should come as no surprise if you look at their personal conditioning history. Objectively speaking, they have managed to become very good, within the top .001% of players, at a relatively difficult game. They have also managed to overcome *all* of those players in the past whom they've surpassed. In a way, it is not unreasonable for them to imagine that they have unlimited potential. But as a result of that conditioning history, many of these players tend to think they are stronger than they actually are, and can beat a much stronger opponent just by pulling something magical out of their well of creativity. This results in an undue sense of superiority, an unchecked ego, and a warped sense of their relative skill level—an easy recipe for trouble.

The opposite pole is a player who has faced more hardships in their career—perhaps they have played lower stakes for many years, or maybe they played higher in the past, but can no longer hold their own at such stakes, or perhaps they are stringent bumhunters. Because of these players' conditioning histories, they are much more likely to *undervalue* their own skill level. They will assume that they should not move up, they'll assume that most other regulars are better than them, and the ones who definitely are, they will assume are *much* better than them. Both the over-inflated and under-inflated players have inaccurate perceptions of their own skill levels. Perceiving your own skill level is difficult, no doubt, but it is essential to pacing yourself properly in the poker world.

You can see how players who have historically done well tend to think that they are really great and capable, whereas players who have struggled tend to think that they are vulnerable and mediocre. These are learned self-perceptions, of course, and they are reinforced in large part by the **confirmation bias**. The confirmation bias is the tendency to search for, pay more attention to, and more easily validate information that confirms your prior beliefs.

For example, the player who thinks he is really great will see every won match as evidence of the fact that he must be really great, and the player who thinks that he is mediocre will take every losing session as evidence that he needs to move down and bumhunt harder—but it may well be that both of these players are winning and losing the exact same percentage of their sessions. The difference is in *how much cognitive weight* they are giving to each of these events. People are much more likely to give cognitive weight to information that affirms their own beliefs, presuppositions, and worldviews, and thus interpret the same set of data differently.

Confirmation bias crops up all over the place in poker talk and theory discussions, but we'll explore that more when we discuss the poker language in Chapter 8.

Fittingly, the last cognitive bias we will look at is the **hindsight bias**. Hindsight bias is the tendency to see past events as more predictable than they really were when they happened—the "I knew it all along" effect. The most salient examples tend to occur in game flow. If someone bets big twice in a row in back-to-back big pots, it is often the case that if you call the second time and he has the nuts, you think to yourself, "God, that was so obvious, nobody ever bluffs twice in a row like that" but if you fold and he shows a bluff, you think to yourself, "I knew it, that was such a good spot to bluff, and my gut was telling me to call, too."

As a word of advice regarding this bias—go easy on yourself. People are often not as predictable as you want to think they are. Like the others, this bias is difficult to overcome, especially so because poker is a game of hypothesis-generating and testing. It's hard to play such a game without operating under the (perhaps delusional) assumption that people and events are predictable if you look hard enough for the pattern. Ultimately, this is just another one of those things that we must temper as best we can, but learn to accept as part of our cognitive inheritance.

The Four Stages of Mastery

The journey of a poker player is long and arduous. At its center, it is about slowly and gradually improving until one reaches the highest level of mastery. The ultimate goal, of course, is to fully scale the mountain of poker. But how does one reach that peak and acquire true mastery?

Mastery is endlessly fascinating to us. From Wolfgang Mozart to Albert Einstein, Gary Kasparov to Michael Jordan, masters have always intrigued and captivated the human spirit. Given how inspiring we find them, it should be no surprise that social scientists have intensely studied mastery over the last 100 years. Compared to the old vague and aristocratic theories of the "natural genius," we now have a much clearer idea of how mastery is

124

actually cultivated. Researchers have posited **four stages of mastery**:

1. Unconscious incompetence

2. Conscious incompetence

3. Conscious competence

4. Unconscious competence

Unconscious incompetence is how one begins any new activity. It is the blank slate. To be unconsciously incompetent means to be bad and to not know you are bad, how you are bad, or why you are bad.

Imagine the first time you sat down at a poker game. You probably were playing hands like Q6 and A3 and 45o, minbetting or overbetting into tiny pots, having little idea whether any of those plays were good or bad. This is unconscious incompetence.

In neuroscientific terms, unconscious incompetence is when your brain is dealing with a new external system and has not yet built an internal network corresponding to each state of that external system. For example, the first time you come to your poker game, your brain has not built up mental associations with Q6o yet to know whether it's good or bad. It is only through the accrual of information and *feedback* that one passes beyond this stage, and the brain starts building up distinct and meaningful categories relating to each state of the external system (such as each poker hand you can be dealt).

The next stage is **conscious incompetence**. Conscious incompetence is when you begin to be aware of your own incompetence. It is to know *just enough* to know how bad you really are.

This is commonly experienced when learning a foreign language. Imagine a language you can somewhat speak, but are far from fluent in. You know you are not getting the accent right, not pronouncing everything correctly, speaking too slowly, etc. You are no longer oblivious to these mistakes, but you are nevertheless incapable of consistently correcting them. Your vocal cords have yet to be conditioned into hitting the right accents, your vocabulary is still disparate and disorganized, and so on. One passes through this stage just the same in speaking a language, or in playing piano, sculpting marble, or playing poker.

The third stage is **conscious competence**. In this stage, if you pay close attention and think consciously about it, you'll know what to do. You are now mostly making the right plays in a poker match—you're no longer calling that flush on the river when the board double pairs, even though you kind of want to. You no longer make decisions that you "know you shouldn't make."

You are aware now of all of the elements that constitute a poker match: betsizing, betting patterns, timing tells, and so on. But these things are all processed consciously. You have to actively think about all of these things. When you are playing well, all of your mental processes are engaged. Neuronally speaking, your consciousness centers (the neo-cortex) are actively engaged in organizing and interpreting the information in front of you. In this stage, if you slip out of conscious focus—if you start zoning out, or auto-piloting, your play will deteriorate considerably.

The final stage of mastery is **unconscious competence**. Unconscious competence is when you are unconsciously doing the right play—you no longer have to "think" about it.

The most obvious example of this is driving a car (or, if you can't drive, riding a bike). Most people who drive have been doing it for many years, and are now in the stage of unconscious competence. While driving, they never have to consciously think about changing gears, which pedal to push and how hard to push it, how to maneuver or effectively signal their lane changes, and so on. They can do things like carry on conversations, daydream, or listen to an audiobook while still driving effectively. This is a signature of unconscious competence.

In poker, the stage of unconscious competence is marked by immediately knowing what you're going to do. You don't stare at the board, try to make sense of the board texture, or imagine how he'd perceive your bets—you simply immediately click your buttons, without giving a second thought. Almost always, this is a sign of an unconsciously competent behavior.

Conscious and Unconscious Thinking

How does knowing these four stages help you?

Actually, the stages of mastery lend a lot of insight into the process of learning poker.

First, you must realize that poker does not progress uniformly through these four stages of mastery. It is not *poker in general* that follows these stages, but rather, individual skills *within* poker. For example, your preflop 3-betting game might be completely unconsciously competent, whereas your flopbet floating game might be at the stage of conscious competence. Every poker player will have a cocktail of skillsets, dispersed over the various stages of mastery. But to really understand the difference between conscious and unconscious competence, we must understand the difference between conscious and unconscious thinking.

To begin with the obvious—in your conscious thought, you are *aware* of everything that you are processing, and you *experience* all of it. In unconscious thinking, you aren't aware of everything that you're processing, and you usually experience only a fraction of what your brain has worked through. For example, you might have some vague awareness of yourself as "playing poker," but if you're playing unconsciously, you're not actively thinking about every bet size, every card on the board, and so on. Things become vastly condensed, the same way they do when you're walking to the corner store, and not thinking about how to coordinate your legs or avoid obstacles.

But most importantly, conscious thinking tends to be discursive. It is process-oriented, and quite often, mediated through language. If you are consciously thinking out how to play a hand, there's a good chance that you're thinking in a step-by-step process: "okay, he raised here, so that means he can only have X, Y, Z hands, but he bet this much on the turn so he can't have Z, and if he had Y then he'd probably have 3-bet," and so on.

Unconscious thinking, on the other hand, tends to be quick. It is prompt and intuitive, and does not generally rely on such step-by-step processes to derive the answer; the unconscious mind directly connects the stimulus to its appropriate response. If you see an A22 flop, your unconscious mind immediately decides what to do; it has one response to that problem, which it applies without need for reflection.

The implication is that conscious thinking, because of this step-by-step discursive process, is *slow*, while unconscious thinking is *fast*. I'll repeat this again, because it's vitally important: conscious thinking is slower, while unconscious thinking is faster. This makes sense—your unconscious mind is what controls your motor skills, internal organs, and so on. It needs to be fast, and needs to know exactly what to do at any given moment. Your conscious mind, on the other hand, can take its time, question itself, and be more process-oriented.

To determine if a situation is being negotiated by your conscious mind rather than your unconscious mind, there are several key signs: if you are experiencing every element of its process, if it is being mediated through language (even if just in your head), if it is taking place step-by-step, and if it is *slow*, then it is probably your conscious mind. If, on the other hand, your experience feels very condensed, if you seem to automatically know the answer, and if it is *fast*, then it is probably your unconscious mind at work.

Self-talk is one way to elucidate what aspects of your thinking are conscious or unconscious. If you try to say everything you are thinking out loud and trace your thoughts verbally (most preferably to somebody else who's also proficient in poker), you'll notice that the majority of what you say will pertain to the conscious spots you're facing. You are very likely to pass over the unconscious parts of your poker thinking, such as interpreting (what to you are) obvious board textures and betting patterns, or making obvious plays. Your conscious mind, because of its tendency toward being discursive and language-based, will be more likely to bubble up to the surface, be easily accessible to your verbal centers, and will end up being most of what comes out of your mouth.

As an aside, you will also notice this phenomenon in poker videos. Oftentimes, when great players talk about poker strategy, they end up talking about the processes of which *they* are conscious. As you can probably guess, first-rate poker players tend to have a *huge* part of their game relegated to unconscious competence. This is because they have played so many hours of poker and so are already situated in very effective habits. The result is that, when they are self-consciously talking about poker, they often seem to say nothing that you actually want to know.

It is easy and intuitive when engaging in self-talk (or narrating a video) to say whatever is on the cusp of the conscious mind. But to be a great teacher, videomaker, or coach of poker requires a wider skill set—you must also be able to probe your own unconscious processes, and visualize how a situation would be rendered through the eyes of a student. You must be able to see a situation the way that a beginner would see it. This is why the best poker players are oftentimes not the best teachers for low, medium, or even many high level players.

Conscious and unconscious processing also shed a lot of light on how to interpret timing tells. Think about it—what is someone doing when they call time to make a decision? They're trying to re-analyze a hand, or in other words, they are re-running their conscious, discursive procedure to try to find a clear solution. They are invoking their conscious mind in trying to process the hand. This means that either their unconscious mind doesn't know what to do, or that they don't have confidence in what it is telling them (perhaps because the pot is big or the hand was weird).

It thus gives us a new way of thinking about timing tells. Why is it that in certain spots, people act really quickly, but in others they slow down? This is why. Conscious thinking is slower than unconscious thinking, and so the spots where people are forced to take time are the spots where they are forced to recruit their conscious hand processing.

This also ties back to centrality—the more central a spot is, the easier it can be dealt with by the fast and self-assured unconscious mind. The more non-central a spot is, the more it's likely to require the conscious mind. Once you leave the circle of centrality, you will often notice a stark difference in your opponent's gameplay and timing. This is largely the difference between his conscious and unconscious mind.

But how different exactly are the conscious and unconscious mind when it comes to the same activity? How often does it really happen that your conscious mind tells you to do one thing, and your unconscious mind tells you to do another?

Remember, for all intents and purposes, the two systems are *structurally separated*. Imagine them as two distinct networks in your brain, estranged in space and neuronal circuitry. Though there is certainly interplay between them, they are architecturally distinct. In a profound sense, there are two poker players inside you—your conscious mind, and your unconscious mind, and were they each called upon exclusively to play for you, they would each have different tendencies, frequencies, and habits.

These are our counterparts to Plato's horses. Instead of Reason and Emotion, we are constantly getting pulled in different directions by our conscious and unconscious minds. Our role as the arbiter between these two forces is to get each to play to their own strength, and cover the other's weaknesses.

The Types of Poker Knowledge

There's an old and tired debate as to whether poker should be considered a sport. For my own part, I think the argument is pointless, but nevertheless, I do believe there is a certain insight that can be gained by thinking of poker as a sport.

If we say that poker is *not* a sport, then we risk thinking of poker as a "purely mental" game. Such a designation implies that since you are not constrained by any physical limitations in such a game, "you can do whatever you want."

This is not the case at all. It's true that, unlike a traditional sport, in poker you are not limited by your physical attributes, such as your height and musculature. But you *are* constrained by the physical limitations *in your brain*. If your brain structures have not been properly calibrated by thousands and thousands of hours at the poker table, then you are, in a literal sense, physically incapable of making the right plays. Making the right plays means to have the right neurons fire in the correct, complex pattern—which they cannot do unless you've already built a dense and properly attuned neuronal network.

From a psychological perspective, there are two very different sorts of "knowledge" about poker that are encoded in our brains. The first is what we traditionally think of as knowledge: fact-based or **propositional knowledge**. The second type is **know-how** (also known as procedural knowledge).

Propositional knowledge is knowledge of a *proposition*, such as: "I should 3-bet KK preflop." It is knowing a nugget of information. Know-how, on the other hand, is your brain's knowledge of *how to execute a behavior*. Rather than a proposition stored inside your brain to be recalled, know-how contains the information about how to send the right signals to motor neurons and muscle fibers, how to coordinate from your perceptual cues, how to calibrate your movement and balance, and so on, in the process of performing an action. For example, how to shoot a free throw in basketball is a matter of know-how. You don't need to know anything propositional about how to make such a shot, such as that you should jump to this height, or make sure the ball rotates in a certain direction to make the best shot. Your body just learns these things automatically and encodes them into know-how, without ever formulating it into propositional knowledge.

Here's the crucial point: playing poker is largely a matter of *know-how*, not propositional knowledge. As you learn poker and become good, your brain is building a network to unconsciously coordinate your perception with your motor reactions—the same things it does in learning how to shoot a basketball. This is not obvious, because we don't think of poker as a physical game, but the *way you learn* poker is nevertheless the same.

If you are a basketball player, it is certainly helpful to learn basketball theory, but the only way you get good is by developing your know-how, your body's internal awareness of the game, which is only done by playing lots of basketball. Though the systems can affect one another, basketball theory and basketball play are not the same. This is also true for poker. The system in your brain that contains poker theory is structurally separate from the system that governs your play.

Let us draw the distinction then between poker theory and poker know-how (or "poker play").

Poker theory is the conscious network that you have in your mind. You should think of it like a computer program that you've built in your neuronal circuitry. You input all of the variables of a hand into your internal poker theory program; it takes it all in, crunches it, and then spits out the answer as to what you should do.

You train and deepen this network by talking about poker, by studying poker videos, by going over other people's hands, by reading poker books, by doing poker math simulations, and so on. Getting feedback from all of these sources (which presumably are attuned to *true* poker theory) helps us calibrate our poker theory network closer toward reality.

This program is slow, as we discussed before, since it is discursive and has to run through many lines of code, so it's unlikely that you'll use this program for every hand you play. But in the really tough hands, you'll generally want to see what it has to say.

132

On the other hand, when we actually *play* poker, we are engaged in something very different. We are not calling upon our propositional knowledge, facts we know about poker, or even the discursive processes contained in our poker theory network. We are executing our **poker know-how**—our unconscious mind's "muscle memory" system that gives us immediate reactions, intuitions about what the right play is, about what a bet size means, about whether this hand is strong enough to call in this spot. This comprises our so-called "gut feelings." Our poker know-how is what instantly moves our fingers toward clicking a button, folding on a turn card, or going all-in.

Our poker know-how is what then constitutes our poker perception. The way we see a J♠9♠8♠ flop or the hand AQo is *created* by our poker know-how. In no small sense, you perceive a hand like AQo *pre-rationally*—mathematics, hand charts, poker theory or your conscious mind never actually come into it. You just have a "sense" of how strong this hand is, of how it works, and how it should be played. Of course, you can try to *reconstitute* the theory behind this perception, by running through your internal poker theory program, or trying to figure out how AQo does against a certain range using PokerStove. But the vast majority of time in poker, you simply function with whatever perception your poker know-how seeds you.

As you'd expect, poker know-how is trained primarily by playing. As with any other physical activity, like swimming or riding a bike, you cannot learn poker know-how by reading a book or by watching somebody else do it. Poker know-how and unconscious reactions are trained almost exclusively by direct experiential feedback—namely, reward and punishment.

Now, these rewards and punishments can be administered in many ways. They can obviously come from making failed or successful plays, but they can also come from criticizing yourself on a play that you think was bad, from getting criticized by a coach, or from watching a video in which the chosen play differs from what you'd do, and so on. With each of these subsequent examples, the further you get away from the actual experience of poker play, the *more* you are engaging your conscious mind, and the *less* you are developing your know-how.

This is a crucial point, so it bears repeating: the further removed a source of feedback is from the context in which you'll use it, the less that feedback will influence your behavior. We will come back to this idea when we discuss learning, but for now we'll leave it at that.

Let's sum up. We can see there are two distinct poker systems that exist within our mind—the conscious system, which is connected to our poker theory and our propositional knowledge of poker; and the unconscious system, which contains our poker know-how, and is what regulates most of our actual poker play. These two systems are distinct, separated in our brains, and are learned and cultivated differently.

The Task of Self-Awareness

You must distance yourself, then, from your conscious mind. You must step off from the throne and inspect the entire system with a Newtonian objectivity. Look. This is who you are. This is how you think. Examine not just the surface, but beneath the surface as well.

After all, your brain was not designed to play poker. Your brain resists poker. Probabilities, uncertainties, cognitive biases, and the ever-present hailstorm of stress and downswings thwart your attempts to wrap your mind around this beautiful and infuriating game.

But you are okay with that. You promise not to get too attached to your mind. You accept this, and will do what poker demands of you.

134

Poker is ultimately a battle against human irrationality. To master poker is to master the brain, the human apparatus. This is also the journey. And perhaps if it weren't so hard, if it were easy for you to truly see yourself, then poker wouldn't be such a dynamic, lucrative, and vibrant game. Perhaps you should be grateful that it is the way it is.

So you must face the task. Survey yourself. Pull back the camera and let your eyes tell the truth, like a spectator's eyes, as though seeing yourself for the first time.

Tell the truth. The ugly truth. What do you want? What are you good at, what are you bad at? What are your failings, your successes? What are you lying to yourself about? Nobody will answer these questions for you. You are alone. You are free to lie to yourself; no one will stop you. There are no shortcuts. There are no secrets.

What do you assume about others? What are you afraid of? What do you want most out of poker? What is it like to play against you? If you can't find these things, ask those close to you. If they don't know, ask your enemies. Somewhere in the middle of all their perceptions and yours is the reality of who you are. You must go searching for this reality.

The question demands itself. Who are you? Poker will ask you this many times over your career. But it is up to you whether you are willing to face that question head-on.

The Illusion of Control

There has been a continuing theme throughout this exploration of cognition. I have continually suggested that we're not in as much control over ourselves as we'd often like to believe.

This might be an uneasy conclusion, especially for an aspiring poker player. Understandably so! It *should* make you a little uncomfortable.

We've used the metaphor of seeing the brain as a computer several times now. Many cognitive scientists believe this is a good analogue of how our brains work, so it's worthwhile to extend it to its logical completion. So far, we've agreed that our conscious poker theory seems to work sort of like a computer program—but really, we can say that our poker know-how is like a sort of computer program as well, one that is more simple, efficient, acts much faster (perhaps more like a database-lookup than a discursive algorithmic process), etc. So when sitting at a table, this know-how program is buzzing away in our brains, ordering our fingers where to click, interpreting our perceptions, and spitting out responses to feedback.

But as with any program, our internal know-how program is constrained by its code. If there are errors in your code which cause you to make mistakes, then in a sense, you cannot "avoid" those mistakes. They will keep happening, over and over again, until you fix how your internal code is written.

You might point out that this metaphor doesn't allow for being able to play better or worse at any given time—which we clearly do. Perhaps you will accuse this metaphor of being overly reductive.

But I challenge you—when you sit down at a table to play poker, what are you really in control of? Realize, at any given moment, all the strategies that you'd use in a response to any situation are already embedded in your neuronal network; that is, the code of your internal program is already written. In the moment of playing, *you have no conscious control over that.* That is, you can't suddenly "decide" to use a strategy that you don't know is a good strategy, or "decide" not to make a mistake in a spot where you're mentally predisposed to making a mistake.

Over time, sure, you can change these predispositions, alter your neuronal networks, rewrite your mental code. But this is a

136

gradual, piecemeal process, as you slowly break bad habits and form good ones.

In any moment, the factors over which you exert *genuine conscious influence* are small. And what are they?

First, you have control over your initial game selection standards—that is, the quality of players or tables you're willing to sit down with. Note the word "initial." If you reach a state of tilt, chances are, your game selection will go out the window. Tilt is triggered mostly by the limbic system, which will forcefully background many of your conscious processes. So all you really have conscious control over is how bad of tables you're willing to *initially* sit in. But if you're a bad tilter, then you have no control over that 5% of the time when you go on bad tilt—it's simply a 5% that may or may not arise depending on how bad you run. You can improve a tilt problem over time, but during any given session, it's simply a part of you.

The second thing you have control over is *when* and *in what state of mind* you start to play. Perhaps you will elect to play mornings, or nights, or days when you haven't had sleep, before you've eaten breakfast, when something stressful has just happened to you, and so on. Each of these variables is likely to affect how well you play, and all of these are fully within your conscious control.

Third, you have control over what rituals you choose to implement before or during playing. This is vitally important. Rituals include things like reviewing hands before a session, watching a poker video, reading something inspirational or instructional, doing exercise, reciting a mantra, stretching or doing a breathing exercise, and so on. It also includes, to some extent, things that can take place *during* a session, such as forcing yourself to take breaks at certain times, or quitting at a certain time or when down a number of buyins, choosing to play without distractions, and so on. Rituals are a valuable means of co-opting your environment to enact your conscious goals. Even if the ritual takes place in the middle of a session and catches you at a point when you're not consciously alert, it will often force you back into alignment with your conscious intentions. We will come back to rituals later, when we discuss how to structure good poker session habits, but they are a good example of places where your conscious mind can directly intervene in your results as a poker player.

So we are not completely powerless. But beyond those few things, almost everything that happens in a poker game is *out of your hands.* Who sits at your table, how bad they are, how long the fish stays, how many kings against aces or aces against kings you get, how many times you soulread the fish, how many times you bluff off a stack to your table nemesis—those things are only in your control inasmuch as these three factors are in your control. Everything else is simply a permutation on what was already there, one of the many possibilities that could happen given your brain at the time you went into the session.

So where does that leave us? What does it mean then to play well, then? And how can we ensure that we do?

We will answer those questions in more and more detail in the following chapters. Though we have explored much in the realm of the mind, there is much left to investigate. Next, we will look into creativity, fear, and the role of emotion in poker.

6

FEAR AND CREATIVITY

If people never did silly things, nothing intelligent would ever get done.

LUDWIG WITTGENSTEIN

In the last chapter, we saw that, even when we attempt to be rational, our cognitive apparatus often fails us. In many ways, we are just not built to be rational. We concluded that the nemesis of rationality is *irrationality*, rather than emotion. So where does emotion fit in?

Before we can answer that question, we must first clearly define the limits of rationality. What precisely does it mean to be rational?

Ideally, we could say that rationality is a kind of optimization. To be rational is to act so as to achieve our maximally desirable results. Note the goal here: "desirable results." How do we *rationally* determine which results are desirable and which are not? A desirable result is just a result that we want. But that begs the question—why should we want it?

David Hume's famous dictum goes, "no 'is' implies an 'ought.'" In other words, no amount of facts can ever lead to an imperative. Rationality cannot determine a course of action unless you first decide what you want. The only way that we can say someone *ought* to do something is by having preexistent values, and values can never be derived *a priori*, by facts, or by "rationality." Rationality may be an optimizing algorithm—but you must first input the *value* you want to optimize for.

This means that rationality and emotion are intertwined. If you have no emotions—that is, if there's nothing that you inherently value more than something else, then there is nothing to optimize for. Emotion is the seed for rationality. Imagine an extremely intelligent AI that exists purely within a computer, but is not programmed to value anything in particular. Would it try to cure cancer? Compose art? Master a game of cards?

If one does not possess values, rationality is a hammer in a world without nails.

Desiring Desires

So what do we value? In ethical reasoning, we value moral equity. In cooking, we value taste. And in poker, since it's what we optimize for, we must value money. Or do we?

There is a long-standing notion that poker players are supposed to be "emotionless" and only care about money. In fact, though it may not be immediately obvious, poker players care about *many* more things than money. We brushed against this idea earlier when we discussed how to placate a tilter. Poker players decide to make monetarily suboptimal decisions all the time!

Consider just a few of the values that they sometimes pursue instead: lowering variance; reducing anxiety (by playing lower or game selecting tighter); having fun; avoiding boredom; chasing excitement; bolstering their egos; feeling better than their opponents; feeling like they are improving; feeling a sense of community; feeling cool; teaching others; getting even; venting anger; competing; sleeping well; having a balanced lifestyle, and the list goes on.

As poker players, we make these sorts of tradeoffs routinely. Though you probably don't think of them in such terms, at core that's what they are. But you should not dismiss these as betrayals against rationality. Instead, you should think of these behaviors as *indicators of your values*.

If you choose to quit a profitable match because it's boring, or choose to play a more aggressive style because it's more fun and interesting, or even if you choose to play for 8 hours straight to try to get even, you should not simply think of those choices as irrationally working against your value of "making as much money as possible". What these choices indicate is that you have *other values* that you are working toward, which you are exchanging for $EV. Now, you may not be pursuing those values rationally (i.e., in a fully optimal way), but that's a separate matter.

You might object, "But when I'm playing a marathon session to get even, I don't actually *value* getting even, I just want to get even in that moment. It's not the same thing." This is somewhat true, and gets at an important insight—not all values are equal. We clearly value money in a different way than we value something like getting even for one session. This distinction is known as **orders of desire**.

First-order desires are the things that you want at any given moment. But the things that you *want* to want, or the values that you *wish* you upheld are your **second-order desires**. For example, if you're trying to quit smoking, then your first-order desire might be to smoke a cigarette to alleviate your cravings, but your second-order desire (what you *want* to want) might be *to not want to smoke that cigarette*. And thus you try to push through your withdrawal symptoms so that you can eventually not want to smoke cigarettes anymore, and change your first order desires.

You might then argue that getting even during a session is a first-order desire, but maximizing money in the long run is a second-order desire. Most of the time, there will be some discrepancies between our first-order desires and our second-order desires. Thus, our major second order desire should be *to align our first-order desires with our second-order desires*. This, at root, is the impulse that makes us scorn ourselves when, in a moment of "passion," we tilt or play above our rolls.

It goes without saying that you should try to adapt your current self to your ideal self. But problems arise when a poker player mistakenly believes that making money is his sole second-order desire. He starts to believe that money is the only thing that he *should* want. But money is not a meaningful end in itself. Money is only valuable insofar as it leads to *happiness*. Happiness should be the second-order desire, with money as a sub-goal, desirable only insofar as it can secure happiness. But happiness is also optimized by other means, such as choosing to play fun matches, avoiding marathon sessions, getting good sleep and taking care of your body, minimizing variance and stress, or even challenging yourself with difficult opponents. We choose happiness over monetary optimization in many ways. And we are right to do so!

This is what I am driving at. There are certainly some emotions that we should wish to avoid, but neglecting one's entire emotional life is a profound mistake as a poker player. Poker takes place within the context of your life—your life! You shouldn't *want* to be an emotionless robot—not only because it's impossible, and not only because it will burn you out (a happy player is a consistent player). You shouldn't want to completely eschew emotion because it won't make you happy, and isn't that the point of the whole damn thing to begin with?

The Hidden Power of Emotion

Even if this reasoning seems sound to you, the intuition might persist that there's a deep opposition between emotion and rationality. You might think, "Sure, I see your argument, but the next time I sit down for a game of poker, I'm still going to see emotion as the enemy. That's just how it is." Let's then look at a second problem with the supposed rift between emotion and rationality.

When we think of emotion as bad, what we really mean by "emotion" is something like "emotions that negatively affect good judgment." It's obvious that emotion can sometimes interfere with and override rationality. But emotion plays many complex and multifaceted roles in human life, which are not always detrimental to rationality. Our emotions are not limited to things like anger, frustration, and envy. Confidence, enjoyment, and playfulness are all also parts of our emotional substructure, and clearly those things are not detrimental.

Neuroscience has taught us that emotions are essential even in what we consider routine cognition and decision-making. Consider an experiment known as the Iowa gambling task. In the experimental setup, a subject is presented with four decks. A subject repeatedly draws cards off the top of one of the decks, and depending on what card is drawn, the subject wins or loses money. It's a game of pure chance. The catch is that that one of the decks is secretly rigged so that it loses more often than the others.

The experiment reveals that before any of the subjects are consciously aware of one of the decks being rigged, before they're even able to articulate any suspicions, they are emotionally repelled from the rigged deck. Their hands may shake, or they may have an elevated galvanic skin response when they hover over the bad deck, and they will tend to gravitate toward the other ones. All of this is pre-conscious, pre-rational; they don't *consciously think* the deck is rigged. They merely unconsciously prefer the other ones, long before the conscious mind processes the same feedback.

However, if you take subjects with damage to their orbitofrontal cortex, a central part of the limbic (emotional) system, experiments have shown that these subjects will *persist* in choosing rigged decks, regardless of their results. Until their conscious minds pick up on the fact that the deck is rigged, and sometimes even *after* their conscious minds do, they have trouble differentiating the bad deck from the others.

What does this mean? It means that *emotion is integral to learning and responding to feedback.* Essentially, the Iowa gambling task hinges on reward and punishment—bad decks punish you, and good decks reward you. But reward and punishment are not merely tallied by your conscious mind, they are also processed via emotions. This makes sense intuitively. In most forms of punishment, it's the emotional recoil, not the conscious consideration, which is more powerful. Poker is no exception. If you consistently make a bad play, one of the chief ways this behavior is adjusted is through the punishment of losing pots. It's your unconscious mind, your emotional system, which is constantly being adjusted by reward and punishment.

Again, imagine a truly emotionless person, a sort of internal zombie. Why would they prefer winning over losing? There would be no reason to. Emotion is how we make meaningful decisions, in both simple and complex problems. In our day-to-day lives, when we talk about emotion, we tend to only mean certain emotions (and in poker, particularly the negative ones). But the role of emotion in our cognitive life is *much* more various and complex than that, and we must take it without simplification.

This is why the idea of being an "emotionless robot" in poker is fundamentally absurd. To not have any emotions would actually impair our ability to learn, to respond to the world, and most importantly, to secure our own well-being. The notion hinges on a misunderstanding of what emotion actually is.

A clever reader might interject, "well, what about a poker playing computer program that doesn't have human emotions and never tilts? Wouldn't that be superior to an emotional human?"

I concede, an AI that was programmed to have equivalent strategy to a human being, but without emotional responses, would be a superior poker player. However—we are not faced with that choice. We are not playing some theoretical version of poker. The game we are playing is *humans playing poker.* And in this game, emotion is an indispensable part of our mental apparatus. Emotion simply *is* part of how we think and learn. We must try to master ourselves, and we must do so *within* the confines of our mental machinery.

So, yes, be as rational as you can. And indeed, try to dampen the emotional responses that are to your detriment. My claim is not that you should embrace all emotions—the bad ones should go, clearly. But to be a good human poker player, you *must* also be emotional. You *must* recoil from losses; you *must* hurt when someone outsmarts you; you *must* have a greedy ego that hungers to improve; and you *must* feel good when you succeed! Without these things, poker would be an empty procedure, a dispassionate ritual, and it would be impossible to muster the energy and desire that it takes to face its challenges. You must suffer and fantasize and become drunk with imagination. The path to true mastery requires nothing less.

The Ticker Tape of the Unconscious

Understand, then, that emotional responses, such as tilting, are not merely random blips. They do not arise without a reason. After all, players tilt in different ways, have different thresholds for tilting, and are tilted by different things. But by taking emotional responses as indications of underlying values, we gain great insight into how to reduce tilt and other unwanted behaviors.

Consider emotional responses as ticker tape from the unconscious mind. If you tend to quit early when you're winning, or tilt when you're losing to someone you think is bad, or if you tend to start splashing around when you're bored, these are all indicators of your values—that is, your first order desires. If you quit games too early, it's likely that you value the feeling of having a winning session; if you tilt against bad players, it's likely that you value the feeling of superiority over others, or feel strong entitlement to winning; if you splash around when bored, it's likely that you value excitement and having fun.

Notice I don't claim you "over-value" these things. It would be impossible for me to objectively claim that anyone over-values anything, because values cannot be "decided" rationally. A person merely has their values and chooses to uphold them. If you value excitement, and are perfectly happy with that value, who am I to say that you should choose money over excitement? However, if *your second-order desire* is that you want to prefer to make money over playing exciting matches—that is, you want to *change* your first-order desires—then at that point, it makes sense to rectify this mismatch.

To fully harness your emotional capacities, positive and negative, you must begin with an honest evaluation. You cannot blindly rebel against the emotional reaction, as though the effect itself is the problem. If you splash around in boring matches, that is only a *symptom* of an underlying desire. To blame your splashing around would be like blaming a cough while ignoring the underlying virus. If you value excitement, then first you must admit to yourself that you value it. If you didn't, then you would simply not splash around to begin with.

Once you acknowledge that you value some emotion at present, you can then work toward rerouting it through a different outlet, or extinguishing the emotion altogether.

Tilt

Tilt.

Just the word, and you're reeling with memories. Dented walls. Broken keyboards. Cups of piss. Marathon sessions. The flattened, aching 5 A.M. feeling of staring up at your bedroom ceiling, having tilted away half of your bankroll, waiting for sleep to arrive. Everyone has a story about tilt. Everyone has a scar. It is our common demon, and perhaps the most painful, exhausting, and human aspect of poker.

Let's talk about tilt.

We discussed earlier how to deal with a tilting opponent, but now we will turn our perspective inward. We will explore how tilt manifests, the various forms it takes, and the most effective strategies for tempering tilt.

As mentioned before, **tilt** is when your emotions negatively affect your normal gameplay. Tilt is primarily caused by five things: losing a pot, failing a play, feeling insulted or disrespected, having an atrophied mental state (such as by being tired, hungry, or hung over), or being affected by concurrent life events (such as losing a job, having a fight with your significant other, etc.).

I also stated before that there are two major manifestations of tilt—hot tilt and cold tilt. **Hot tilt** is the aggressive, angry, try-to-win-it-all-back-right-now type of tilt, which is emblemized by the blind all-in preflop shove. **Cold tilt** is more of the resigned, tired, just-let-me-get-aces-one-time type of tilt, which is emblemized by the player who's been playing for twelve hours straight and is folding to all of your 3-bets. For more discussion on hot tilt vs. cold tilt, refer back to Chapter 3, Tilt and Emotional Dynamics.

We discussed the "pot of boiling water" as a metaphor for tilt. Briefly, your tilt level is like a pot filled with warm water. As bad (or tilting) things happen to you, they each deliver a unit of heat to the pot of water. For a while, the heat won't affect you, and your internal state will remain stable and calm. But after a certain point—at your boiling point (i.e., your tilt threshold), the water will start to simmer, and as more heat is added, begin to boil violently.

To take the metaphor a little further—like with a pot of water, once you turn off the heat (i.e., step away from the poker game), that doesn't mean that your tiltedness diminishes to zero. A pot of water taken off the stove retains some of its heat, which we call **accumulated tilt**. This is essentially the residual tilt from a downswing. The result is that the next time the heat is turned on, it is easier to bring the pot to a boil. Accumulated tilt can be naturally resolved by simply letting the pot cool down for a while (i.e., taking a break), but there are also other methods for attacking accumulated tilt, which we will discuss in the proceeding section.

That gives us a simple definition of tilt, and accounts for when it happens. But the question remains—*why* do we tilt at all?

Let's start at the neurological level. If tilt is when our emotions negatively affect our normal gameplay, then we can restate this at the level of the brain. Tilt is when our limbic system (part of our unconscious mind, which regulates emotional responses) inhibits our conscious mind (which is supposed to be regulating our unconscious poker game with its theory). When a player goes on monkey tilt, he essentially experiences a flight or fight response—due to various neurochemical reactions, his unconscious mind, with its impulsive, instinctual reactivity, takes control over his poker decisions. The conscious, discursive mind is essentially overridden and shut down.

Recall the distinction we made before between conscious competence and unconscious competence. Essentially, what happens when you're tilting is that your conscious mind is getting pushed out of the picture, leaving your unconscious mind in control of your behavior. Therefore, when you tilt, you are performing at the level of unconscious competency, without the self-regulating conscious mind looking over your shoulder. This has the effect of dumping all of your consciously competent skills. To put it another way, *what you do when you tilt is equivalent to your unconsciously mastered game.*

Have you ever wondered why people behave so differently from each other when they tilt?

Let's take two players, Mary and Joseph, who are at the same stakes and skill level, but tilt very differently. Say that they both become equally infuriated and start tilting. Mary starts 3-betting more aggressively and 4-bet calling off with medium pairs, making more desperate hero calls, stuff like that. But Joseph, despite being no more aggravated than Mary, open shoves ace-rag into four players, checkraises and triple barrels with a gutshot, and starts overbet-shoving rivers.

Clearly, these two players tilt very differently. A naïve observer would dismiss this by saying, "oh, Joseph is just a monkey." But let's be precise. If, in fact, tilt is a paring down to one's unconsciously competent game, this implies that when Mary takes off all of her conscious mental checks, the only thing she is unconsciously *able* to do is to elevate her 3-betting frequency, 4-bet/call more, etc. Mary, in a sense, *cannot* open shove A4o preflop like Joseph can. Her unconscious mind won't let her. She doesn't even perceive it as a possibility, or a decision she's allowed to make. In other words, Joseph need not be "more tilted" than Mary in order to make "tiltier" plays—it is simply an indication that Joseph's unconscious mind is less restricting of the available moves in poker space. Joseph's unconscious sees open shoving A4o preflop as a potential play, and so in his frustration, he takes it.

Tilt causes your mental shackles to be shattered, one by one. Your most unrestricted conception of what is possible in poker comes out. But most people, myself included, have too much mental inhibition to ever open shove a hand, no matter how tilted they are. I have monkey tilted many times in my career, but I have never open shoved a hand preflop—I have never even been close. This is not because I have not "tilted as bad" as someone else, but simply that my unfettered unconscious mind did not even consider doing such a thing. But, believe you me, it nevertheless did all it was capable of doing.

When tilting, some play looser, some 3-bet more, some make hero shoves. But your unconscious mind will only do things that it *believes might work*. Chances are, if somebody is open shoving preflop, he unconsciously believes that he might end up winning (and it is likely that if this behavior has not been eradicated, it was rewarded at some point in the past). Or, alternatively, if someone is open shoving hands preflop, it's possible that what he actually wants is to lose (we will discuss the desire to lose and reset your narrative later in this chapter).

Emotional responses always arise for a reason; they are vestiges of the substructure beneath them. To dismiss them as

149

merely random blips is to simply throw away information. There is no such thing as "just tilt." There is always some underlying value, desire, or belief to which tilt is merely the response, the symptom. If you want to correct your tilt, you must first understand your underlying emotional structure and incentives.

Here, then, is a one of the problems with the term "tilt" as it's commonly used. We've defined tilt as "emotions negatively affecting our gameplay," but we already know that "emotion" runs a large gamut. Two players can both say that they have tilt problems, and yet have almost nothing in common in terms of their emotions, triggers, or behaviors. One player may tilt because he feels like he never gets to win a flip, and the other may tilt because he's tired, or has been playing too long, or his ex-wife has been elected head of his PTA. So when you say, "I tilted bad today," it fails to express anything about *why* and *in what way* you tilted. In fact, by having a word such as "tilt," it gives us license to dismiss any inquiry into the underlying cause. When someone tells you they tilted, you're not supposed to ask, "Well, why did you tilt? What specific emotion did you feel? What did your tilt make you do at the table?"

Of course, poker players are eager to discuss strategic mistakes—"I was 3-betting too much and trying to win too many pots," or "I kept calling all his river shoves when he was actually really nitty," but never will you hear a poker player tell someone else "I was tilting because I felt like I deserved to win, so I decided to try to force big pots and increase variance by moving up."

This should be no surprise, though—poker culture discourages shows of emotion and vulnerability. Through its hyper-masculine veneer, it places no importance on emotional self-awareness. Although poker strategy has evolved tremendously in the last five years, as a result of open, rigorous discourse and exchange of ideas—widespread development of emotional skills has not followed alongside it.

There is an implicit taboo against talking openly and vulnerably about your own tilt. Though we quickly admit to our strategic errors, we are more likely to laugh off our tilt. We will joke about our degeneracy among friends, and sulk over our failings in private.

Emotional skills are developed no differently than strategic skills. And in order to develop them, it takes time, discipline, and most importantly, the unwavering acuity to see yourself and your failings honestly. As you go further on into this book, you will see more and more emphasis placed upon emotion skills over strategic ones. I truly believe that the biggest edges in poker come not from cutting-edge strategy, but from emotional resilience and self-mastery.

It is problematic to group the many species of tilt under the same umbrella. Jared Tendler, in *The Mental Game of Poker,* lists what he thinks are the six main types of tilt: injustice tilt, hate-losing tilt, mistake tilt, entitlement tilt, revenge tilt, and desperation tilt. These are expedient categories, but ultimately, tilt spans a spectrum, and there is no generalized rubric of tilt that will apply to everyone. Each tilter has their own emotional profile, beliefs, and values.

Thus, there is no universal answer to the question, "why do people tilt?" Each person tilts for a good reason, but it is a reason specific to their emotional incentives. Whether it's for venting, or justice, or maintaining egotistical homeostasis, we all tilt for our own reasons, and each in our own way. There is no single answer that addresses everyone, and so we must each try to understand how we ourselves are emotionally constituted.

Now, let's say you're already in a session, and you realize that you've begun tilting—what can you do to allay your tilt? Well, as long as I have your ear: quit. But, of course, you're tilting, so that's probably a futile suggestion.

The first line of effective techniques for alleviating tilt is **breath control**. There are literally hundreds of different breath control techniques; which you choose is unimportant. If you are not familiar with any, I would recommend simply this—when you realize you are on tilt, first lean back in your chair. This will open up your diaphragm and support your lower back. Relax your body as much as you can. Then close your eyes, and take ten deep, long breaths. As you are taking these breaths, try to internally scan your body. Try to think, "Hmm... let's look at what sensations I'm feeling. Let's see what this tilt feels like. Where do I feel it? What does it feel like in my body?" As you are taking these long breaths, look objectively at what internal sensations you're experiencing. Continue doing this until you feel calm, relaxed, and aware of the state of your body.

The very act of calmly examining yourself will defang many of the emotions you'll be feeling. Hopefully the mental distance will let you convince yourself to quit, but even if you sit back in and continue to play, you will be more centered, calm, and self-aware.

There are a number of other things that can help with tilt problems: mantras you can recite to yourself, pre-session rituals, taking breaks, visualizing, hypnotism, and so on. The list is endless, and there is no solution that is going to work for everyone.

But for most people, tilt is a very difficult issue to correct on your own. It's not impossible, and most players will naturally improve at it over time. But having seen many, many players trying to improve naturally, I've noticed that tilt tends to be the most recalcitrant part of a poker player's game.

When someone is a complete tiltmonkey, it is usually obvious, even for them. And those people, if they hit rock bottom or get the wind knocked out of them enough times, will often seek help. They know that they are tiltmonkeys. But for most people, tilt is like a bear sleeping beside them—they never know when it will wake up and bite them again. But because it is usually asleep, most of the time they feel like tilt is not really a big problem. In a way, most players would be lucky if instead of only tilting in small, intermittent episodes, they tilted continuously, only a little bit, all the time—they would be constantly face-to-face with their own emotional weaknesses.

Seeing a tilt coach or mental coach is often the best intervention for dealing with tilt problems. But if your tilt problems are very serious and are causing major negative effects on your life, then you should consult a psychologist or licensed therapist. Although a mental coach can help you to understand your motivations, your tilt profile, and help you to work through tilt and develop better habits, it is a short stumble from a tilt problem to a gambling problem. If you're unsure where you lie on that spectrum, I would urge you to consult a licensed mental health expert.

Weathering your Downswings

Two things are inevitable in poker: downswings and taxes. (Unless you're British, in which case you can subtract the taxes and add funny accents.)

As successful as you think the greatest players are, part of their greatness comes from the fact that they have braved downswings deeper than almost anyone else. It is a statistical certainty that the longer you play poker, the more likely you will face a downswing of truly titanic proportions.

We are naturally inclined to think of ourselves as poker players in terms of what we're like when things are going well and we are successful. But how you face those downswings is just as big, if not bigger, a part, of your true capability as a poker player. I say again, *how you face your downswings is a vital part of your skill as a poker player.*

I emphasize this because it's a direly important point. Being a great poker player isn't just about capitalizing on upswings, nice graphs, taking shots and moving up. A huge part of the journey of a poker player is *how you brave* your downswings. It is gritting your teeth, taking punishment, again and again, day after day, and holding fast. Being a great player when you're winning is not enough.

You must know that it is always possible a storm of variance will hit you, a storm so large, so powerful, so destructive that you will not survive it, so ruthless that it will break you. And someday, if you keep playing poker, you will face that downswing, and it will be one bigger, deeper, and longer than you ever thought possible. This is a statistical certainty. No amount of playing good, or praying, or good karma will protect you from it. It is only a matter of time and chance. The question, then, is this. How strong are you, really? How big of a storm will you be able to weather?

There are scores of players who were fantastically skilled when they were sailing out in the open waters of running-good. But when they could not handle the storm that hit them, they went broke. It is the oldest story in poker, and though it happens again and again, this story always goes untold, unremembered. Narratives in poker revolve around the successful, the upward spiking graphs and the smooth, continuous winrates. The masses of poker seek these stories out, they selectively inundate themselves with these stories, as though to blanket themselves from reality.

But this is the way it is. Poker is a fickle mistress.

So let us say this—skill and winrate in poker should not be measured merely by how good you are when you are running well, but also by how good you are when you are running poorly. Your running-bad winrate is part of your overall winrate, when abstracted over the long run. This seems obvious, but in fact, most players unthinkingly do the opposite when they calculate their winrate. When you look at a sample of your winrate while you're playing well and running well—that winrate isn't your true winrate, because it's skewed positively.

When you are downswinging, you will always play worse. How much worse? That depends on your emotional skills in being able to brave downswings. So we must ask the more pressing question. What tools do we have for handling our downswings, and how can we strengthen our emotional skills?

Imagine your worst downswing. Take a moment and try to remember. Think about the weeks, or months that it dragged on. Losing day after day. Constantly having to lower your sense of progress—you'd lose one day, hoping to recuperate it the next, but then you'd only lose more, and more the next day, on and on.

Maybe you weren't good anymore, maybe you had been wrong all along, or maybe you lost the skill you once had, or maybe everyone else got better. It felt like poker was punishing you, a feeling of overwhelming, indiscriminate injustice. But worst of all, it felt like you were moving backwards. Like you were no longer climbing the mountain. That you were beginning a slow and indefinite descent downward, and that things might never turn around.

These feelings create a feedback loop. Because you are running bad, you lose confidence, making you believe you're never going to win again, making you play worse and tilt more, making it all the more likely that you're going to continue to lose. The cycle self-perpetuates, feeding itself like a snake eating its own tail. I call this phenomenon **Poker Hell**.

Once you descend into this cycle of losing, tilting, and more losing, how do you ever break out of it? Obviously, you have to run good—but because you're in Poker Hell, you're inherently going to play worse, and your winrate will be depressed. Thus, you would have to run *better* than you would otherwise, since any positive variance is tapered by these negative effects. So the better question is this: how do we counteract the negative effects of Poker Hell, so we can achieve the escape velocity for our upswing more easily?

To answer that question, let's pull back and analyze the constituent mental processes that go into downswings. There are two major types of negative effects caused by downswings—the first type is a short-term negative association, and the second is a disruption in one's self-narrative.

First, we will look at **short-term negative associations**. A downswing is a stretch of time over which you are repeatedly given negative feedback, regardless of what you do. You are going to learn—at least in the short term—certain things that are simply incorrect, but which have been impressed upon you by repeated negative reinforcement, e.g., "aces never win," or "my bluffs never work." Thus, a downswing is a severe deviation from perfectly calibrated feedback (which would occur by rewarding correct behavior, and punishing bad behavior). This results in your senses being significantly miscalibrated. These are short-term negative associations.

For example, a common thing that people learn while they're downswinging is that "they always have the nuts," or that "I never win with [x] hand or in [y] situation," or even more obtuse claims like "I lose every flip." Of course, to a non-downswinger, these claims sound silly. But to the downswinger, these claims are actually the product of his conditioning. He has *learned* these things by the feedback that poker is giving him, simply through trial and error. And, in a sense, such a thought is not stupid—it is what his unconscious mind, which is constantly receiving and responding to feedback, has learned in the short-term.

Because the unconscious mind can adapt quickly to new information and changing dynamics, the player "feels" many things are true that a non-downswinger knows are not true. Even if his *rational* mind knows that objectively it's not true that he never wins flips, he still cannot resist his unconscious premonition. You've likely experienced this yourself. Such a player can't help but *feel* like he's going to lose every flip. It looms over him, and affects his expectations, his behavior, and his emotional responses.

The behaviors that are engendered by downswings are, for the most part, risk-averse. Downswingers tend to stop making high-variance bluffs, they stop being as creative or experimental, they prefer low risk-reward situations to high ones, and they try to avoid getting into situations where they can make mistakes.

In animal psychology, there is a related concept known as "learned helplessness." In one (very old) experiment, researchers took a dog and placed it on an electrified mat that delivered electric shocks at random times. Although at first the dog would scramble for safety, once it realized it could not escape the electrified mat, the dog essentially underwent a depression. It hunkered down, stopped expending energy, and simply accepted the pain that it was going to receive. It learned that it was helpless, and therefore not to expend energy or to take any risks.

In a downswing, you experience very much the same thing. Because your unconscious mind has learned that "nothing works," you stop trying to make plays or take risks, and simply hope to wait it out until the good side of variance arrives—or until your suffering ends. Exerting dominance over your opponent is integral to good poker, but this is the first thing to go out the window in a downswing.

This is problematic. What can we do to circumvent it?

To some extent, the problem is intractable. You cannot prevent your unconscious mind from learning from short-term patterns—it is too absorbent for that. The mental distortions caused by downswings are thus inevitable, and no functioning human brain can escape them. They are simply part of our fate as poker players. But although we cannot exorcise them completely, there are a few things we can do to mitigate these effects.

First, *win*. This sounds simplistic, but it's profoundly important. Once you start winning, your unconscious mind will shed its distorted negative associations. But you might think that's the catch-22—if you're downswinging, you have no *control* over whether or not you win. In fact, there are a few things you can do to give your winrate an extra nudge forward.

First, you can move down. For some, I would recommend even moving *way* down. Don't hesitate to do this just because your bankroll is large. If you're playing $2/$4 and going through a brutal downswing, a week of playing $.50/$1.00 would likely do you a lot of good—it will make it much more likely that you win, feel a sense of control and mastery over your opponents, and thus it will straighten out a lot of your negative mental distortions.

Secondly, you must force yourself to start taking more creative risks, in order to re-sensitize yourself to a range of possible actions. A downswing is naturally going to clip your wings when it comes to creativity, because your creativity is being consistently punished. When you're playing lower, it'll be easier with smaller amounts of money to make creative plays, and forcing yourself to take such risks is going to undo that short-term conditioning.

A third thing you can do is game select harder. Again, this seems obvious, but it's worth stating. This, too, will have the effect of nudging your average winrate higher.

And lastly, you should shift your focus away from results and more towards *process*. This is a bit abstract, so I'll explain what I mean.

Poker naturally rewards and punishes us by making us win and lose pots. However, if you were getting rewarded and punished by *playing well* and *making the right decisions* rather than winning or losing pots, this would alleviate a lot of the negative effects we're talking about, wouldn't it? This is precisely what focusing on process aims to do. If you are process-oriented, then even if you're downswinging, your self-reinforcement will be based on whether or not you make good plays, regardless of whether you lose the pots. On the other hand, if you're results oriented, running bad is going to cause you continual negative reinforcement, even if you're making the right plays. Being focused on results causes you to undergo a higher degree of variance in your mental feedback—the right play will always be the right play, but it won't always end up winning the pot.

A good analogy is in an EV graph, in which your winnings and all-in-EV lines deviate substantially from each other. It would be nice, of course, if your winnings line were glued to your all-in-EV line. The same can be said of mental feedback. Your mental feedback has its own winnings vs. all-in-EV line, but we would call winnings "results," which has more variance, and we would call all-in-EV "process," or "making the right plays," which has less variance. So if you could make your mind interpret *only* whether or not you made good plays, rather than their results, this would greatly dampen the effects of a downswing (though it's impossible to fully stamp them out). This is a very important idea in poker, which will be reiterated and explored further when we discuss learning.

The second major aspect of how we are affected by downswings is **disruptions in self-narrative.**

Self-narrative is a central concept in the psychology of identity. According to many theories of self, the primary way that we make sense of who we are as individuals is through constructing personal narratives. Even if our bodies change, or we undergo dramatic shifts in consciousness or personality, the narrative thread that winds through all of our life nevertheless unifies our sense of self. We carry this narrative continuously in our minds, adding to it, bit by bit, as time progresses. This is how we make sense of who we are—through the stories we construct about ourselves.

Our humanity is negotiated through narrativity. He who controls the story controls reality. The very same is true is poker.

As a poker player, your identity is tied to your success in poker. Poker is what you do. When you succeed at it, you are validated, and when you fail at it, you fail yourself—if not consciously, then unconsciously.

So in a downswing, your self-narrative becomes disrupted. Up until now, poker has been the story of your ascent. You started off with nothing, not knowing even the rules of the game, and now here you are, half-way up the mountain. Not a week of playing poker has gone by in which you did not learn, improve, and change. But a downswing represents a reversal in that narrative. In a downswing, suddenly you feel like you have gone backwards. You have somehow lost progress. Your self-narrative, instead of one of growth and ascent, becomes one of stagnation and degradation.

That self-narrative affects you deeply! It's more than just what you think about when you passively reflect on your life. Your self-narrative is where you *feel like* your life is going. It's your sense of tomorrow when lying in bed at night. It's your internal compass of purpose and growth. It's essential to your life as a human being.

In a downswing, it feels as though this narrative has gone backward, and in a literal sense, it has. But for most good players, downswings are aberrations from their true winrates. They *should* be winning, but that fact provides no comfort. All they feel is the down-ness of the downswing. They lose their optimism toward poker, along with their sense of well-being, safety, and motivation. This in turn affects their monetary EV, and much more importantly, affects their happiness.

So how can we defy these effects?

159

Mental Frames

To take control of our stories, we must harness the power of **mental frames**. A mental frame is simply a perspective or interpretation with which to view reality. Mental frames are enormously important in poker (as in life), and so we'll explore them in great detail.

For now, let's start with the stereotypical example—a half-filled glass of water. You can see such a glass as being half-full or half-empty, depending on your mental frame. A simple shift in interpretation makes all the difference in one's attitude toward the glass of water.

In the same way, self-narratives rely heavily on mental frames. A downswing will generally create mental frames of "nothing is going right; I am getting punished when I should be rewarded; I don't deserve this; I am going downhill; I'm losing money," and so on. It conjures emotions of entitlement, victimization, and decline.

But we can reverse these perspectives, solely using mental frames. Using the exact same set of facts, we can interpret and contextualize them such that they're more to our advantage. Let's say that instead of thinking, "I am getting punished when I should be rewarded," the entitlement frame, we replace it with, "how I brave this downswing defines me as a poker player," which is instead a frame of challenge. Then instead of, "I don't deserve this," a victimization frame, we replace it with, "everyone has downswings; this one is mine; I knew it was coming eventually, and now it's simply here," an acceptance frame. Then we can replace the decline frame, "I am going downhill," with the progress frame, "I am making progress through *this downswing.*"

I call the combination of these last two frames the **fog of variance frame**, and it's very powerful at dealing with downswings. One of the reasons why downswings are so difficult is because we believe we are the *only* person getting punished unfairly. No matter what we do or how well we play, when we're downswinging, poker seems to punish us, and only us.

In poker, there are two competing frameworks that describe variance—first, that we alone create our own graphs, but second, that we are victims to variance's whims. People tend to vacillate between these two ideas, never really choosing one (and the truth is no doubt somewhere in between). But the most fruitful answer is to fully take on both.

Instead of imagining that poker is a monolithic entity that treats one person fairly and another person unfairly—some murky, mindless god of variance—instead, imagine variance as being isolated for each individual person. When you are facing a downswing, instead of thinking, "that's not fair that poker chose *me* to face this downswing," instead take on the frame that, "this downswing was inevitable. This downswing is part of my mountain. Eventually I would have to face a downswing of this exact proportion and length; it just happens to be right now."

It is analogous to climbing a mountain and noticing that an upcoming segment is going to be especially difficult and time-consuming. Does a mountaineer curse and say "I don't deserve this part of the mountain; this is unfair that the mountain did this to me"? Of course not. To a mountaineer, that is simply *part of the mountain.* It makes no sense to talk about climbing that mountain if you're going to exclude its hardest parts.

But why does poker feel different?

It feels different, because in some part of our mind, we imagine that we don't *have* to have downswings. Things *could* be different. Variance could simply "choose" to be kind to us.

And there is, in fact, some truth to that! Variance simulators, forum posts showing perfectly shaped graphs, and all those rags-to-riches stories seem to reinforce this idea—were poker but kind enough to us, things could be easy. But though it may be technically true, that perspective, that mental frame, is extremely deleterious.

It is imperative that we choose the fog of variance frame. We must imagine that, in fact, our graph of variance has already been written for us. There is no moment-to-moment re-deciding or re-shuffling. No—the variance that awaits us is like a mountain that we have already begun to climb. We cannot see the variance that we are going to have to face; it is obscured by a layer of fog when we look up. But nevertheless, we must know that it is going to be there, that it is simply *part of what it means to play poker*, and therefore that we inherently accept it the moment we choose to play.

There is one problematic mental frame, and that's the frame of monetary decline—"I'm losing money." You might interject, "how could I re-frame that? If I'm losing, I'm losing, that's just a fact. I can't delude myself on that point."

Think for a second how we delineate downswings. If a particularly edgy player loses over a week, he might announce, "I've been downswinging for a week." But why? Notice, this person is defining the start point of his local self-narrative at the beginning of *this* week. But let's imagine he's won the previous three weeks. Why do we accept that he's having a week-long downswing? Why don't we say that he's breaking even over two weeks? Or on a three-week, or four-week upswing? It's completely arbitrary where we draw the starting point of our current self-narrative. This is true even drawn over a month, or two months, and so on.

So if your lifetime career graph has been going up, and for the last month it has been going down—why are you deciding that you are on a downswing? Why not instead choose to say that for the last four months, you have been winning? Or, why not further— that you have been on a steady rise since the beginning of your career?

This powerful mental frame is what I like to call "**it's all one long session**." Because it's completely arbitrary where we begin or end what we call our downswing (our local self-narratives), once

162

we acknowledge this, we can choose to draw those lines anywhere—so let's choose at the beginning of our careers. So every session you play, you're not entering into any new upswings or downswings; there are no special episodes dividing up your experience. You are simply in the same continuous stream with which you began, which is your entire poker career. Therefore, you do not need to take responsibility for individual days, or weeks, or months being bad or good. You are free from that burden. You do not need to experience those fluctuations as separate episodes of pain or glory. Instead, accept the entire story, from beginning to end—all the time.

It sounds nice, right? It's easier said than done, of course. Can you actually *identify* with your entire poker career? Can you actually sit there after a losing session, and think to yourself "well, my lifetime career has gone pretty well"? Clearly, it's not easy. But holding this frame is a skill that can be cultivated, given honest and deliberate practice.

Resetting your Narrative

In the end, everyone at a poker table is fighting for something. Some are fighting for money, some are fighting for engagement, some are fighting for self-respect—there are many motivations that drive a poker table and keep the blinds posting. But what about the person on monkey tilt—that furious, violent, bet-the-farm kind of tilt? What is it that person wants?

Money? Not really, no. When a tilter is on furious tilt, he is generally in the worst possible position to make money. Oftentimes, he even moves up to higher stakes, and plays people against whom he *knows* he's not a favorite. Let's say that there's a 70% chance that he loses a lot, and a 30% chance that he gets even. We might just assume that he's being irrational in trying to make money. But this is too simplistic. What if we assume that he knows what he's doing, and is actually acting according to his incentives—if that's the case, then what is it he really wants?

What he wants is precisely this: he wants to alter his self-narrative. He wants to escape the story he's living. For the player in a downswing, his entire downswing will feel to him like one continuously painful event, which is tied to his previous high point. But a session of violent tilt changes all that. On the 30% chance that he gets even on the day, he can escape that pain, and end this downswing—but even on the 70% chance that he loses a great deal of money, he will lose so much that he's no longer in the same situation, and can no longer be really tied to his previous high point—he will **reset his narrative**.

Have you ever lost so much money that you felt like you were in a new place? That everything changed? That suddenly, you had to re-take stock of yourself and start over?

This is resetting your narrative. It is pushing so hard through the other side that you feel, perverted as it seems, almost... refreshed. It is forcefully creating a new chapter in your personal story. You no longer have to associate with the decline you were feeling before—everything has started over. It's like throwing out your old wardrobe, or moving into a new apartment, or making a list of New Year's resolutions. It's an arbitrary place that makes you feel like everything's brand new, another starting point. It might sound bizarre to describe it that way. But as arbitrary as it sounds, this is how we really experience it—it's the feeling of being released from your story. In many ways, it's a relief!

A player who violently tilts thereby ensures that he will experience a **mental reframe**. *That* is what he is fighting for. He wants to be relieved from his story, and in a way, that's a very sensible incentive. The only problem is, from a second-order perspective, it's not a good way to go about doing this, since it sabotages significant long-term goals (namely, making money). Rather than sacrifice all that to reset our narrative, we'd much rather try to impose *our own* mental reframes.

If self-narratives are the stories by which we make sense of ourselves, then mental reframes are rewritings of our own stories. We've seen many such reframes that are advantageous to adopt—but how do you really adopt a new story for yourself?

Simple. By telling it over and over again. Why did the ancient Greeks believe in stories of Zeus and Apollo, never having seen any evidence for them? They believed it because of the power of the storytellers themselves. Stories gain their power by being told, again and again. With enough sincere tellings, the story itself becomes more and more powerful, more and more convincing, to the point at which you have no choice but to suspend your disbelief.

So consider the stories you keep telling yourself. They may not be obvious, but if you turn them over in the light, you can reveal them to yourself. Examine these stories, and consider how you can revise them to better frame your mental life. And therein, with some practice, you can rewrite the experience of your journey.

Reference Points and Periods

Consider this classic gambling experiment from behavioral economics. A subject starts with no money, and he is told that he has two choices. He can either take a 50/50 gamble between winning $20 or $0, or he can choose to go home with an assured $10. The EV of these two propositions is the same obviously, and you'll probably have no trouble guessing that the vast majority of subjects choose the assured $10. This seems to suggest that people are mostly risk-averse.

Now, let's switch around some of the variables. Let's say that instead of starting with no money, the subject *begins* with $20. Again, he's told he has two choices—he can take a 50/50 gamble to either keep his $20 or lose it all, or he can accept a guaranteed loss of $10, which will leave him with $10 remaining. Which of these do you think most people choose? Turns out, most people choose the former. Most people choose to gamble in this case, and try to keep everything. Perhaps then, in some cases, they're risk-prone.

But if you are an astute observer, you will notice that actually *both of these experiments have the exact same outcomes*. In both cases, if you take the gamble, you have a 50/50 chance of walking away with either $20 or $0, and if you don't take the gamble, you're assured $10. Not just the EVs, but the *actual outcomes* are equivalent. Yet, in one case most people avoid risk, and in the other case, they seek it. Why is this?

We could just say that people are irrational, but this tells us nothing useful, and merely dismisses complexity. We would do better to assume that this behavior is arising for a good reason. At its essence, risk aversion means that winning a certain amount *feels less good* than losing that same amount *feels bad*. Simply framing something as a loss or as a win changes our emotional response to it. Examples abound in poker: when you're faced with the option of a slightly +EV flip that is so big it would make you anxious, you'll often forego that flip. But that decision is not necessarily irrational—you are simply optimizing for your feelings rather than for money. In the same way, these subjects *are* responding rationally to their incentives—their incentives being to maximize for their feelings (since the EVs are all the same).

These experiments show the power of framing something as a loss or a win, but there's also a more subtle point to be made. Notice how in each experiment, we gave the subject a different amount of money to start with. Of course, the starting amount is immaterial—the subject's outcomes will be exactly the same. But if you tell a subject he starts with $20 as opposed to $0, this gives the subject a **reference point**. Reference points are mental and emotional anchors by which we orient ourselves. They set the initial conditions, like the first chapter of a story. By controlling the reference point, we can control the mental frame with which we view an object or a situation.

Even experts can be swayed by reference points. In one experiment, medical professionals were proposed hypothetical procedures with a "90% 5-year survival rate", or "10% chance of death within 5 years." Even though the two are functionally the same information, the experts reacted to them very differently, preferring the 90% survival rate procedure over the 10% death rate procedure.

The way information is presented strongly affects how it is processed. Framing and adjusting reference points are widespread tactics in advertising and politics, as well as in rhetoric and persuasion in general. But for our purposes, we will narrow our focus on poker, on money, and on EV decisions.

These experiments suggest that there are patterns to risk-seeking behavior. When people perceive that they are even, or starting from scratch, they are more likely to be risk-averse. But when people are already up, but are being threatened with losing those winnings, they're more likely to be risk-prone—they would prefer to try to protect their winnings and risk more, rather than accept a definite loss.

Of course, in practice, the relationship between risk-aversion and risk-proneness is player-dependent. It also depends on how tilted the player is, whether they are at risk of wiping out their winnings or simply diminishing them, and so on. But reference points play a big role in risk-taking behavior.

Now turn this back on yourself. When do you tend to be risk-averse? When do you tend to be risk-prone? Everybody has triggers that will dispose them toward one pole or the other. I encourage you to examine what situations trigger such a shift in your own risk behaviors.

Ultimately, in a game as complex as poker, risk-taking behaviors are not as simple as in the aforementioned experiments. In fact, most of the time when you're down a lot, you will be especially risk-prone, and when you're up a lot, you'll usually be more risk-averse. This is because of attachment to specific reference points over the course of a session, like "even," or "up 5 buyins."

For example, let's say you're up 2 buyins and are put in the situation to make a large 3 buyin bluff. If you're getting somewhat +EV odds on the bluff, but you'll wipe out all of your winnings if called, then most people will avoid making that bluff. They will be risk-averse, because they can effectively still protect their winnings by folding. On the other hand, take a different scenario: you're up two buyins, but now you're really deep, and there's a huge pot with over 400bbs already in it, and so a fold would put you down to even on the session. In that case, most people are going to become risk-prone to try to protect their being up (which is analogous to the situation in the initial experiment). However, in poker, this latter situation is rare; it's much more likely you'll experience the former when you're up on a session.

So if put in a position that risks their winnings, most poker players will readily fold, avoiding the +EV risk. But the irony is that if they would simply wait 6 hours and start a new session, they would likely be okay with taking that very same risk. They will become more risk-prone by simply including a 6-hour gap between two hands.

This shows how one's "current total" functions as an implicit reference point. But where we draw the lines around our "current total" is arbitrary. Some people use as their reference point a single session, and others use the entire day's session. Thus, if two players played multiple sessions a day, one player might pick new reference points for each session, while another player might carry over the same reference point from earlier in the day (and do things like try to protect his winnings from earlier). The units of time between which new reference points are chosen are called **periods**. Periods of different length produce different risk-taking behaviors.

So how can we manipulate reference points and periods to our advantage?

There is no intrinsic reason why we should choose any specific period over any other; periods are all arbitrary lengths of time. But we don't *arrive* at our specific period arbitrarily—it arises out of our mental conditioning. Programs like PokerTracker and HoldemManager, daily graphs, Excel sheets, and the simple ritual of telling somebody else how much we're up or down on the day—all of these help to reinforce the idea of the *day* as being the natural period, and thus suggesting we adopt daily reference points.

But is this to our advantage?

Theoretically, we should be an optimal level of risk-taking for each of us, dependent on our bankrolls, our emotional stability, and the types of games we're playing in. We don't want our behavior to deviate from that optimal level. If you think about it, having reference points tied to your daily session is going to cause frequent fluctuations in your level of risk-proneness (since your reference point will continually change) and therefore it will create deviations from the *optimal* risk-taking behavior, as well as put you through more emotional swings.

Instead, you should try untangle your local self-narratives from your daily winnings. Stop thinking about how you do on any given day as "what you're going through." Try setting your PokerTracker or HoldemManager to show you your weekly results by default, or your monthly results, or your lifetime results even. With some practice, it's possible to break the paradigm of daily results as how you experience poker.

Again, a new narrative can be imposed over an old one by repeatedly being told in its place—so tell yourself this story, again and again: how I do today doesn't matter. There's nothing special about today. It's all one long session!

Quitting behaviors are also influenced by reference points. There was a telling experiment done on this using New York City taxicab drivers.

Cab drivers were surveyed as to how many hours they worked during busy days, and how many hours they worked on slow days. Obviously, a cab driver's hourly earnings are going to be substantially higher on busy days, so it would seem to make sense that they should work more on busy days and take it easy on slow days. But this is the exact opposite of what was observed. Instead, almost all of the taxi drivers worked *fewer* hours on lucrative days, and *more* hours on slow days. Why?

It all has to do with reference points. For the taxi drivers, their internal reference point was the average amount of money they'd make in a given day. In other words, they were unconsciously aiming to get *about the same amount of money every day.* On busy days, they'd quickly make a lot of money and then take the rest of the day off, and on slow days they'd work long hours to try to ensure their usual paycheck. Their reference points were causing them to pursue very suboptimal behaviors in order to satisfy their expectations.

Poker players do the same thing. People love to quit when they're up past a certain threshold, which feels like a "good win," and they hate quitting when they're down, or when playing a tough session—often they will keep playing indefinitely, until they're forced to stop. The reason is the same. Unconsciously, they are aiming to win about the same amount money every day, and to play about the same amount everyday—when clearly that is not necessarily optimal.

The optimal strategy would be to play as long as you can on the days when you're winning, and then to quit early on days when you're losing. On winning days you'll likely be on your A game, feel especially confident, are more likely to be playing bad players, tilted opponents, etc. Continuing a losing session pales in EV to continuing a winning one.

Again, consider your own mental life. What are your quitting patterns? What amount of winnings feels like "a good enough win" for you, that you're comfortable quitting on it early? How much of a loss is so small that it doesn't really feel like a loss, and you can quit essentially even?

We each have a constellation of these internal reference points—but ideally, we want to do away with them altogether, and to act purely disinterestedly in our poker decisions. If we keep playing through upswings and quit early when we're taking a beating, we can maximize our winnings in the long run.

The solution, again, is to adopt the frame of "it's all one long session." Whether you're in a losing session, or a winning session, it doesn't matter, because it's just the tail end of your massive lifetime graph. If you can see it this way, and choose when to play and when not to play based on the quality of your games, then your life as a poker player will be a lot easier.

If you truly adopt this perspective, playing marathon sessions to get even will make no sense. What would it mean to "get even?" If you're down 10 buyins in one night, what's so special about trying to win another 10 buyins tonight? Why not try to win them back tomorrow? Or tomorrow and the day after? The next 10,000 hands of your graph will be dealt to you regardless of when you pick them up, so what's so special about this night? Except, of course, that tonight you will likely be playing worse—implying that the logical answer is to get some sleep, and play again the next day, and the next.

Another effective mental frame is that of **winning your hourly**. Let's say you know that your average winrate is $100/hr, and let's say you're down $1,500 on the night. If you wanted to get even, according to this perspective you should say to yourself— "well, if I want to get even, I'll need to play for 15 hours. If I play for three hours, I'm only making $300 on average (plus, I'm tilted and tired, so it's probably less than that. Is that really worth it?" The answer: probably not.

So there are a variety of strategies for trying to reframe our periods and mental reference points. But inevitably, one of the difficulties with shifting these reference points is that it's impossible not to, on some level, know how you're doing during any given session. Even if you've decided to repudiate your daily session reference points, even if you shut off your tracking program and don't look at your bankroll, if you're minimally observant, you're always going to have a pretty good idea of how much you're up or down. So how can you resist not wanting to finish up or down?

Well, this is the raw challenge. There are no further tricks or shortcuts—you simply have to force yourself to frame reality differently. This takes time and practice, of course. But if you understand the power and vitality of mental frames, then you must face your responsibility to master yourself, and use them strategically to alter your perception.

The Role of Ego

"Ego" can be a dirty word in our society. It's obvious that ego drives many poker players. But there's also a widespread feeling that it's not good to be driven by ego—that it's perhaps juvenile, or even immoral.

The truth is, most of the great men and women of history were driven by ego. Not exclusively by ego, of course. But the desire for greatness and self-creation is one of the oldest and most powerful human motivations. Poker players are no exception to this. Money is not nearly as motivating, as aggravating, or as electrifyingly exciting as the process of self-creation.

I don't mean to proselytize on behalf of the ego, or to say that it is "good" to be egotistical. My point is merely that ego drives an *enormous* amount of the work and energy that great players pour into honing their games. We should acknowledge the existence and power of ego, which means not only to sometimes curb it, but also to harness its momentum when we can.

Almost all of the great players I have ever met were driven more by their egos than by money, at least initially. For a long time, I wondered why that is. When I was coming up in the poker world, playing low stakes, I ran across many people whose only goal was to make a lot of money, to become ballers, to afford a luxurious lifestyle, and all the rest. But few of those people ever seemed to make it. Why is that? What is it about ego that makes it a more sustaining motivation than money?

I suspect that it's because, in reality, poker is not a very easy way to make money. This sounds counterintuitive, because chances are, if you're reading this, you're fully sold on the notion that poker is a great way to make lots of money—you may have

172

even made some yourself. But in reality, most people don't make money in poker in the long term. Not only that, but most people end up busting their entire bankroll once, twice, or many times before they end up becoming successful. Poker is not easy. And if money is the only thing motivating you, there are numerous points along the average poker career at where poker will simply not seem like the best route to financial success—for most people, it will make more sense to invest one's time in school, work, or other endeavors to try to make money.

But maybe it's even more than that. Why is it, after all, that we don't see great poker players emerging out of poverty? Why don't they come out of the slums of Brazil, or China, or India? Why isn't it that out of the billions of people who truly would *need* the money, who are most desperate for it, among whom many must be intelligent, hard-working, steadfast, it simply doesn't seem to happen?

You might argue that this is because online poker culture hasn't disseminated into those areas—but you observe the same thing even in the first world. Online poker players don't emerge out of the lower class, and a great many of them are post-adolescents with no dependents.

There's something about ego that makes it a more powerful driving force than money or fame. I don't know for sure why that is, but it seems to be true.

Ego plays a role in all of our lives. In the context of poker, ego is essentially the sense of ourselves as being better than others. We inherently want to be better than other poker players. In psychology, this is known as perceiving skill **horizontally**, as opposed to **vertically**.

If you think of skill horizontally, you are evaluating your skill relative to other people in your field. On the other hand, if you think of skill vertically, you think about how you're improving relative to where you were yesterday, or last month. (Generally, it's said that men think of skill more horizontally and women think more vertically). In a sport like sprinting, it's quite easy to think of your skill development vertically. You simply measure your own personal best times, and try to beat them. But in many ways, poker forces us to think of skill horizontally.

How high your winrate is, how stringently you game select, which opponents you isolate, even what you choose to study—these are all contingent on your skill relative to your opponents. Somebody who's successful in one situation against certain opponents may not be successful against other opponents, and the same level of skill may mean a lot less 6 months down the road. So to some extent, thinking of our skill horizontally is inescapable, because it's tied to the structure of poker.

It's starting to sound like ego is inherent to poker, then. We've also noted that it is a strong and sustainable motivator. What's the problem then? What's the downside of ego?

The downside comes when your ego gets insulted, of course—primarily by losing. If a poker player has an extremely strong attachment to his ego, he may even react violently or aggressively against the possibility of being worse than he thinks he is. He may tilt, have an outburst of anger, or make other detrimental decisions when his ego has been threatened.

Not only that, but ego often clouds our attempts at accurate self-evaluation. If you have an unchecked ego, you will tend to think you are better than you really are, you will often play in bad matches, not recognize your own weaknesses, not quit matches when you're losing, be unwilling to admit that you're the weaker player, and on and on. Ego clearly causes many players to spew money in the long run.

So there's a large downside to ego as well, but ego cannot be done away with. It is too important to poker. Although ego can be harmful when unchecked, at its best, it can be a powerful force to our advantage.

Let's not throw ego out, then, but temper it.

I have always believed that self-awareness is the single most important skill for a poker player. To be self-aware in this sense is to accurately be able to look at yourself and say, "This is who I am. This is what I'm bad at. This is what I'm good at. This is who beats me. And I could be wrong about this, too."

When you're playing a match, the most powerful thought you can have is: "this guy might be beating me." No matter how bad he is, or how much you think that he misunderstands some important concept, or how badly he played this hand or that, you must *always* be willing to accept that it's *possible* that in this match, right here, right now, you are losing.

Notice how I speak of "losing" or "beating," rather than "being worse than." It is unfruitful most of the time to talk about "being worse than," except in cases of drastic differences in skill, because poker skill is non-linear. You might have a positive winrate against 3-4 strong regulars at your stakes, but lose to the worst regular, simply because something about his game exploits you and you're just not adjusting correctly. Don't think about skill as being linear— not only because it isn't, but also because it creates unnecessary tension on your ego.

Rather than trying to dissolve your ego, subvert it. If you are losing against someone, it's not necessarily because "you are bad." It's simply that your style has a negative winrate against that particular person's style, and so you need to do your homework and figure out the match. But the fact that his style beats yours needn't be integrated into your ego. It's not a fact about "you." It's just how your game happens to interact with his right now.

I repeat this again, because it's such a vital point: you must always be able to acknowledge the possibility that you have a negative winrate. Then, you must be able to quit that match with grace. And after you quit, you may not even be sure whether you were actually losing that match—that's fine. When you walk away from that game, your ego is going to be burning, driving you to improve, to figure out what you did wrong, and to mend your weaknesses—so that when you return to that person's table, you will be ready to rise one step higher.

And yet, the idea persists, even for me, that ego is somehow a bad thing. Sure, maybe everybody needs a certain amount of ego when coming up in the game—perhaps without it, nobody would be motivated to get over the initial plateaus of becoming a serious poker player. But once you get a foothold, once you start climbing the mountain, what use is ego? Maybe *then* it should be extinguished.

Don't get me wrong—I'm not claiming that ego is the be-all-end-all, or that selfishness is the highest value man can pursue. But there are two senses of ego that we need to disentangle here. One is ego as a motivation, as a driving factor to become better, higher, more respected. The second is ego as a personality trait—as narcissism and self-centeredness. Clearly, the latter is undesirable. And the two may be correlated, but they are not the same.

Ultimately, the struggle toward greatness, indeed, the path toward self-actualization, cannot be divorced from ego.

So yes, let us try to be good to people. Let us be honest, let us be genuine, let us care for others around us. But this does not mean we should extinguish our ego—instead, let us partake in a different kind of ego. A selfless ego.

To become a great poker player requires inspiration. You must push yourself through darker depths, and into deeper fugues of concentration than ordinary people put into just about anything. It is not about money. No poker player becomes great because of money. It is about *you*, it is about creating yourself—and at the same time, it has nothing to do with you, it is only poker, it is only the climb, only the mountain. Selfish and selfless at the same time.

So take ego seriously. Be ready to lose to many people, over and over, throughout your career. No matter how successful you've been, and no matter how bad you want it, no matter how smart or precocious you are, you are going to lose to people, and that's okay.

But hunger nevertheless. Hunger to be better—to be the best. Let that steaming desire bubble up in your belly. It is good for you. It is the spring from which you draw your energy. It will guide you to grow into the kind of poker player you want to be.

Creativity in Poker

Poker, at its highest level, is an art form. Traditionally, the notion of art is restricted to things such as painting, music, and the like. Yet, you will occasionally hear people speak of a beautiful baseball swing, or a sublime mathematical proof. In poker, we also speak of beauty, though we sometimes use different words for it—"sick play," "a soulread," and so on. What we apprehend as beauty in poker, I would argue, is the masterful demonstration of creativity.

Where does creativity in poker come from? What role does creativity play? And how can we be more creative?

In a sense, it's natural to be creative. When you first began playing poker, just about everything you did was creative. You experimented, you made plays you'd never made before, and you were unafraid. It was only over time, after you learned what you shouldn't do, that your creativity began to be stifled. By the time you become a fully capable and disciplined poker player, you are no longer even aware of just how restricted you are by your conditioning—at that point, you can no longer even see all of the available possibilities. When you are dealt AA preflop, you don't see limping as a possibility—it has been culled completely from your perception.

Imagine, for a moment, the landscape of poker as a wide-open field. Your "game" is a pattern of trails etched on top of this open field, restricting the space available to you. Instead of simply being able to roam freely, you now only move inside the paths you've delineated. This is for good reason! You put up these trails to protect yourself from unsafe, –EV plays. These structures become your self-imposed map, insulating you from the dangers of losing money.

But once you reach a basic level of proficiency, you realize the pattern you've constructed is not perfect. Hypothetically, there is some better shape that your trails can take, the shape of a perfect poker game, but your pattern doesn't capture that shape—you suspect it extends out too short in most places, and perhaps too far in a few.

Where does creativity come from? Creativity arises naturally from the simple process of trial and error, of making plays and learning from their results. And while you are in the process of creating the structure of your poker game—when you are deciding where to draw your trails—it is natural and easy to be creative, to test your limits, and to take risks. That is the easy part.

It is after those parts of your game have hardened, when the trails have been established so long ago that they are now impressed deep into the ground, that creativity becomes a true challenge. If you perceive limping AA as an unacceptable choice, if you have removed it from any of your potential paths, how are you ever going to find out if limping AA is in fact the best play?

You might wonder why I'd use such an obtuse example— "of course limping AA is never the best play," you might say. Ah, but that is precisely why it's a good example! You and I both know that open limping AA is never good in a cash game. It is outside the trails that both you and I have built, and this pattern probably aligns perfectly with the shape of +EV play. However, *you don't know* which of your trails is misaligned with +EV play—it could be a trail that seems just as obvious as to you the one that dictates you should never limp AA. Since it is a solidified part of your game, it is something that you pass over in silence; it is a tacit assumption; an unasked question.

When you have overstepped your bounds, it is usually obvious. When you are making bluffs that don't work, or plays that get easily countered, you immediately receive negative feedback, and so you know where you should step back. It is hard not to be aware of such problem spots in your game. But most of the time, the EV that we're hemorrhaging in bad spots are dwarfed by the swathes of EV that we *could* capture. This is the EV we're not aware of, of course. You don't receive any negative mental reinforcement for missing out on EV you didn't even know existed; the only effect of understepping your bounds is a smaller winrate (than it could otherwise be).

You *can't know* where you're understepping your bounds. This is the state of nature for a poker player. You are missing value, and you don't know where.

To be creative, then, is to go exploring for that value. And the only way to explore new spaces for value is by *pushing past your mental trails*.

So how does this manifest in reality? What does it mean to "push past a mental trail"? The transgression of a mental trail manifests in your game as fear. It is the feeling that something isn't right; it is discomfort. It is the same thing that stops you from overbetting the pot by 2 buyins if I instructed you to do it. It's not that you'd think to yourself "this is –EV," although maybe you'd be able to convince yourself of that if you thought about it—but viscerally, the moment you moved the slider all the way to the right and considered clicking, before you ever did any mental math or digested the theory, your *body* would recoil. It is this physical, psychic wince that I want to focus on.

I call it **the pang**. The pang is what happens when a potential play scares you. It's the stone that drops in your gut. It doesn't matter what you label this feeling—fear, discomfort, whatever. If you are a poker player, then you know what I'm talking about.

Of course, the pang is tremendously useful. It is what prevents you from making plays you know to be bad! Without the pang, you'd probably go off and do every stupid play that ever occurred to you out of boredom, or curiosity. Using the conscious/unconscious framework we discussed before, the pang is basically the unconscious mind's method of regulating your play. Where the conscious mind disagrees with you, you will feel stupid—where your unconscious mind disagrees with you, you will feel the pang.

If the pang is what happens when you transgress a mental trail, then to be creative in poker is to push past the pang. To overstep your bounds, you *must accept* that the pang will come. The pang is merely a signal that your unconscious mind thinks you're making a mistake—that is, it is the signal that your internal mental trails forbid you from making such a play.

But you *know* that your mental trails are imperfect. Thus, if you want to move toward a perfect game, you must acquaint yourself with the pang. To feel the pang is to knock on the door of creativity. If you are making a genuinely creative play—if you are doing something you've never done before, a call you've never considered, or a raise that your unconscious mind has trained you against—the pang is the signal that you have come up against the edge of a mental trail.

You must *want* to feel the pang, then. The fear, the pain, the discomfort—it's the only way to know you're making progress. You must flirt with it. You must lean into it. And finally, when you are ready, you must step with resolve over your old trail, and start to erect new one. This is the way that poker evolves. There have always been rules that seemed ironclad—the way to play preflop, rules of betsizing, hand selection—but one by one, all of those trails were abandoned and rebuilt, always a little more daring, always a little farther out.

The Fear Response

Poker, by its nature, is a fearsome game. No matter how good or experienced you are, there are always some plays you are going to be afraid of. But there are obvious differences among us in how much fear we feel when playing poker.

Feeling a pang of fear when about to make a big check-raise bluff or a river 3-bet is normal. It is completely healthy feel fear when moving into uncharted territory, or when making extremely risky plays. So you shouldn't worry if making a big 3-buyin bluff scares you; it scares everyone.

But what about being afraid of a specific opponent? Or fearing flips? The more idiosyncratic a fear that a poker player has, the more likely it is to be toxic to their game.

We'll start with the fear of specific opponents. It's very common for newer or weaker players to be afraid of well-known or established opponents. This was a phenomenon I faced a lot in my poker career. When someone would take a shot at me, very often, they would immediately psyche themselves out. They'd put me on crazy bluffs and outlandishly tricky strategies, and they'd consistently either play overly crazy (because they thought there was no other way to stand up to me) or they'd play extremely conservatively (because they were afraid they couldn't handle my aggression). Quite often, I would just sit back and play a very normal, uncomplicated game, letting my opponents do all the work of exploiting themselves.

There is no reason to fear players whom you've never played. All poker players are beatable, even at the highest levels. As much as it seems that people like Phil Ivey or Phil Galfond possess godlike poker games, I assure you, they are riddled with faults. They have tells, they have patterns, they make mistakes, and they can be exploited. When I was coming up in high stakes and started playing against many opponents who used to be my heroes when I played low stakes, I quickly learned this lesson. Everyone whom I had idolized... was just another poker player. The amazing stories that I had heard about them made no difference in the end. They gave off tells, had bad habits, and were just as manipulable as anyone else.

So if you are facing an opponent you've never played, remind yourself—this is just another poker player. If I can figure out their habits, I will win. Simple as that.

But then there is the matter of a table nemesis. If you consistently lose to a specific opponent, quite often you'll start to fear them. Slowly, you'll see them as a sort of giant, someone who crushes you without trying. This happens to everyone. I had a number of such opponents who other regulars beat easily, but who seemed insuperable to me.

There will always be some opponents who, by pure chance, always run well against you. It is a statistical certainty that you'll encounter such players periodically over your career. But then there are those opponents who just seem to always get the better of you. Maybe they are closely attuned to your habits and weaknesses, or maybe you are utterly mistuned to theirs. We will often be afraid of opponents like this. That fear is going to affect our perception of them, and in turn, affect the routine judgments we make during hands.

My advice is usually to simply avoid such players. There's no reason to try to play them and push through your conditioned fear (unless they are exceptionally fishy opponents). The fact that you're afraid of them just means you're already at a huge disadvantage—it's pointless to fight an upward battle. There is no shame in throwing away an opponent. There are always more fish in the sea.

But what about being afraid of specific poker events like flips, or river bluffs? During my career as a mental coach, I have worked with a number of poker players with these issues. Even when they were running normal, they would consistently expect to lose every flip, or expect every river bluff to fail. If the situation would trigger a full-blown fear response, they would try to avoid those spots altogether, even at the cost of EV.

Fear responses can be insidious, because they prevent us from accurately collecting data. Due to the innumeracy bias, it is already difficult enough for our unconscious minds to monitor frequencies—fear responses make the problem even worse. Being afraid in a certain situation will make your thoughts more psychologically salient, and will cause you to over-represent it in your memory. It will skew your perception. How will you ever figure out that a river bluff is 50% likely to work if you're deathly afraid of it, if it makes your heart pound, or if you're already convinced it will fail? You must overcome your fear before you can objectively take account of what's really happening at the table.

And how does one overcome fear? There is no universal answer; fear is a very complex web to untangle. But there are generally two aspects to fear—the cognitive aspect, and the emotional aspect.

The cognitive aspect of fear derives from your beliefs. This is usually the easier part to change, but it requires some self-analysis. If you are afraid of flips, you might realize that your underlying belief is that you expect to lose every flip. This is obviously an irrational belief. So if that's the case, you need to try to supplant that belief for a more rational one—"I'm going to win about half my flips, so it's neutral EV in the long run." If you first acknowledge that the old belief is irrational, and then repeatedly remind yourself of the new belief, you can effectively replace the irrational belief with a rational one.

The tougher part of fear is the emotional aspect. Generally, this is a conditioned, unconscious response, rather than a conscious one. For example, you might run completely average, but have a consistent emotional reaction to flips—you just feel a pang of fear at every flip, and in your gut, expect to lose. Let's say that you've done the work to alter your cognitive belief, but you still feel that visceral fear. In such a case, there are two ways to deal with this emotional response—emphasized de-conditioning, and strategic avoidance.

Emphasized de-conditioning means that you basically try to condition yourself in the other direction. If you are deathly afraid of river bluffs, then you might move down to micro stakes and do lots of river bluffs, *forcing* yourself to get conditioned by your bluffs sometimes working.

We call it "emphasized" conditioning, because in certain cases, like for flips, you can't really force opposite conditioning—I can't make you win a lot of flips—but you can *emphasize* the under-represented aspects of that conditioning. For example, if you're afraid of flips, then the next time you got into a flip and won, you would emphasize that win by reminding yourself, "See, I do win flips. That's not an anomaly; that's normal." Because that event is usually mentally underemphasized or ignored, emphasizing it conditions you in the other direction. Another way of reversing your conditioning would be to go through your hand database, and acknowledge all of the flips that you ended up winning, and even tally up the percentages.

Strategic avoidance is the less sexy, but still essential, tactic for dealing with fear. Strategic avoidance entails trying to, as intelligently as possible, "work around" your fear so you minimize its effects. For example, if you're afraid of flips or river bluffs, you might collapse or minimize your tables every time you flip or make a bluff so you don't have to sweat over the outcome, and can focus on other hands in the meantime. For different kinds of fears, you might just avoid them altogether (such as playing a certain player, or certain stakes). This is something of a temporary band-aid, but it's wise to incorporate nevertheless, as it will increase your bottom line as you work toward extinguishing the fear response altogether.

As you can see, there is a trove of techniques for dealing with fears, which are all highly dependent on the specific individual and the nature of the fear. But the bottom line is that fear causes distortions of reality, and as poker players, reality is our currency. Thus, we must constantly work to extinguish our fear responses, and close the gap between our perception and the truth.

On Style

You have probably heard the term "style" used in poker. "Style" is based on the notion that what that what works for one person's game may not work for another's. There are many plays that other people make that you don't. It's likely you attribute this difference to your "style."

I'm here to tell you—style is a myth.

"Style" is merely a justification people use for not incorporating new plays into their repertoires. A poker player might say, "Oh, that's not my style. Maybe it works for him, but not for me."

Admittedly, it is true that different game structures will require different plays. However, what I challenge is your *a priori* ability to differentiate them *without trying them out.*

What would happen if you flatted AA to 3-bets instead of 4-betted it? What would happen if you started minraising everything preflop? Or limping everything? What would happen if you started overbetting every value hand 1.5x on the river? What would happen if you started min-4-betting your opponent's 3-bets?

If you don't know—accept that you don't know. *Try it!* Experiment! Style is nothing. Experimentation is everything.

Venture past your mental trails! This is the essence of creativity in poker. The greatest poker players I have ever known are the players who are unafraid of taking stupid risks. They are the ones who are suspicious of every trail they have built, until they have proven its deservedness with their own feet. They are ceaselessly curious and transgressive.

Yes, they make stupid plays—and often! But through constant reinvention and innovation, they learn what works, and they don't take things for granted that haven't been proven by their own experience. They are not impressed by poker dogma. They don't care that "they were supposed to go broke there," or "that hand was supposed to be uncallable." The greatest players are the ones who make uncallable calls, and unfoldable folds—*not because they know they are right, but because they need to know whether they are right.*

And, yes! To be such a player, you must sacrifice some EV now and then. You must accept that sometimes you will make terrible plays, and you will lose huge pots. You will be unsafe. You will move into the landscape of fear and uncertainty. But it is by pushing through that fear, by leaping into that darkness that you will understand how poker truly works. It is through creativity, and through taking risks that you reach out and, for a moment, graze against the raw structure of poker.

Fancy Play Syndrome

While most poker players commit the mistake of understepping their bounds, there are a few who consistently overstep them (a sin we are all guilty of occasionally). This is commonly called **FPS**, or **fancy play syndrome**. As the name suggests, it is the error of trying to make a complex or fancy play where the simple and obvious one would be better. As far as being a *consistent* error, chronic FPS is relatively rare.

So what can we say about FPS?

Despite the widespread use of this term, I think the name "fancy play syndrome" is a bit deceptive, because it seems to suggest that being FPS-y is being "excessively creative." In fact, I would contend an FPS-y player usually has a shortage of creativity.

If you are making a play dubbed as FPS-y, what it really means is that you are attributing to your opponent some kind of thought process that is incongruent with reality. The most common example of this is the suicide bluff—a spot where your opponent puts a huge part of his stack into the pot with a clearly strong hand, and by going back over the top you try to make him fold it, despite giving him good odds on the call, because you think a play of such power will force him to put you on the nuts.

Now, here's the problem I have with calling this "creative": chances are, if somebody is doing a lot of suicide bluffs (and hence is termed an FPSy player), really, he's not actually doing anything

186

genuinely *inventive*. He simply has an overall tendency to misattribute other people's ability to fold huge hands (and also probably an over-attachment to investment). He's not making lots of different experimental plays—he's simply making the same speculative play over and over again, hoping eventually it will work, or that he'll stumble upon the perfect situation for it.

Creativity, on the other hand, is *trying out new stuff*. It takes some introspection, then, to realize whether what you think is your "creativity" is actually just you justifying bad play. But taking stock of this is part of the challenge of self-awareness.

If you an FPS-y player, then I would suggest two mental frames to keep in mind: "people usually have it," and "people don't fold when they have it." If you keep reinforcing these two frames, you will likely relax a lot of your excessive and misguided aggression.

But if you are called an FPS-y player because you are genuinely creative, then I would say—keep on. Don't let the label deter you. As long as you are *learning* from your experiments and consistently trying new and challenging things, then wherever you are in your poker career, you are going to evolve. Of course, chances are good that getting a good poker coach or mentor to help temper your experimentation would be a good idea. But either way, you must do your best to learn as much as possible from your experimentation, and not to let failed attempts go to waste.

I'm reminded of words a wise gentleman once told me— "you should make every possible mistake once, but only once."

The Poker Face

If, in the midst of small-talk, you ever tell a stranger that you're a professional poker player, you'll probably experience a familiar routine. They might tell you about their friend's sister's ex-tennis coach who plays poker, or that-one-time-they-were-in-Vegas; they might ask you if you've ever been on TV, what your parents think about your career, or if you are really good at math. But the one that always gets me is when people say, "Oh, you must have a really good poker face."

The "**poker face**" trope is so widely recognizable in our culture that it has become practically wedded to the game. If you know what poker is, you know what a poker face is. But the poker face represents more than the role it plays in poker. What we call a poker face would be familiar to the Roman stoics, to Zen samurais, to warriors and mystics and gamblers and thieves throughout all of human history.

The poker face is an inimitable human symbol. It is the mask of emotionlessness worn over one's face, concealing the person beneath. The poker face floats somewhere far above the game, detached from the fear, the anger, and the elation that the rest of us seem to feel. It is part of the reason why "poker player" is such a fascinating, almost superhuman vocation to so many.

So when people ask me, "how can I have a better poker face?" I feel like I should have an answer. But what can I say to that?

The truth is, there is no way to have a better poker face—or rather, no special way. Sure, mental frames can help, and there are many little tips and tricks that one can use to mediate tilt and emotional potency and so on. Sure, you can practice in a mirror, visualize stuff, whatever. And yes, you should close your mouth, relax your muscles, be aware of your eye movements, stare straight ahead, breathe consciously, don't talk, and all the rest. But really, these are small things. If you are somebody who has a lot of emotional weaknesses, then these morsels of advice aren't going to transform you any time soon.

Emotions are like the cliff-face of your mind. Formed by years and years of erosion by the forces of world, the contours of your cliff-face reveal your personal history. Some players, before they come to poker, have smoothed out their emotional edges and have good poker faces, whereas others are still jagged and coarse, and seem to betray everything. This is simply part of the genetic and environmental lottery. At this point in your life, you have little say in it.

If you want to have a good poker face, then you first have to stop feeling those emotions.

But once you have come to poker, the only way to smooth the texture of your emotions is by the force of nature. The wind, the passage of time, the thousands of hands of poker grazing against you will sand down your mind. That's it. So, yes, be conscious, be self-aware—learn how to mentally frame, co-opt environments, and other various techniques to try to ameliorate the effects of tilt and control your expression—but, in the end, all you can do is wait. Keep playing, feeling, and hurting. If you stay here long enough, eventually your features too will get sanded away. It takes time. Be patient.

But how can I teach you to be patient?

In the end, this is the only virtue that is fully in your domain. Be calm, let be what will be. If you are emotionally weak, that's okay, be emotionally weak. But keep playing. Keep trying, keep messing up. We were all once where you are now. If you return again tomorrow, and again the next day, then someday it will change for you as well.

Organizing your Sessions

So far, we've been examining these mental aspects from the top down, but we haven't looked so much at the actual experience of playing poker. Let's lift up the hood during a real session and think about what we actually experience, as well as how to regulate those experiences. Here I will offer some practical and straightforward advice.

Remember, a session always begins before you ever sit down to play. Before you play your first hand or load up a table, you have already tacitly agreed to two things: that you will play at the time of day you are playing at, and that you will play with the mental state you are in. Those two factors have significant bearing on your expected EV, and you should experiment with each, to see at what time or in what mental state you tend to play best.

Also consider the schedule that you have in place leading into your session. Have you just exercised, eaten, stretched, meditated? These all tend to be positively correlated with a good state of mind and brain chemistry, and are likely to be good times to start playing poker. Playing after waking up or after a stint of watching TV is likely to induce the opposite. Try to place your poker sessions at optimal times, and follow them up with similarly de-stressing activities to cool you down afterward.

And still, your session has not yet begun until you've completed your **pre-session rituals**. These are things you do immediately before a session begins to get yourself into the right state of mind. They can include light stretching, breathing exercises, visualization, hand review, repeating a mantra to yourself, reviewing your goals, listening to motivating music, and more. It is not especially important that you do all or any of these things in particular, but I would advise experimenting with each to see what you find particularly effective, and to implement at least one. If you continually use these pre-session rituals before you play, you will effectively condition yourself into a state of concentration (à la Pavlovian conditioning). Thus, you will be more likely to stay on point and not get distracted.

Okay, so we're ready to *begin* our session. Let's look at what happens next.

Maintaining your A-Game

Generally speaking, most of your sessions will begin near or on your A-game. Being on your A-game means a few things:

1) you're highly conscious and actively using your rational analysis
2) you're (for now) fairly resilient to tilt
3) you're capable of quitting when appropriate

The last two are linked to the first, so let's examine this in detail.

First, what do I mean that you're using your conscious mind? Recall the distinction between the conscious and unconscious mind that we talked about before. Conscious thought processes are discursive, mediated through language, and tend to be slow. They are also highly correlated with poker-theory analysis.

However, it is incorrect that when you are playing on your A game, that you are *only* using your conscious mind. Even when you are playing your best, you are *always* employing your unconscious mind on the majority of plays. Your conscious mind is simply too slow and laborious to actually compute all of the hands you get dealt. (And to be honest, you would probably find that process excruciatingly boring—imagine having to explain every c-bet or every preflop raise to someone.)

When your conscious mind is sharp and fully at attention, it is generally doing three things: one, it is doing background-processing on high-level things like game flow, reads, and opponent psychology; two, it is "on call," in case a hand that needs direct analysis pops up; and three, it is keeping tabs on your own mental state and how the match is going. There are a few little odds and ends that your conscious mind might attend to, but these are the main things. When you are playing your A game, your conscious mind is skillfully maintaining this juggling act.

But what happens when you're playing your B game, or C game? The conscious mind doesn't simply get thrown out at this stage. It's still there; it's simply more tired, less sharp, and is doing less work—it might only be juggling three balls, rather than four. Perhaps it doesn't update its reads on game flow and psychological profiles as often; perhaps it stops checking up on your mental state and lets you play a longer session because you're down; or, perhaps the threshold for hands that it's willing to stop and analyze has become higher. Of course, it's not as though it *won't* analyze any hands—when your unconscious mind doesn't know how to deal with something, it's going to hand it off to your conscious mind no matter what, but *slightly* or *somewhat* strange hands won't get double-checked as often, and you're more likely to simply take your unconscious mind's intuitive answer. You're also going to be less resistant to cognitive biases, and less likely to think about how those biases might affect your first conscious response (which requires extra processing).

And what happens when our game degrades to our D game? At this point, our conscious mind has probably checked out—it's no longer paying attention to our mental states, it's not trying to model our opponents, and it's certainly not going to be double-checking our standard hands. Occasionally when we try to feed it a hand that is so big or strange that it needs solving, it will offer us an answer—but chances are, that answer is going to be highly biased, since our unconscious motivations will bleed over into our discursive thinking. These motivations might be such things as wanting to get even, wanting to avoid risk, or not wanting to be embarrassed. At this stage, it is no longer easy to quit. Usually, it is only when our unconscious mind wants to quit that we will finally quit—when we feel so bad that we don't want to play any longer, or when we have given up all hope of getting even.

Notice that there is a continuum, a gradual process. In poker, we often speak of "going on autopilot," but there is no single autopilot point, no on-off switch. The sharpness of your conscious mind will wax and wane over a session, and this process tends to be incremental. So instead of speaking in binary terms like "on your game" vs. "autopilot," we should instead consider your session a process of **conscious decay**; the natural deterioration of your conscious acuity over a session.

Remember, your conscious mind is also your primary defense against tilt. But you probably know by now that most people are really bad at realizing when they're on tilt. This is another cognitive bias: most people tend to think that they're more immune to tilt than they really are. This includes you and me, no matter how smart or tiltless we think we are.

Being on your A-game will make tilting events affect you less, but it does little to help you *recognize* once you've reached your tilt threshold. This is another catch-22—starting to tilt is going to make your unconscious mind overpower your conscious mind, preventing you from objectively realizing your tilt. In other words, the point at which our *conscious mind* will conclude we are on tilt is usually a while after we've already reached it, and our conscious mind has checked out.

That doesn't bode well for us. How can we improve our likelihood of recognizing and avoiding tilt during a session?

First off, there is a mental frame that is very useful here. If you are a habitual tilter, it is helpful to note to yourself before a session begins, "I might tilt today, and one of my challenges is to stop myself before I tilt; if I quit before tilting, I will have accomplished one of my goals for the day."

Think about what it's like to be on tilt. When you're tilting and don't want to quit, your unconscious mind has two choices: quitting and feeling bad about your loss, or continuing to play and *possibly* feeling good by getting even. Again, don't dismiss this behavior by calling it "irrational," but instead assume that the behavior is simply responding to a different incentive structure than you'd like. By adopting the frame that *quitting before you tilt* is an inherently valuable goal that you can *feel good* about, you are actually making quitting more attractive. You are creating the possibility that quitting *feels good*, which will make it more likely that your unconscious mind will naturally choose it.

The second way to ameliorate tilt is the environmental method. Rather than hoping your internal overseer will catch you before you tilt, instead you employ external fail-safes to override your tilt. One example might be to you force yourself to quit after being down a certain number of buyins, or after a specific tilt trigger (such as being soul-read, or losing a big flip, or being up a lot and getting back to even). By co-opting an external mechanism that determines when you quit, you avoid the inevitable lag before your conscious mind admits you're tilting. But, of course, you must be able to obey the external rules you create. Programs such as *Tiltbuster*, or temporary self-exclusions (3-6 hours) are excellent mechanisms for self-policing. But the more low-tech (and versatile) method is simply creating hard rules for yourself to follow—"I have to quit as soon as I get soulread," or "I have to quit as soon as I'm down 3 buyins."

Environmental mechanisms can be very effective, but they do little to address the underlying emotional weakness. I encourage you to use a mix of both in your poker game (and in your life).

Through our study of poker, we have covered many domains of skill—theory, which is controlled consciously, play skills, which are controlled unconsciously, and now emotional skills, which draw upon both conscious and unconscious processes. But in the next chapter, we will explore how to best learn and cultivate these skills—that is, we will explore the complex processes and strategies that go into learning.

[For further reading into tilt and emotional self-regulation, I strongly recommend Tommy Angelo's *Elements of Poker*, Larry Philips' *Zen and the Art of Poker*, and Jared Tendler's *The Mental Game of Poker*, which informed some of my thinking on tilt and its antidotes.]

7

Learning How to Learn

"How long does it take to learn poker, Dad?"

"All your life, son."

MICHAEL PERTWEE

We all come to poker with a blank slate. No one arrives knowing how to identify a SA/WB, read a flop texture, or spot a cooler. We learn these things through the feedback that poker provides us. And yet, though poker gives us all essentially the same feedback, some of us become proficient and others do not. One of the strongest determinants of how good a player will become is in how well they learn.

How does one become better at learning?

This question probably seems odd on first glance. Learning is fundamental to how we humans negotiate the world. It feels strange and reductive to take it aside and interrogate it. But if you play poker, learning is an essential part of your vocation. To become a great player, it is imperative that you optimize your learning.

As a poker player, you have all sorts of resources readily available to learn from—videos, forums, books, and so on. Yet no amount of watching videos or reading forums will, on their own, make you good at poker. Why is this? Isn't poker, after all, a purely mental game? It's not like football or tennis; in poker, all you have to do is *know* what the right play is, and then do it. Yet why doesn't it feel that way?

The Three Types of Learning

Although we may learn from playing, from watching videos, or from reading forums, the modes of learning involved in each are fundamentally different.

Let's enumerate them again briefly. First, there's *poker theory* or *knowledge*—what we might call *propositional* learning. This is the kind of thing you generally absorb from watching a video. It is your ability to talk about poker, all of your ideas about exploitation, combinatorics, game theory and so on.

Then there's your *know-how* or *procedural learning*—the ability to play unconsciously. This is your ability to click buttons for two hours, instantly to think of the right play in the moment, your raw poker intuition.

Third, there's *emotional* learning—often termed "*the mental game.*" This is your ability to take losses, to play consistently, to follow your own rules and monitor your mental states. Although all three of these kinds of learning are essential and mutually reinforcing, they are importantly distinct. If you want to develop your poker know-how, it is unlikely that engaging in an activity that develops your theory or emotional skills will be much help (although they may still bolster your overall game).

Imagine each of these as being separate networks in our brains. While each of these networks contributes to the overall effect of playing good poker, these networks are distinct; each is grown and strengthened in a different way, by different stimuli, and are exercised differently.

To draw an analogy, if you're a boxer, being good at your sport involves developing your stamina, your punching, and your footwork. Although all of these skills together might be called "boxing," they are distinct abilities, developed differently, and none of them individually could be called "boxing." Yet they are each essential to the final boxer.

As poker players, the skillsets that we have to develop are our poker theory, our poker intuition, and our emotional skills. How do we develop each of these individual skills? What's the best way to learn them?

In order to answer these questions, we will have to delve into a deeper understanding of the process of learning. This leads us to the three most powerful techniques for optimizing learning.

Risktaking

In Chapter 5, we discussed how the brain is composed of networks of neurons. The interconnections that form among these neurons are strengthened by repeated firing, and are inhibited by inactivity. Through this continual firing and non-firing, these networks gradually emerge and change. These networks are our mental building blocks—all of our knowledge and capabilities are ultimately stored in these networks' structures.

We can define learning as *any change to the connections in our neuronal networks.* Whenever a connection is strengthened or weakened—in any way at all—we will call that learning (barring changes caused by injury or attrition). You might protest that this seems overly inclusive. After all, sometimes your neuronal networks will be conditioned to make you play *worse.* If your brain convinces you that J4o is a lucky hand, that's a change to how your neurons interpret J4o, but do we really want to call that learning?

Absolutely. It's imperative that we don't prejudge learning, or take learning only to mean productive learning. Learning involves trial *and error*, so learning incorrect plays is an inevitable and important part of the learning process, especially early in the development of your mental network. For every bad habit you learn, however, the goal is to learn two good ones.

Now, let's posit that there is some *ideal* neuronal structure. We can call this the "optimal network." That network is essentially the brain of a perfect poker player—it is the structure of the perfect poker game. Your own network has its own shape, probably simpler than the optimal shape. If you superimposed your structure onto the optimal structure, like laying a tracing over an original, all of the inconsistencies between your game and the perfect game would be apparent. What we want, then, is to train our neuronal networks toward hammering out those differences.

This training happens naturally. Because the optimal network is the shape that makes the most money in the long run, and you're getting conditioned by what makes money, you will automatically gravitate toward the shape of this network. The process is akin to natural selection. And yet, it is unlikely to ever get all the way there on its own. If it did, just everybody who has played millions of hands would be a great player. Why does it get blocked in its movement toward that optimal shape?

There are many reasons—lack of selection pressures (not playing in tough enough games), persistent cognitive biases and misperceptions, lack of critical awareness, being motivated and reinforced by factors other than money (such as excitement, etc.), and, sometimes, hurdles of complexity (such as a risky play that's only effective when gotten exactly right, but catastrophic when miscalibrated). There are many obstacles facing an undirected learner.

Imagine, for a moment, that learning poker is like mapping a minefield. When you start, your map of the terrain of poker is very naïve—you have no idea what's good or bad; everything just looks like an open field. The underlying reality (that is, the optimal, real map of poker) is very complex, but you're oblivious to all of that. You just see the blank map. The only way to get more information and fill in your map of poker is by exploring. You must uncover where the mines are, and as you travel through the terrain, you uncover mines (bad play) and safe areas (good play). But in poker, unlike in a real minefield, you do not lose a limb when you stumble on a mine. You might lose a pot, sure, but you are allowed to continue. At worst, you take a slap on the wrist.

In this way, poker encourages us: take risks! Make mistakes! Spread out as far and wide as you can, to figure out what works and what doesn't. The more data points you have, the better and faster you will learn the terrain. The ideal approach to learning is one that uncovers the underlying field as quickly and diligently as possible.

Learning poker is hard. If it weren't, it wouldn't be lucrative. But this understanding of what learning poker *is* (that is, tempering the shape of our networks toward the optimal network), gives us valuable insight. The process is one of trial and error, continual feedback and calibration. Our goal in learning, then, is to speed up and optimize that process as much as possible. We want to maximize our data points, increase the rates at which our neuronal networks are trained, and increase our retention of that training (i.e. make the learning *stick*). This is true in almost any skill—if you are not continually testing your limits and challenging your boundaries, you are not growing as a learner.

There was once a study of Olympic ice skaters, which showed that the athletes who achieved the highest skill level were the ones who took the *most falls* during practice. Rather than taking mistakes to be a bad sign, take it as a sign that you're pushing the threshold of your skill level—and that is exactly where you should be!

So the first key to learning is that *we want to have a strategy that takes a lot of risks*. You're playing a game of Minesweeper, except you effectively have infinite lives. Click around. Make mistakes. In the end, every mistake is an opportunity to gain new knowledge about the terrain, and to use it to your advantage in the future.

Blueprinting

Of course, there are many differences between poker and a game of Minesweeper. One of these differences is that as poker players, we are not forced to start with a blank slate. We are given access to maps that other people have already made.

Articles, videos, books, interacting with poker friends, or even just watching hands play out—these all give us valuable insight into *the way that other poker minds are structured*. Although looking at such things from the outside does not make us capable of emulating their poker mind (no number of hours watching Phil Galfond videos will make you play like Phil Galfond), it does allow you to see the overall *structure* and *organization* of their game. It gives you an idea of what a good map looks like, what it's composed of, and how different elements relate to one another. Instead of simply throwing darts on a blank board, looking at other people's maps allows you to have some idea of approximately where and how things should be allocated, and what a final map probably looks like.

This is the second key to learning: *to use blueprints to accelerate the shaping of our games*. With blueprints, you are able to learn significantly faster, and guide your learning in the right direction. Videos, articles, hand histories, and relationships with other poker players allow you easy access to very powerful blueprints.

So how do we best take advantage of blueprints?

Consider the education of apes. In certain species of ape, when a young ape is trying to learn how to properly crack a nut, the mother will put her hands around the hands of the infant. It will then *manipulate the infant's hands* to make it crack the nut correctly. This is called **shaping**. Rather than simply demonstrating visually by cracking her own nut, the mother is able to directly imprint on the infant's mind the proper technique, muscle memory, and timing of cracking a nut. It primes the infant to learn the correct technique on its own. Such shaping is much more powerful than mere demonstration, because it gets the technique "into the learner's body."

How can we take advantage of shaping in poker? The most prominent example is getting sweated. Being sweated by a stronger player is one of the most effective methods of learning in poker, for the simple reason that it *instills the learning into your body*. If you are being sweated and the person sweating you tells you to make a check-raise you'd never ordinarily do, this is very different than having someone merely point out that checkraise on paper. The simple act of clicking the button (and getting all of the table feedback of watching your opponent thinking, calling time, eventually folding his hand, you winning the pot) primes your poker-playing-mind to be able to make such a move again in the future. In other words, rather than appealing to your propositional knowledge, it conditions your know-how. Of course, a sweat is more than one check-raise—in an extended sweat, you will sometimes assimilate a completely different player's style, logic, and attitude toward poker. Inhabiting the space of another person's mind will allow you viscerally to explore their blueprint of poker, and let its possibilities mesh with your own.

Unfortunately, while sweating may be ideal for learning, real-time sweats may not always feasible, or ethical in many cases. So when we can't do a real-time sweat, what *can* we do? Well, we can *simulate* sweating. We will talk about this in the subsequent section on elaborative rehearsal, as the ideas go hand-in-hand.

Language is another invaluable aspect to incorporating your poker blueprint. The *way* that someone talks about poker reveals a great deal about the way that his blueprint is organized. Try observing the differences between the ways Phil Galfond, Sauce, and Jungleman talk about poker hands in their instructional videos—what are the first things they mention? What concepts do they particularly like to invoke? What do they *not* talk about? By analyzing these things, you will reveal a lot about the way they think about poker, and what concepts they give the most priority.

Although these three players would reach many of the same conclusions about certain hands, they have very different blueprints of how poker should be played and organized.

The point is this—start speaking with the right kind of language, and the structure of your poker thinking will follow. If you start speaking about poker the way Phil Galfond does, chances are, your structure will start to gravitate toward his. Language is important. But how exactly does one learn to speak the language of poker?

Apes are not the only creatures that shape their young; we humans do it too. When parents hear their children tell stories, they will actively guide their child toward the right structure for telling a story. Children tend to rattle off facts—they have not yet learned how to create coherent narrative structures. So a parent will lead them: "why did Billy do that?" "And then what happened to Billy?" "So what did you learn in the end?" This is called **scaffolding**—the teacher provides a skeletal framework that leads the student towards the right kind of structure.

Ideally, a competent poker coach will engage in the same sort of scaffolding. "Why are you making this bet?" "What do you think he perceives your range to be?" "What inference should we make from the hand he just showed down?" and so on. This kind of questioning is often known as **the Socratic Method** in teaching, and its strength is that it leads the student toward having the right *structure* of thoughts, and primes him to follow a pattern of logic. But as in any scaffolding, it doesn't actually "create the story." It merely provides the skeleton to which stories can be grafted.

Blueprints must be utilized in conjunction with exploration, risk-taking and, as always, acquiring lots of data. No matter how well you're following a blueprint, your poker game must be fleshed out with experience. The path to perfection, as always, is paved by playing hands, hands, and more hands.

Elaborative Rehearsal

This brings us to the third key concept of learning: rehearsal. Specifically, **elaborative rehearsal**. The concept of elaborative rehearsal entails that when you are trying to learn something new, you should not only practice it, but also practice it through as many modalities as possible, relating it to other things you already know. The elaborateness of your rehearsal will maximize the retention of new learning.

Say, for example, that you're trying to memorize this list of six words: "cat / farm / blue / chip / pave / tree." If you try to memorize this list using a shallow rehearsal then you'll simply repeat the list of words to yourself until you can recite them from memory. It will probably take you some time, and won't be very efficient.

If instead you learn this list of words by creating a *story* or an image and relating the pieces of information to one another, such as: "There was a cat farm littered with blue chips and paved with trees"—by *elaboratively engaging* all of the information and activating structures of meaning, you will learn the information faster, and retain it for longer. So instead of just a list of disconnected words, it is now an elaborate and multifaceted image, which can be remembered more easily. Or perhaps instead of simply reciting the words out loud, you practice writing them down, or creating a melody to accompany them. The more elaborate the rehearsal, the more effective it is.

By engaging with the information presented to you in different modalities, you create stronger interconnections within the networks that already exist in your brain. Rather than forging completely new network of knowledge (an auditory list of disconnected words), you should take advantage of all of your other pre-existing networks, to reinforce this knowledge and retain it more easily.

You want your rehearsals (that is, your practice) to be *as elaborative and engaging* as possible. This principle is essential to optimizing your learning as a poker player.

Say that you are reviewing some of your hands in PokerTracker or HoldemManager. Your review method is probably to find your biggest losing hands, read them over, decide mentally if you made a mistake or not, and then move on. This is a very shallow rehearsal—there is a limited modality of engagement here, which is *reading a hand history*. The rehearsal becomes more elaborative if you do things like:

♦ write down what you think your mistake was
♦ replay the hand in the hand replayer
♦ imagine yourself playing it again

Just taking the time to visualize the hand again will engage many more mental networks (ideally, the parts that are activated while actually playing), and is likely to make the learning stick.

I should also mention, at the risk of stating the obvious, that reviewing past learning is essential to retention. Once in a while, go back to your marked hands from last month or three months ago, and read some of them over again to remind yourself of what you've learned. Once in a while, read over all of your notes on your table nemesis, even if you feel like you know him like the back of your hand. Review is essential to solidifying knowledge—don't short-change yourself, even if you feel confident in your reads.

There is a second principle to elaborative rehearsal, however, and that is **practice like performance**. According to this rule, you should make rehearsals as similar as possible to the conditions of performance.

If, for example, you are going to be tested on your ability to write down the list of words we mentioned earlier on a test, what do you suppose is the best way to practice for that? By the principle of practice like performance, you shouldn't read a list of the words again and again until you remember it, or try to memorize reciting the list verbally. The best way to improve your test performance is by testing—that is, by *simulating the conditions under which you'll have to perform your knowledge*. Studies have repeatedly shown that if you practice for a qui by repeatedly testing yourself similar to the way you will be quizzed, this vastly improves testing scores over any other method of learning.

This insight extends naturally to poker as well. After all, in poker, what are you studying for? What's the final performance? The performance is *actually playing poker*. This means two things: one, we should deliberately practice our skills *while* we are playing poker, and, second, we should make our external practice *as close to the reality of playing poker as possible*.

Consider how most people watch videos. They sit idly, listen to the video-maker speak, and zone out until they see something really cool or something they disagree with. If something exciting happens, they are engaged—but their engagement is primarily with the theory part of their mind. This is why watching a video is primarily good at developing your theoretical muscles, but not as good at engaging the *know-how* or *procedural* skillset.

Remember when we discussed the value of sweating? Well, videos provide an excellent platform to mentally *simulate* sweating. If you watch a video and imagine that you're actually playing the hands on screen—if you can really visualize that—it will activate a totally different network in your brain from the passive video-watching, theory network. You might then imagine that the video-maker is directly speaking to you and telling you what to do. In fact, I encourage you to click the actual button on the screen, as though you were actually playing the table. This sounds silly on first hearing, because we are married to the idea that poker is a "mental game"; that knowing what to do and doing it are one undifferentiated skillset. As we've discussed, this could not be further from the truth.

Every video is an opportunity wholly to inhabit the mind of another poker player, and test your physical and mental boundaries in a safe environment. All it takes is visualization and commitment.

Remember the power of fear and mental boundaries—remember how difficult it can be to merely click a button! You might think it's something trivial, but the difference between making a bluff that popped into your head and not making it is sometimes no more than *having experience clicking that button before*. If you've seen a certain bluff made in many videos, yet have never made it yourself, it is often simply the fear of hitting that button that holds you back. Respect the physicality of poker! Something as simple as rehearsing going all-in or making a ballsy bluff by clicking a button on a frozen video can make a difference in your next session.

Practice like performance. Anything you can do to make your practicing, studying, and preparation as close as possible to actual poker will maximize your learning gains. Your brain is not as smart as you—it can be tricked easily. Take advantage of visualization, multiple modalities, and elaborative rehearsal in your learning.

Finally, let's look at **isolation drills**. If we want to make practice close to performance, then we should deliberately practice our skills *while* we are playing poker. Isolation drills provide us a way to do this.

The first and simplest isolation drill is simply **isolating attention**. If you want to practice 3-barreling, make it the focus of your session. Pay extra attention every time you barrel someone and there's a chance for a third barrel. In short, make your session unofficially "about" doing third barrels, and put everything else on the backburner. This might seem simple, but it's very effective when trying to hone a specific skill.

Remember the three types of learning we talked about—theory, know-how, and emotion. By isolating your attention, you can foreground your theory network or emotional network while playing. Let's say you have the emotional problem of expecting to lose every coinflip. You might play an isolation session, in which you practice mentally imagining that you'll *win* every coinflip. If you know you are weak in a certain situation and you can isolate and counteract your natural reaction, an isolation session will powerfully enhance your learning and development.

The second type of isolation drill is an **artificial experiment**. In an artificial experiment you temporarily create artificial rules for yourself, designed to practice or emphasize a very specific skill for some period of time.

For example, say you have a lot of trouble fighting 3-bettors out of position. You might design an artificial experiment by moving down a couple stakes, and playing a session where you call *every* 3-bet out of position and try to play well postflop. By isolating and continually exposing yourself to the situation, you will quickly increase your sensitivity and experience, as well as force yourself to challenge your preconceptions about what it's like to deal with such spots. Artificial experiments are not just valuable for gaining experience and understanding of the map of possibilities, but they can also challenge and break down recurrent negative cognition, such as a belief that "it's impossible to play well when you call a 3-bet out of position."

If you have a good strategy coach or mental coach who is guiding you in your learning process, ideally you will have a learning regimen that incorporates all of these techniques in tackling your poker weaknesses. But even without a coach, as long as you have the knowledge (and a little creativity), you can engineer a plan to bolster your weaknesses yourself. By incorporating ample risk-taking, proper blueprinting, and effective rehearsal, anyone can optimize their growth as a student of poker.

The Road to Mastery

How do we become masterful in poker? In previous chapters, we have skirted around the concept of mastery, but let's now face it head on. As poker players, the one goal we all ultimately have in common is the mastery of our craft.

A definition of **mastery** can be elusive, since it's subjective what we each consider masterful. After all, to a 5¢/10¢ player, any

$1/$2 regular might seem masterful, whereas to Phil Ivey, perhaps *no one* seems masterful. The exclusivity of "mastery" depends on your vantage point.

But for simplicity, we'll accept some ambiguity in our definition. We'll say that mastery is "reaching the highest level of proficiency in an art." So a master could be a concert pianist, a chess grandmaster, a professional athlete, or for poker, let's say a consistent mid-high stakes pro.

The science of mastery was famously explicated by Malcolm Gladwell in his book *Outliers*, which was largely based on the research of Swedish psychologist Anders Ericsson. According to this research, rather than being due to innate skill or natural "genius," mastery is acquired as a result of a supportive environment and continual, consistent effort. More recent studies have posited two key elements to acquiring mastery: 10,000 hours of deliberate practice, and a capable mentor. (We will focus on the first element now and discuss mentorship in a later chapter.)

10,000 hours is an intimidating number. If we take this number literally, for someone who's been playing poker for five years, playing 360 days a year, in order to have reached 10,000 hours, they'd need to have played about 6 hours a day, every day. If you've been playing poker for eight years, that number adjusts to about 3½ hours a day. These numbers might seem daunting, but it's important to remember that there are different levels of success in poker—you can be a top $2/$4 regular, or a mediocre $10/$20 regular, and there are many shades of success in between.

Furthermore, studies have shown that the 10,000 hours rule famously touted by Gladwell isn't so clear-cut—depending on the field, that number may range from 8,000 to 25,000 hours. For poker, chances are, it's on the lower end, since it's a relatively young game, and many masters of poker have been playing less than ten years (whereas the best concert pianists have been training all their lives). Ultimately, you should take this not so much to mean that there's a magic number of hours that you need to play, but more that you just need to play *a lot* to get to the highest arena of the game.

But the dictum goes, "10,000 hours of **deliberate practice**." What exactly is deliberate practice? Ericsson theorized that it is not enough to merely perform a skill a large number of times; *how* you practice is the key to whether you will attain mastery. Here are some of the essential properties of good deliberate practice:

1. Breaking down skills into smaller chunks, and rehearsing those specific skill chunks
2. Continually practicing the skill at more and more challenging levels
3. Being very attendant and conscious of feedback and mistakes, with the intention of moving toward mastery

What makes practice "deliberate" becomes very clear—it is rigorous effort with the intention to dissect a skill and master every part of it.

This is all well and good for mastering a piano sonata, but what about poker? In poker there's no such thing as "practicing"— you can only *perform* (unless you take play money, but that's nothing like the actual thing). A concert pianist can practice his piece a hundred times before a recital at Carnegie Hall, but it's impossible for a player to practice taking a shot at Jungleman unless he actually *plays* Jungleman. Or is it?

This problem troubled me for a long time. What does practice mean in a game that is all performance? Is poker some kind of exception from the conventional concept of mastery? I eventually came to the conclusion that although poker has some particular nuances of its own, the same rules must also hold true for poker.

Poker has some counterparts to deliberate practice, like studying or watching videos, as we've discussed earlier. Ultimately, however, they are not enough. The only thing that qualifies as true, deliberate practice is *deliberate play*. Play *is* practice in poker. Every session in which you are paying your full attention to your errors and trying to learn from them, in which you are actively training a particular weakness, such as to take more risks, play more conservatively, or learning to play deepstacked—when you are listening as closely as you can to what poker is telling you—*this* is deliberate practice.

Thus, it is not enough to have done 10,000 hours of mindless grinding or 24-tabling. It *must* be deliberate. You *must* be listening to feedback from poker, and using it to inform changes in your game. In order for each session you play to count towards your goal, it must be a conscious, intelligent, and measured attempt to improve and monitor your weaknesses. Of all the players who are able to quickly shoot up through the stakes, I have only seen two types—those who put in astronomical hours in a short time, or those who are profoundly rigorous with their playing and studying habits. Experience and rigor are the only viable paths to mastery— genius alone always falls short.

Orienting Yourself Toward Feedback

We've already discussed things like isolation drills and elaborative rehearsals, which can make our practice more deliberate. But on the whole, practicing poker is trickier than practicing most other things. If you are practicing a piano sonata, you can usually hear whether or not you've misplayed a note, but as a poker player, you don't always know when you've made a mistake. Poker is constantly giving us feedback, but that feedback is noisy and chaotic. This is partly why poker is such a difficult game to learn.

Feedback is what causes mental conditioning—positive feedback will reinforce a behavior, while negative feedback will discourage it. Imagine your brain as a rabbit in a cage, being either fed pellets of food or shocked by electricity. Usually, you get fed pellets for making good plays, and zapped for making bad plays. But in poker, both pellets and shocks sometimes come down randomly. It can often seem like there's no rhyme or reason—

pellet, shock, pellet, shock, shock, pellet. With all of this chaos, you're bound to get confused, and come up with all sorts of strange and outlandish narratives for why pellets and shocks appear. Unsurprisingly, this is exactly what novice poker players do. When I was playing NL10, after losing a few big pots with aces against 25o and 34o, I started to believe that playing low cards was smart, because an opponent with a big pair would never guess that I'd hit two pair or trips with such a hand.

This is the basis of being **results-oriented**. If you are results-oriented, you will respond to the surface-level feedback that poker gives you. For example, if you make a bluff that fails, you'll get discouraged and assume that it was a bad play. Being results-oriented means that you're conditioned by what poker does in *this* instant—whether it shocks you or feeds you a pellet. But poker is capricious, and as experienced and thoughtful players, we ought to be conscious of this. So instead of letting poker shock or feed our brains, *we* must take hold of the lever, don our lab coats, and ourselves become the scientist feeding or zapping our brains.

We want to be **process-oriented**. Instead of focusing on results and winning every hand, we focus instead on going through the right decision making process—on making plays that will be good *in the long run*. This allows us to make plays that may lose the pot, without becoming negatively conditioned against making that play again. *It gives us control over our own conditioning*. Being process-oriented allows us to circumvent some of the stochasticity and chaos of poker, and more directly shape our brains toward an ideal game.

So how do you *become* process-oriented? How do you stop feeling bad when you lose an individual hand? There are two answers—the first is that it gets easier with time. Lose enough hands and you'll become desensitized to losing, as well as the negative conditioning that often comes with it. But the second answer is a bit more complicated, and it brings us back to the realm of cognitive biases.

Loss Aversion and other Feedback Imbalances

The **loss aversion bias** states that people are inherently irrational in risk-taking—they overvalue avoiding losses, and undervalue making new gains. For example, if you're in a 300bb pot, and you have 200bb behind with which to bluff shove the river, and you think that he's folding 50% of the time—would you shove, or would you fold? Even with these assumptions, many people check back this river because their mind is inherently biasing them toward keeping what money they have. The 200bb they already own have feels *more valuable* than the 300bb in the middle. Losing that 200bb feels worse than winning the 300bb in the middle feels good.

Of course, in reality, every dollar should be equal to every other dollar (in most cases). A dollar gained should be equally as good as a dollar lost is bad.

This bias is one of the most difficult to overcome because it is grounded in emotion, and emotion plays a huge role in how we make internal decisions in poker—not simply in terms of strategy, but also in terms of how we play, when we play, and who we play. For combating this bias and becoming more process-oriented, one of your most valuable tools is self-talk.

Self-talk is the process of mentally "talking to yourself" while you're performing an activity. It's a ubiquitous feature of our mental lives; we are constantly praising, reminding, and chastising ourselves as we act in the world. There are three basic types of self-talk: positive, negative, and instructional. Positive self-talk is self-reinforcing, such as "I've got this in the bag," or "I'm so sick!" Negative self-talk is self-rebuking, such as "I'm such a donkey," or "how could I make that call?" Instructional self-talk, on the other hand, is a mental reminder or walk-through on how to execute something, such as "okay, call this turn and then shove any blank river," or "don't tilt, be patient, and wait for him to 3-bet you again."

Unsurprisingly, positive self-talk is vastly better for performance than negative self-talk. But, interestingly, studies have shown that instructional self-talk is even more effective than positive self-talk for improving performance. Thus, it is in your interest to talk to yourself and, in a sense, to *coach yourself* through your poker game. This is not to say that positive self-talk doesn't serve an important function—it does, as we'll soon discuss. But instructional self-talk is the best remedy for loss aversion bias.

Using instructional self-talk, we can help our rational mental processes overcome the biases of our unconscious mind. "It's okay I lost two buyins, because I had a good shot at three buyins, and that bluff was hugely +EV"—by simply saying this to yourself enough times *you will learn to accept this as a satisfactory justification.* By repeatedly contradicting your natural loss aversion through self-talk, you can counteract the natural impulse of your mind to inhibit the behavior that led to that loss.

Thus, in places you haven't extinguished your loss aversion, you must continually engage in self-talk. Every time you make a good bluff or call that fails, you must mentally tell yourself that you made the right play, and try your best to accept the justification. With enough repetition, you will eventually start to overcome this bias. In fact, you can do the same thing to counter other cognitive biases, such as first-impression bias (your tendency to cling to first impressions longer than you should). Self-talk is an invaluable tool for a poker player, and a skill that needs to be actively developed to truly master the mental game.

As you can see, quite often our brains interpret different kinds of feedback with unequal weight. I call these **feedback imbalances**. Due to these feedback imbalances, our brains impose another layer of noise over and above the distortion already inherent to poker.

Consider **negative events**. A negative event is when you decide *not* to do something you were considering doing. Negative events happen all the time, although we rarely think about them—you elect not to 4-bet, or decide against a flop checkraise. The problem with negative events in poker is that we rarely allow them to condition us.

Say, for example, you're in a big pot, you've barreled two streets, and you're deciding whether or not to bluff the river. If you barrel the river and he folds, you win the pot, you feel really good, and get a big chunk of positive conditioning. If you bluff the river and he calls your bluff, you lose, and you get a big chunk of negative conditioning. But what if, after some consideration, you *don't* bluff the river, you lose, but he shows the nuts? What do you feel then? You might feel a little sense of relief, but probably you'll feel relatively neutral, and perhaps even a little irked that he had the nuts and won the pot.

There is a feedback imbalance here—when you make the right decision by barreling and he folds, you get a lot of psychological reinforcement that it was a good play. But when you make the right decision by checking and he wins with the nuts, you get very little reinforcement that you made the right play. The latter doesn't *feel* like a win, when strategically it should be.

Another prominent feedback imbalance is in hero calls. Think about the last time you made a hero call with ace high in a big pot. If you were right, you probably felt amazing—heroic, even. You received an enormous surge of positive feedback when you won the pot, which was multiplied every time you showed that call to a friend. But what happens when you call with ace high and lose? Well, some of the time you might feel really stupid, especially if you get berated. But most of the time, you'll probably just think to yourself: "well, I knew I was beating his bluffs, and he happened to have it this time. I still don't know if it was a good call." Or, if he had a bluff that beat you, you might think to yourself, "damn! I knew he was bluffing! So sick!"

This one might not ring true for you, but it certainly does for many players. Hero calls carry a lot of psychological weight, because we glorify them in a way that we don't other poker hands. It's almost as if they're exempt from the normal rules of poker diligence. As a result, failed hero calls tend to get relatively little negative feedback, while successful hero calls get overwhelmingly positive feedback. In terms of the emotional calculus, you can see that your brain *incentivizes* you to make outrageous hero calls. After all, it doesn't feel that bad when you lose, and it feels amazing when you win. Hence, hero calls introduce a troublesome feedback imbalance.

So what can we do to equalize all these feedback imbalances? The answer comes back to self-talk—and here's where positive self-talk comes into play. Using positive self-talk, you can reinforce behaviors that poker does a poor job of reinforcing.

For example, after checking the river in a big pot and electing not to fire the final barrel, if he shows down the nuts, instead of simply allowing yourself to feel bad or neutral that he won that medium-large pot, you might instead mentally tell yourself, "Good job not firing that river bluff. He would've called. Good play."

With hero calls, you can do a couple of things to equalize the feedback. First, you can engage in negative self-talk (followed by instructional self-talk) to make a failed hero call more likely not to get brushed over by your brain: "damn, I shouldn't have made that call. Bad play. Be more careful with hero calls."

Second, you could try to dampen the positive reinforcement you get from successful hero calls, to even the playing field. For example, you could make a rule for yourself that you're not allowed to show off your hero calls to any of your friends. This would remove a large part of the psycho-social incentive to making the hero call to begin with, and make you more likely to simply focus on making the immediate best play.

Closely related to feedback imbalances is the concept of **indicative strength**. Indicative strength is how much information a given fact (such as a shown hand) gives you about your opponent's game. I'll illustrate with a non-poker example, for simplicity.

Say you have a vase full of marbles. You know that there are 100 total marbles inside, but there are two possible configurations for its contents: they are either 95 red and 5 blue, or 65 red and 35 blue. You don't know which of these configurations it is, nor the probability of each configuration, but you are allowed to draw out one marble. So let's say you draw out a marble and it's red—this is an event of low indicative strength. That is, it doesn't tell you much about whether the jar is 95% red or 65% red. It could easily be either. But if you draw out a first marble and it's blue, this has high indicative strength—it makes it *more* likely that it's the 35% blue configuration.

With marbles, this concept might seem obvious. But in poker, the confluence of emotions, noise, and complexity make it much more difficult to properly assign probabilities. For example, in a spot where you call top pair because you think your opponent has either the nuts or a missed draw, in the event that he shows you the nuts, you are usually very strongly negatively conditioned—"god, I'm such a donkey, I should've folded." But quite often, his showing down the nuts is an event of low indicative strength—he would have the nuts sometimes whether you thought he was bluffing with his draws or not, and so you shouldn't take it as a very meaningful data point. When your unconscious mind loses a big pot (because it naturally wants to find significance in everything), it rarely accounts for that. It simply sees you lose the pot, and rings the hurt bell.

Our unconscious minds are very poor at processing data for its indicative strength, and so we must use our conscious minds to calibrate our reactions, and thereby, our self-conditioning. Self-talk, again, proves an effective remedy. By telling ourselves: "I knew he might have the nuts either way; that doesn't tell me anything about whether my play was good," we mollify some of the negative conditioning that comes with losing that pot.

We must always be consciously vigilant, and orchestrate the dialogues in our heads. Eventually, with enough practice, your unconscious mind will learn to interpret such events in a way that takes into account their indicative strength, and you'll no longer need to consciously regulate it (in other words, you'll achieve unconscious competence at this). But until then, you must be rigorous with your mental dialogue and calibrate your own self-conditioning. Self-talk is one of the few things over which you have genuine control in poker, so you must wield it as best you can.

The Pitfalls of Hand Histories

There are some pitfalls to the architecture of our brains that are more deeply entrenched, and often, more difficult to see. One such pitfall is **context-dependent memory**. Context-dependent memory entails that what is learned in one context is much better retained, retrieved, and performed within the same context. In short, if you want to remember something, you should put yourself in the same environment in which you learned it (e.g., go to the same place, listen to the same music, engage the same senses, put yourself in the same physical or mental state). This might seem obvious, but it has one very important consequence to the learning of poker.

If you thought of hand histories, you're exactly right. Hand histories are, in a very important sense, *alien* to the context in which we actually play poker. A hand history is a big, meticulous, awkward block of text. It has no sense of time, it (usually) has no visual cues at all, and it is completely static. An actual poker hand involves movement, action, experience, emotion—the way you experience a hand history is completely different from the way you actually experience the living hand of poker. Thus, the context-dependence of memory suggests that the learning you gain from a hand history (or books or forums) is not going to be fluidly exported when actually playing poker.

This partially explains the existence of players who offer robust analysis on hands, but whose poker games are actually quite weak. There are various names for this phenomenon: "theory crafters," "keyboard jockeys," among others—these people have learned most of their poker skills in the context of hand histories, reading forums, or sweating players, but they cannot retrieve that learning during an actual poker game.

How can we avoid this pitfall? To some extent, our psychology makes the problem intractable. The further we move from the context of learning, the more difficult recall will be. That's just the way it is. But there are a few things we can do to make our learning more effective in light of this problem.

The first and most effective thing to do is *to try to emulate the native context*. I.e., do everything you can to make a hand history more like an actual hand of poker. Try to put every important hand in your hand replayer, so you get visual feedback more similar to a real hand of poker. This might seem simple or a waste of time, but the visual cues it activates make it much more likely you'll be able to retrieve the learning in a real game.

But even more powerfully—try visualizing the hand *as though it were real*. Try to invoke the poker-playing part of your brain to accept the stimuli you're receiving. Focus your eyes and imagine the money amounts, what they would mean to you, the timer ticking down, and making the right play. The closer you get your experience of hand histories to the actual experience of playing poker, the more effective your learning will be. Go out of your way to make this happen! It's a pain, and it can often seem awkward or cumbersome, but doing this will dramatically improve your learning and retention in the long run.

A second thing you can do is to try to boil down your learning from hand histories (or from forums and books) into cues that can be imported as self-talk. For example, let's say you read a hand history that shows a great river 3-bet bluff. Instead of simply thinking to yourself, "I'm going to do that next time" (a commitment that will usually never materialize), write down an actionable piece of self-instruction. For example, write: "when you can rep a backdoored flush, 3-bet bluff the river." Keep that piece of paper with you the next time you play a session of poker; ideally, read over it periodically to remind yourself of this piece of self-instruction. This will make it much more likely that in the moment that 3-bet bluffing the river is a viable possibility, this hand will come back to you, and you'll be more likely to make the novel play.

What We Talk About When We Talk About Feel

So far we've explored a lot of the mechanics behind learning, but if we want to fully understand its role in this game, we cannot ignore the concept of the Feel Player.

A vague and shadowy mythology surrounds the Feel Player. He is a genius of mysterious origins. No one can explain how or why he is good at poker—not even the Feel Player himself. He is like a low-born squire who pulls a mythical sword from its stone. He is a fluke, an exception. He is not supposed to be great, yet somehow he is.

Perhaps it is his impossibility that so excites us. Or perhaps it is the dream that we, too, could be great like him. What, in the end, could be more democratic, more reassuring, more feel-good than the possibility of the Feel Player?

Unfortunately, it does not hold up. The notion of a Feel Player is a myth.

But before I can explain to you why that is, we need to define clearly what we're talking about when we talk about "feel".

What is Feel?

The hallmark of the Feel Player is how he justifies his plays. When you ask a Feel Player why he made a bluff, he'll answer, "it felt right." The origins of his answer are a mystery. Where the rest of us invoke combinatorials, betting logics or notes we've taken, the Feel Player invokes the god in his head.

But somehow—incredibly—the god in his head is usually right.

There are many poker players who have embodied the myth of the Feel Player. Personally, I have always seen Ilari Sahamies (Ziigmund) as the foremost exemplar. There are many others, of course. And while I have seen many Feel Players come and go, few have lasted the test of time.

It is commonly believed that Feel Players have a unique style of thinking. While most players are analytical and focused on theory, Feel Players are intuitive and feel-heavy. "Feel" is seen as a thinking style, like the difference between auditory and visual learning. Then perhaps Feel is a sort of shorthand for intuition— pure unconscious competence. We've talked about this concept before, but let's examine it in a little more detail.

Feel and Consciousness

As we've seen before, there are four phases of learning in the process of mastering any skill:

1. Unconscious incompetence (inattentively being bad)

2. Conscious incompetence (attentively being bad)

3. Conscious competence (attentively being good)

4. Unconscious competence (inattentively being good)

Consider **autopilot**. In poker, what we call autopilot is another way of referring to the sum of your unconscious competence—your poker "muscle memory," so to speak. When you are autopiloting, you are essentially restricted to only your poker skills that are unconsciously mastered—skills in the fourth stage of mastery. Everything that is not mastered to that level (skills in which you are only consciously competent) will be missing from your game.

So if, when on autopilot, your flop checkraising game crumbles, this tells you that your flop checkraising game is still not yet mastered to the level of unconscious competence. Although autopiloting is often seen as a bad thing, it is invaluable for elucidating which parts of your game are completely automatic, and by implication, which parts are not.

When you are *not* autopiloting—when you are playing your A-game—there is a thread of conscious chatter that's running through your head. This conscious thread is what gives you access to all of our consciously competent poker skills. "This is a good spot to checkraise," or "he has it here, this is a fold." Notably, the goal in poker is *not* to remove all of the chatter from your mind. This is unlike other activities, such as juggling or dancing, in which the goal is to "get out of your head" and "just be in the moment." The chatter we experience when playing good poker is *essential* for invoking the skills in which we are only consciously competent.

The neurological differences between conscious and unconscious processes are not well understood, but we do know that they are distinct, and understanding their differences is crucial to managing performance.

Consider, for example, driving your car to work in the morning, compared to driving your car in a thunderstorm. On a normal day, you drive very inattentively, perhaps listening to music, or talking to a passenger. But during a thunderstorm, you likely turn the music down, lean forward in your seat, and fully focus on the task. By fully attending to your driving, you recruit all of the subtlety and attention you have to your handling of the car. Skills like fine handling, reactionary decision-making, and adjusting to weather and visibility conditions, most drivers *don't* have unconsciously mastered. We intuitively recognize that this stretches the limits of our unconscious competence as drivers, and so we adjust our concentration levels according to the needs (and dangers) of the task at hand.

But perhaps you might argue that poker is a very mental game—it's not a physical activity like driving a car. How is it that such a mental game can be automated into our mental muscle memory, such that we don't even have to think about it? One process that explains this is **chunking.** Chunking is the process by which larger and larger patterns of information are condensed or "chunked" into single mental units.

A good example of this is in the assessment of starting hands. The first time you ever played no-limit Hold'em, perhaps you looked at a hand like A7o, and processed it as "I have an ace and a seven." Perhaps you considered how each of those cards could hit a pair—a pair of 7s, or a pair of aces, and maybe you figured this to be pretty good. But now, as an experienced poker player who's been dealt thousands of A7's, you treat A7o as not two separate cards, but one distinct "chunk" of a hand. You think very fluidly and quickly about how A7o does against other chunked hole cards—A5, AJ, 78, KQ, etc.

The more we play poker, the more we are able to chunk bigger and more complex patterns of information into single units. As you continue to gain experience, you will start to chunk flops— such that J♠8♠7♣ will become a flop that you will play so many times, you will no longer analyze it card-by-card, but will see it as one discrete thing. And when the turn comes down 2♦, a blank, you will not have to analyze that card separately either, because you know exactly how you're supposed to play with your JT on J♠8♠7♣+ low blank. Once something is chunked, it no longer needs to be consciously analyzed, and your hand processing speed increases exponentially. You're not thinking anymore "what do I beat and what don't I beat on this board? How many hand combos are ahead of me?" but instead, you just unconsciously "sense" the relative strength of your hand on this board, and play it accordingly.

Once a skill becomes unconsciously competent, it is almost always chunked to a high degree. And because chunking requires a great depth of experience, the only way to reach this level of unconscious competence is by putting in thousands of hours and consciously analyzing them so many times that the analysis becomes crystallized into chunks. The spot can then eventually be dealt with as a single unconscious unit.

So when I ask you, "why do you think A♥8♠3♣ is a bad board to checkraise?" you might not have an immediate answer— perhaps, for you, you just know this intuitively. It's part of your chunked sense of A♥8♠3♣; you "feel" it. But if you take a minute to think about it, you can probably retrospectively explain—"well, if I checkraise that board I'm repping very few hands, most aces I have will just check/call, and he has more big aces if he's raised preflop," and so on.

We all have some of our decisions relegated to "feel," but most of us can still *reproduce the theory* needed to derive them again if they need to be analyzed. Yet according to the popular mythology, this is precisely what a Feel Player cannot do.

The Evolution of the Feel Player

So how could such a thing as a Feel Player ever arise? How could someone who doesn't theoretically analyze their hands ever become good at poker?

It's not as unlikely as you might think.

First, let's remember that poker is a **stochastic** game—that is to say, it's non-deterministic. Poker gives you *partially random feedback* to your plays. E.g., if you make a *good* checkraise, your feedback might still be negative (the checkraise fails and you lose the pot) 40% of the time. Not only that, but there's second-level stochasticity—your checkraise might be good against 80% of players who've given off the same reads your opponent has, and bad against 20%, so even if you've made a bad checkraise against *this* player, one of the 20%, it might be good on average. Add to this stuff like getting sucked out and coolers, and you can see how poker gives chaotic and unreliable feedback.

But the idea we have is that the Feel Player is *purely responding to feedback.* He is not using theory to temper his learning. He is simply listening to what poker is telling him—little *yes*'s and *no*'s—simply being conditioned by the feedback of winning and losing hands. He is like someone learning to balance on one foot, gradually getting better and better, his body continually nudging him in the right direction. Perhaps this seems a little farfetched to you. Isn't poker too messy for a player like that to ever get good?

Let me provide you with a hypothetical (which is known as a Monte Carlo simulation). Imagine a group of 1,000,000 "theory" players, and 1,000,000 Feel Players. The theory players are those who using poker theory to negotiate the game, whereas the Feel Players are learning purely from poker's stochastic feedback. Of course, a lot of those theory players are going to fail; maybe they're not smart enough, or they're too tilty, or just unlucky—but let's say that only 30% of them succeed as poker players. That gives us 300,000 surviving theory players. For Feel Players, on the other hand, *tons* of them are going to fail—poker is so random and their learning is so undirected, the vast majority of them will drop off like flies. But given the sheer numbers and the fact that poker might, in its random feedback, mold some of those players into really good habits, let's say that 0.5% of them succeed. That gives us 5,000 successful Feel Players.

That's a ratio of 1 Feel Player for every 60 theory players. That's a pretty lopsided ratio. But it's enough for most people to have run into many of them, and we would not be surprised if a couple Feel Players randomly rose to be among the best 300 players in the world. But the "Feel Player" seems like a prominent phenomenon; surely there are a lot more than 1 in 60, you say.

In reality, Feel Players are overwhelmingly rare at the highest levels—we just tend to notice them a lot more. It's a sort of availability bias; Feel Players are mentally overrepresented.

Theory players are everywhere. They're boring, mechanical. But Feel Players are sensational, rare, and fascinating, so we pay more attention to them. We hang on their every word, we watch them in games, and we root for them. Why? Perhaps because they are like us. Feel Players take crazy risks. They tilt. They make plays no one would ordinarily make. Just the idea of being a Feel Player, of thumbing your nose at the meticulous and boring process of poker theorizing—this is an exciting attitude in and of itself. The Feel Player appears to show us that anyone can win at poker. It doesn't take a genius, or having spent thousands of hours studying the game, or the ability to do GTO simulations or combinatorial calculations.

So we follow him. We tell his story. We, in a sense, create the myth of the Feel Player.

The Luck of the Draw

Now think, how many Feel Players do you really know of? Make a mental list. And of those, how many *are you really sure* are Feel Players, and not just players whose poker theory you find to be suspect, or simply don't know? I'd be surprised if you knew of more than five who are still successful.

A mental Monte Carlo simulation can account for the existence of Feel Players. But this doesn't mean that one should take them seriously. As with any thought experiment, the point isn't whether it actually happened. The point is that being a Feel Player is not a reliable way to become good at poker. It's not a learning style, or a way of being. We are better off thinking of Feel Players, rather than as geniuses or heroes, as simply being really, really lucky.

It's strange, I know, to call someone who is highly skilled "lucky." We reserve that word generally for people who are ostensibly bad. But in fact, if you are looking at the top 0.1% of Feel Players—the ones who are very successful—their getting conditioned by poker in the exact right way to produce good habits was purely a matter of luck. It was out of their hands. Even though they may now be good, solid, consistent cash game players, they still may have been, in a way, just as lucky as a first-time fish who binks a bracelet, depending on the EV and unlikelihood of those events. Feel Players have little control over their development. They don't "choose" to get good. If you took 100 simulations of their career, with all of their decisions held constant, they would succeed in only one iteration, whereas a theory player might succeed in 20 of them.

And that is also why Feel Players are going extinct. You don't hear as much about them now as you used to. Feel Players in general have very short lifespans. After all, if your conditioning and learning was mostly random, what makes you think it's going to continue to keep up with evolving games? In that sense, they are like comets. They may burn brightly for a time, and that draws our eyes to them, but they go out just as fast and foolishly as they arrived. This is not to mention that the chance of a Feel Player reaching the highest levels is becoming more and more unlikely, as poker continues to get harder and more players are employing complex strategies, guided by game theory and exploitation. Strategies that you could've stumbled into three years ago and taken a run at high stakes with are now not enough to break even in $2/$4 games.

Poker is changing. The fact that you're reading this book probably means that you're on the right side of that change. It was merely 10 years ago that basic poker conversations we have nowadays would've been scoffed at as reductionistic, nonsensical, or "not what the game is about."

Don't get me wrong. I'm not suggesting that intuition is not important, or that "feel" doesn't play a role in most of our decisions. It absolutely does. There are many things that our unconscious minds are better at processing than our conscious minds will ever be. Theory can only do so much. It is slow and lumbering, and we often have no time to work through the full calculations in a hand before we must make a decision.

Further, there are games like PLO, which can become so complex that it's impossible to do EV simulations in many flop scenarios. We are always navigating poker unconsciously, and often "feeling" out the terrain with our guts before our brains. But we must also remember that, as poker players, we are tasked with the responsibility of doing *everything we possibly can* to become good.

Poker, rake, and randomness are all working against us. So we must enlist every tool at our disposal—theory being perhaps the strongest. All theory players use feel; without it, they would be uselessly slow. But properly oriented, theory is the driver, directing the raw power of feel.

One of the greatest benefits of theory, perhaps, is its ability to reduce the stochasticity of poker feedback. Without theory, you might be conditioned not to make that checkraise again—but with a solid understanding of theory, you may realize that even though this hand gave you a *no*, in terms of EV, it was really a *yes* in the long run. With theory, you don't have to swallow the randomness and noise that poker is feeding you; you can instead you shape your game in closer accord with the real mechanics of poker.

In reality, there are probably no true Feel Players at high stakes anymore. The binary opposition of theory against feel is a bit of a fantasy—it's really "theory *and* feel," in constant orbit of one another. Every serious, modern-day poker player has some form of theory that's guiding his play. Some, like Ilari perhaps, just have relatively less compared to their peers. And how do I know Ilari is a feel player? I don't, really—maybe he is a theory player who just doesn't seem that way. Inevitably, these things are hard to quantify, and in truth, a lot of it just comes down to perception. But whoever is or isn't a feel player is beside the point.

The point is: feel is not a reliable way to become good. Feel is not a learning style. Feel is ubiquitous, and necessary for every poker player, and always has been. But in the end, feel alone is just luck of the draw.

So how *do* we become good? Is theory ultimately the answer?

The Hubris of Theory

So far, I have ardently extolled the virtues of poker theory and rigorous study. But I should also make clear that I don't believe theory is all-powerful. Some players, especially ones who are mathematically inclined, have a rosy conception of how poker works. In their minds, poker is just a mathematical construct—a puzzle, with a definite solution. They imagine that, if locked in a room for 20 years with a calculator, they could develop a poker game so robust that it could take down the best player in the world.

These players imagine poker consists merely of figuring out a set of strategies, as though writing them out on a note card— "how to play poker"—and having the right stuff written on your note card will make your game impregnable. Of course, that's not how poker works. Poker must be *learned*; you must absorb that learning into your bones. Your brain must get conditioned into the right network, which takes many hundreds of thousands of hands. You needn't worry about mapping out all of your strategies, or obsessing over the mathematics. Focus on getting the learning into your fingers. I have known countless players who were more mathematically capable at describing poker than I was, but who couldn't stay afloat in a $1/$2 game.

Imagine a difficult poker hand you've played. You might believe that there's some way to theoretically break this hand down and trace the "right answer," as though you are a scientist looking down on a lab rat in his maze. You might believe that theory will show you that answer—the way things really are. But why do you believe that?

You want to see it from up there, the scientist's view. But in reality, you are the rat in the maze. You will never be the scientist. You're trapped, and there is no way to not be trapped. You don't have access to perfect theory, and you don't know how your theory is imperfect. And it's possible that, in everything that you know, it's *impossible* for your "theory" to lead you to the optimal solution.

You might believe in some part of your mind that poker is a beautiful, righteous, mathematically pristine game. But you, the learner of poker, are but a rat in its maze, and you must find your way out. Reason will not always save you.

8

THE LIMITS OF POKER THEORY

The poker player learns that sometimes both science and common sense are wrong; that the bumblebee can fly; that, perhaps, one should never trust an expert; that there are more things in heaven and earth than are dreamt of by those with an academic bent.

DAVID MAMET

The call of "poker theory" is inherently seductive. In a game full of chaos and uncertainty, poker theory beckons us, promising comprehensibility and control. But while theory is powerful, it is not a panacea. That's not to say that theory in and of itself is flawed—rather, that *we* are.

Human beings are only boundedly rational. We only approximate logical thought. And yet, we often take it for granted that in any situation, theory will show us a path to the answer.

In this chapter, we will analyze the limits of poker language and logic.

It is critically important that we are attentive to our language and the concepts it implies. There is a temptation to think about poker theory the same way one thinks of theory in physics or chemistry. By the end of this chapter, we will see that theory serves a profoundly weaker (and fundamentally dissimilar) function in poker.

The Power of Heuristics

Most of our play in poker is unconscious. This is true even when we are playing our A-games.

We have spoken before of playing on "autopilot," as though autopilot is a deviation from your normal poker game. To be more exact, autopilot is more like the *skeleton* of your normal game. Your "autopilot"—your unconsciously competent skillset—is always running in the background when you're playing poker. It's just that when you're on your A-game, there's a lot of extra conscious activity buzzing on the topmost layer. But your unconscious autopilot is always running beneath it; it remains constant, even when you're playing really well.

Our attention in this chapter will be on that topmost layer—the thoughts that arise when we are consciously thinking about our play. Specifically, we want to look at the stream of *internal dialogue* running through our head.

The chief characteristic of poker theory is that it is mediated through language. So any engagement with poker theory will almost always be processed through our conscious brain. (Or to be more exact, it is mediated by symbols, including both linguistic and mathematical ones.)

When we are on our A-game, we are constantly invoking **heuristics**. A heuristic is, simply put, a rule of thumb. It is a not-quite-perfect-but-good-enough script that we follow, which usually gives us good results. A practical heuristic would be something like, "don't check-raise bluff a board like A49r, just float it," or "never c-bet air on QT7s," or even something more general, such as "in a SA/WB situation, try to minimize the pot size." A heuristic is not a mental breakdown of a hand—it is merely a prefabricated rule to help you get to the answer to a hand without having to think about it.

How do you know when you're using a heuristic, rather than "just playing"? After all, we are constantly making good decisions in poker when autopiloting. Most of those decisions are purely unconscious. The mark of using a heuristic rather than merely using your unconscious perception is that there will usually be some conscious, linguistic thinking involved. If the phrase "SA/WB" pops into your head, or "draw-heavy," or whatever mental language that you happen to use to describe these situations—this is an indicator that you're invoking a heuristic. They don't always have to be explicitly linguistic; they may be merely symbolic. For the most part, heuristic use is easy to spot.

Heuristics are essential to how we play poker. For spots where we haven't achieved unconscious mastery, it would take impractically long for us to fully process every scenario and figure out the best play. Heuristics provide us pre-formulated, simplified rules to quickly process these situations and approximate the best answer. But because heuristics are so widespread, we must be very attentive to how we use them. Bad, unexamined heuristics are often the source of some of our most consistent mistakes.

I used a particular heuristic for a long time without ever realizing it. Whenever a good player overbet, I almost always assumed they were valuebetting. If you asked me why I assumed this, I likely would've cited the language that went along with my heuristic: "an overbet is a risky and unpredictable bet, so people usually make it when they're sure of their hand."

Now, certainly, this qualifies as a rationale. It is poker-logical, so to speak. But I wasn't *thinking through this* every time I folded to an overbet. I was simply consulting this heuristic that I had and applying it (or, after long enough, not even remembering the heuristic and simply folding to overbets because I unconsciously perceived them as strong).

Remember, a heuristic is a mental shortcut; it simplifies the processing of a hand and conserves our mental energy (which is limited when playing a long session, multi-tabling, or battling a difficult opponent). But when you use them unreflectively, you run the risk of crystallizing bad play. In reality, good players *were* overbetting me with bluffs, but because my heuristic was so entrenched, it took me a long time to realize this and discard it.

232

Every player has some of his consistent mistakes and biases embedded into his heuristics. This is why creativity and defying your mental trails are so important: in order to break free of suboptimal heuristics (which are usually quite old and deeply ingrained), you must go over them with a magnifying glass, you must *really* see them for what they are, and you must challenge them one by one.

Not all Theory is Created Equal

We might think of heuristics as prefabricated molds of theory. While theory is fluid and dynamic, heuristics are frozen and static. However, heuristics do initially *derive* from theory. So what about theory, then? Where does theory come from?

There are two fundamental types of theory. The first is **discrete theory**. When I tell you to imagine poker theory, this is likely what you'll think of. It is discrete, mathematical, and involves things like delineating hand ranges, combinatorials, GTO analysis, breakdowns of stats, and so on. It's the type of thing you do in PokerEV or PokerStove. It involves math, modeling, and explicit assumptions.

But contrary to the popular imagination, discrete theory is a miniscule part of the poker theory that we actually use.

By far, the largest chunk of poker theory we use is not discrete. It is rather what I call **narrative theory**. Narrative theory is not mathematical, but *descriptive*. It tells a story. It is not scientific, logical, or deterministic—rather, we might call it literary.

A narrative does not outline all of its assumptions or convert a hand into an analytical model. Instead, it uses established conventions to tell a story that leads toward the answer. Narrative theory lies somewhere between heuristic and discrete theory. And it is, by far, the most commonly used type of theory. I would conjecture that almost all of the theoretical thinking that we engage in is narrative. And yet, few poker theorists and writers acknowledge the role it plays in shaping our approach to poker.

It is comforting to pretend that all theory is equally robust. But if the vast majority of poker thinking is narrative rather than discrete, then our faith in the comprehensibility of poker might be unearned. It suggests that the vast majority of poker theory (and our understanding of this game) is *not* scientific, logical, or deterministic. Poker becomes more an art than a science. And that is a deeply uncomfortable thought for those who want to believe in poker as being a chess game.

Narrative Theory: Wittgenstein's Poker

Take this nugget of theory, taken from an actual explanation of a poker hand: "His range here is weak, and he just lost a couple big pots, so this is a good spot to bluff." This seems on its face like valid reasoning, doesn't it? This is a very typical example of what is going through our heads when we're thinking through a poker hand—and it is also very typical narrative theory.

Narrative theory has a few hallmarks:

- It is not immediately falsifiable (and sometimes never falsifiable); in other words, it would be difficult to point out a single fact that would prove the narrative incorrect

- It tends not to explicitly state the assumptions and variables on which it hinges

234

♦ It tends to be much more concise than discrete theory

To discretely analyze a spot involves complex math, the mapping of assumptions and forking paths through a hand. Narrative theory collapses these complexities. And, as it turns out, that is precisely where its strength lies.

Go back to that original example: "his range here is weak, and he just lost a couple big pots, so this is a good spot to bluff." What if perhaps instead the opponent knows his range is weak, and thus will be calling more? Or, what if losing big pots is going to make him more call-y? These are two possible counter-narratives that would directly challenge this one. The question is—how do we decide between them?

There are no numbers to compare, nothing to multiply or divide, no pot odds to analyze. How do we decide between the first narrative: "villains who just lost big pots tend to call more," and "villains who just lost big pots tend to give up more"? In a very real sense, both of these are valid. If the line of reasoning went, instead: "his range here is weak, but he knows that and he just lost a couple big pots, so he's likely to call down light here," this story would also sound convincing, wouldn't it?

It can be frustrating, but such ambiguity is inherent to narrative theory. Its strength is in its ability to transform a hand into a story—a simplified narrative that efficiently organizes and condenses the information in a hand. Imagine if we laid out all of the assumptions behind something like "I'm going to slowplay my set here because a raise would look too strong." We'd have to first say what his range is going into this hand, what our range is, how we think he'll perceive a turn flat, the likelihood that he'll bluff or valuebet any given river card, how he is going to react to a turn raise, and so on and so forth. Really, when it comes down to it, actually *breaking down* a hand is enormously complex. It involves a lot of paperwork. Narrative theory is, in this sense, a kind of deferral, a form of shorthand.

Behind narrative theory lies the claim, "there is some discrete theory that justifies this. I don't have it on me, and I can't show it to you now, but it exists somewhere." Actually doing that discrete theory during a poker hand would be prohibitively taxing, in terms of mental processing and of time. We can't discretely analyze every hand we play. So we must take shortcuts. Narrative theory is the only practical way that we, as human beings, can efficiently organize and recall our knowledge of poker theory.

But how do we actually *generate* a thread of narrative theory?

Narrative theory is composed of building blocks, which we might call **poker memes**. Things like "checking back for pot control," or "maximizing stack-to-pot ratio," or "extracting max value," or "betting to induce a bluff." These memes describe interpretations of events in a hand which we, poker theory users, view as possible. We all agree these are things that really happen in a hand—they have a discrete theoretical basis. That does not mean that they happened in *this particular hand you're describing*, but we all agree those are valid concepts.

Here are some (usually) invalid memes: "I raised for information," or "I bet because he was challenging me," or "I folded because the hand might be weird." We don't consider these memes to be grounded in discrete theory, so we dismiss them. Unsurprisingly, the language of valid narrative theory has changed as poker has evolved (and thus, as discrete theory has evolved).

Narrative theory, then, is a social phenomenon—in the words of Wittgenstein, it is a "language game." This game is created by the community of people who want to talk about poker, and it is through that community that we regulate what is valid narrative theory and what is not. This gives it a genetic quality—generally, very strong players (especially vocal ones who make videos or talk openly about their poker thinking) create new memes and foreclose less useful ones, and most other players tend to follow their examples. Thus, changes in narrative theory disseminate not through poker itself, but through the *poker community*. And these changes are not broadcast through playing or changes in gameplay, but rather through *social and linguistic changes* that are amplified by prominent community members.

Narrative theory is, in a way, much more interesting and organic than discrete theory. Discrete theory should be identical for two people on opposite sides of the world, even if they're in totally different player pools. But narrative theory is always different. It is fluid and changing. It adapts to the needs and worldviews of its users. Reading a forum thread from top players just five or six years ago reveals just how much narrative theory has changed in recent years.

One realization that came to me late in my poker career was this: one of the most valuable things communicated through poker videos is narrative theory, and this is why videos are invaluable for learning. In fact, most of what I think I gave away in the videos I was making was not actually my poker strategy, or the individual plays I made. Rather, it was in how I talked about poker.

Think about it. There are some videos that discretely analyze situations in hands, break things down into math and EV simulations and so on, but really, they are the minority—the majority of videos see a hand, quickly give a narrative explanation, and then move on. Most videos function purely through narrative theory.

Of course, once you start to see this, your instinct might be to think this is some kind of rip-off. Discrete theory is what you really want, isn't it?

On the contrary. One of the most important things we learn from videos is *how better to apply narrative theory.*

Narrative theory is much more important than discrete theory when it comes to regulating our play, because we rarely have the time to apply discrete theory during an actual hand! If 95% of our play is regulated by narrative theory, then simply being able to listen to other people's narrative theory, examining and absorbing their language, and internalizing the *rules* with which they combine and chain together memes, we learn to become better narrative theorists. If Phil Galfond checks back top pair on a flop, his breaking down the math and discretely analyzing the hand is, actually, of little value. But what is immensely valuable is learning the memes, the rules of narrative theory that Phil Galfond is applying, and learning to apply them yourself. It is a curious thing—you take a bad player, teach him to simply *talk* about poker better, and he suddenly becomes a better player.

It would be incorrect to claim, however, that narrative theory is *all* that we're doing when we're playing poker. There is also some discrete theory involved, especially as your game advances to a high level. Estimating pot odds, optimizing against a specific hand, logical hand-elimination, or even strategizing how to allocate your hand range over a certain spot—these may well fall under the purview of discrete theory, which strong players are continually applying during their play.

But no matter what level you're at, narrative theory is always the dominant mode of theory we employ in poker hands. There is simply no other method as efficient at encoding the large swathes of information contained in poker. Narrative theory, you might say, is the human antidote to complexity.

Arguing over Stories

So let's say that you begrudgingly accept the validity of narrative theory as I've presented it. Okay, you say, maybe this is how it works. So what?

I've been steadfast in claiming that narrative theory has many advantages, and is essential to our ability to parse the complexity of poker. But, of course, narrative theory has its weaknesses.

Inherently, narrative theory cannot be logically argued. There are a *few* narrative disputes that can be resolved verbally, such as when two inconsistent memes were strung together, and the rules of narrativity were broken. For example, there might be a narrative that includes both "he couldn't have had a draw on the flop, because he loves to checkraise them" and "on the river he never bluffs big, so he had to have hit his draw." The rules of narrative theory disallow this combination. Inconsistencies like this, however, are not terribly common once you reach a certain level of mastery over poker theory.

More often, when people are arguing about a poker narrative, it will not be resolved by the narratives themselves. Narratives are incommensurate—they cannot be evaluated objectively, and each participant will usually believe their own narrative. This should come as no surprise. When we share hands, we even label ourselves the "hero" and our opponent the "villain."

So when disputes arise, they are often resolved by an appeal to authority. The players will go to a third party, another trusted poker player, to decide which narrative is best aligned with the authoritative narrative.

In fact, once you recognize this phenomenon, you will start seeing it everywhere, especially in poker forums. What happens in a typical strategy thread, after all? An opening poster shows a hand, and then every subsequent poster takes a shot at communicating their own narrative of what's going on in the hand. This *should* become chaos, a soup of competing narratives. And yet when we read such a thread, we usually have an idea of which narrative "won." How do we decide that?

There are three ways such threads are decided. First, if there is no consensus, we tend to ally ourselves with the narrative that most closely resembles our own. Second, if there *is* a consensus, then we choose the narrative that is most popular with the best players (a sign of its fitness). This is often the way that narrative theory is evaluated. We observe a narrative somewhere in the wild, and from the fact that it's thriving—by the principle of natural selection—we assume it must be strategically fit.

This is the basis of what I call **ecological learning.** There are three modes of learning in poker: learning through theory, learning via direct experience, and learning through observing others— ecological learning. Through this type of learning, you learn from "what's out there" or "what people are doing," under the presumption that weak strategies would be culled out from the population. Thus, through ecological learning, popularity is an effective measure of a narrative's fitness.

Going back to how we determine which story won the thread—the third possibility is that a poker authority weighs in to choose among the narratives presented, or possibly even offers his own. Let's say, for example, that Sauce or Jungleman weighs in on a thread. If they say something like "this is a definite fold," that doesn't really qualify as narrative theory; that would be merely a determination of the best play. But if they *do* offer an explanation of the hand—their narrative—then that narrative becomes the dominant one that later posters accept.

Rarely are these things decided by application of discrete theory, comparing mathematical models of the hands and assumptions and so on. Really, once you start seeing this, arguments about poker can seem almost simplistic.

If you are anything like I was, as a student of poker, you will get into many arguments with fellow poker players. When you find something you disagree with, or which doesn't seem to make sense to you, I encourage you to challenge it. Debating poker theory will nourish your mind. But, especially as a developing player, you should be wary of arguments that begin and end in narrative theory.

The Importance of Being Discrete

At its core, all of narrative theory is supposed to carry an implied warranty. The warranty is: "somewhere out there, someone did some discrete theory to prove this works." Usually, this warranty goes unquestioned. But if you are engaged in a debate about poker, it is time for you to call up this warranty.

When someone makes a narrative claim that you deeply disagree with—challenge them to prove it. Don't accept it at their word! Or, if you have good reason to trust their authority, then take the time to prove it for yourself. As much as I've been stressing narrative theory as essential to our development, the ability to do discrete theory is also vital. Especially now, as poker evolves and games get more and more rigorous, the precision in strategy that can be captured by narrative theory is often not enough.

To reach the highest levels, you must gain a mastery of both discrete and narrative theory. And the only way to do that is to practice them. Learn how to run simulations. Learn how to use PokerEV, or StoxEV. If you don't know how to run basic programs like PokerStove, or how to do fold equity calculations, or how to calculate a GTO river strategy—learn them.

Discrete analysis is always the bedrock of theory. In the end, narrative is only a stand-in, and so you must be willing to call others out when their stories don't add up, as well as scrutinize implicit assumptions in your own game. Narrative theory is merely the roadmap we sketch atop the deeper terrain of discrete theory.

And yet there are some situations that, no matter how hard we try, are insuperably complex. They simply cannot be broken down by discrete theory. PLO has many such situations. When you have a pair and a mediocre draw on a flop, is it better to lead out, or check/call? Is it better to flat it in a 3-bet pot, or raise the flop? What if stacks are deep? All of these variables will certainly affect the answer—but we can't know *how*. We have no idea where any of the cut-offs are for these variables, because PLO is such a combinatorially complex game. Mapping out a decision tree would be effectively impossible.

I remember once getting into a very basic PLO flop situation. I couldn't figure out how to analyze the hand, so I took it to a number of world-class PLO players I knew. To my surprise, I kept getting different answers on the best way to play it—it baffled me that there could be so much disagreement about such a seemingly simple spot! I was frustrated, but also fascinated. In reality, nobody who I took the hand to could actually break down the hand—mathematically, it would be too overwhelmingly complex to even try. Flop hands in particular suffer from this, because the number of possible routes the hand can go after the flop is astronomically large.

The only way to defend a particular way of playing that hand was through narrative. Essentially, I realized I was being told two different stories—and the only way I could decide between them was to eventually pick one and go with it.

Even with all its complications and imperfections, we need narrative theory. Although it can seem hopelessly convoluted at times, we have no alternative but to engage in the circus of narrativity, debate, and reason-giving. It is our only hope for navigating poker's astronomical complexity.

You could say that it's incidental that math can model poker. After all, you can mathematically model a game like tennis, but those mathematical models have little to do with the process of actually learning tennis. I suspect that the same is largely true of poker. Most of the learning that we do in poker has little to do with the so-called chess match underneath. What we are playing is something vague and broad. It is played in wide strokes of thoughts. It is not transmitted through equations and proofs, but through stories and emulation.

If poker couldn't be modeled by mathematics, then storytelling would be all we'd have to make sense of the game, would it not? Perhaps that scenario is closer to reality than we think.

In the end, poker theory tells us about a lot more than just poker. It tells us about ourselves, the way our minds work, and the way that we interact with other members of our community. In the next chapter, we are going to look at this latter phenomenon, with an eye toward the practical. Poker is an intensely isolating and isolated profession, and yet, we would be helpless without a community of peers to guide our learning in the right direction.

What kind of relationship should we have with the poker community? How can you successfully develop and foster a poker network? And how can you stay sane in a less-than-sane culture?

9

THE POKER COMMUNITY

At the gambling table, there are
no fathers and sons.

CHINESE PROVERB

For a game of poker to be dealt, you must have other players to battle, to deceive, to outmaneuver, to control. In poker, you are surrounded by people. And yet, every hand of poker you are ever dealt, you will play alone.

No one else is in your corner. You may find sympathy in others, encouragement, words of wisdom. But you know they have no stake in your success. You are the only one who will feel your swings. Your ups and downs belong only to you.

And yet, there exists a poker community—a society of self-interested individuals who nevertheless teach one another, share ideas and stories, and empathize in each other's failures and successes. They sacrifice their time, their knowledge, and their EV to help one another. Why?

In this chapter, we will try to make sense of the poker community.

Perhaps the most fundamental axiom of poker is "always maximize EV." We internalize this from the beginnings of our careers. So why does something seemingly so at odds with that—

the poker community, with its sharing information and dedication to helping players—exist in the first place?

Why Money Matters

Poker culture offers us a strange system of values. First, we are meant to be dispassionate toward money in poker. They're just chips, we're told. We are supposed to be detached and objective. And yet, at the same time, we are supposed to be driven, to the point of obsession, toward maximizing our EV.

If we're not supposed to care about money, how can we be monomaniacal about EV? And more importantly, why would we be?

Poker culture teaches us to protect information, to look out for ourselves, to be indifferent to ups and downs. Here, the ideal human being is the ruthlessly selfish one. The game of poker, by its nature, drives us apart. After all, when you win a big pot from someone, there is no fanfare, nobody to congratulate you, no handshake at the end. Once you win a pot from someone, the only recognition you get is the new enemy you've made, sitting across the table from you.

Money is not important, we are told. Money is not the end. Then what is?

It is as with every human endeavor—*other people* are the end. It is only through the *poker culture* that having a 6bb/100 winrate, or making an amazing hero call, or being the biggest winner at $2/$4 for a month becomes a meaningful accomplishment. Without other people to care about those things, they would simply be arbitrary facts. But here, they mean something. The poker culture instills us with a value system; it gives us a reason why money is important. It gives us a reason why bb/100, non-showdown winnings, hero calls, marathon sessions, minute questions of poker theory—why they all matter. This is how the stories of poker are created and imbued with meaning. As human beings, we need actualization, and poker culture gives us that.

This is why the poker culture *must* exist. Through it, a simple monetary gain is transformed into an accomplishment, something laudable, even noble. It is through the poker culture that your success truly matters. Your skill, your fame, your journey—in reality, they mean little to the wider outside world.

Yes, you would be making money. But in a vacuum, making money means very little. Poker culture is the logos; the source of values. I contend that, without the poker world, much of poker would be meaningless.

I'm not claiming this is good or bad. It simply is how it is. This doesn't mean that you must derive *all* of your values from poker culture (there are some who do, and many who don't). But all of us who participate seriously in the journey of poker are in orbit of the poker culture. It's the sun that both propels us in different directions and pulls us together.

The Value of Sharing Information

Somewhere in your education as a poker player, you learned that you have to protect information. You probably can't pinpoint where exactly where you were taught this. I certainly can't. It's one of those ideas that's so deeply ingrained into the culture of poker that it seems to have always existed.

Of course you should protect information. Information is important. It's EV, money. We realize the wisdom of this caution, and so we generally follow it. But we don't always. We *do* share information sometimes. We gush to other people about our poker ideas. We show hands instead of mucking. We discuss theory at the table. We trash talk. We post hand advice in forums and help out our friends when they have a tough spot. The truth is, we share information all the time.

Our desire to share information stems from our desire to commune—to participate in the poker community. In a sense, sharing information is the only way to puncture the veil between yourself and another human being. Those are the moments we brush our minds against others—we get to *feel* poker. After all, the game is little fun without other people to play with.

This is not to suggest that you shouldn't protect information. It's important. You probably shouldn't show hands, you really shouldn't trash talk, and you definitely shouldn't discuss theory at the table (unless, of course, any of these are done strategically). But sharing information on the whole is very, very important. In fact, if you want to become a great poker player, it is absolutely essential, because it is the only real way to build a healthy and supportive network of poker minds around you.

How to Build a Village

When I first started playing poker, I was alone. I had no one to share my ideas with. While many others I knew started with a friend or two climbing up poker alongside them, I was completely on my own. After a while, I finally started gaining companions, but it would always happen that, as I improved and climbed up the stakes, I'd soon become the best player within my circle, and would have to search for stronger players to discuss poker with.

I was not lucky in how I started poker. I knew none of the right people. It took me a long time to find good resources. I never won any tournaments, and didn't have the resources to deposit more than once. And yet, I quickly became successful. If you asked me why I think I became good at poker, I would give a few answers—obsession, competitiveness, intelligence. But really, those things alone are not enough.

What truly saved me, I believe, was my ability to make connections with other poker thinkers. I wasn't great at it, by any means. I was 16 when I started playing poker, and had all the adolescent density to go with it. But if I did not possess this skill, I suspect I would have had no chance at all of success.

You *must* reach out to people. You *must* find people to talk poker with. People to bounce ideas off of, to learn from, to encourage you and make you feel less alone in this game. There is probably no single greater determinant of a poker player's success than the people with whom he talks poker.

Well, say you agree with all of this—but you don't really know anyone. You've learned poker on your own, you have no poker friends who are on your level. This was the position I found myself in time and time again. The task seems daunting. How do you start? How do you create your own poker network?

The answer is simple: *give.*

Find someone whose game your respect—they might be a regular in your games, a poster on a forum, a friend of a friend, whatever. Offer them something. Share information. Reveal to them what you had in a hand and what you were thinking. Tell them some of your reads. Offer your own tips that you think they'd find helpful. Offer to help them review hands, or to let them know when good games are running. There are many things you can do, even if you're an unknown player, that can give value to another player.

You might think, "Why would I do that? Just give away information—especially to someone I play against? I might as well set money on fire!" When I was coaching particularly isolated students, I would often hear responses like this. And almost every time, although the protest sounds pragmatic, it is usually not motivated by EV. More often, it is motivated by a fear of rejection.

Try it. Just see what happens. Allow yourself to be pleasantly surprised.

There are times when you really don't have much to offer someone. Perhaps they are so much better than you—and you both know it—that you have little in the way of insight to offer. In that case, compliments go a long way.

I know—it sounds trite. But as I was rising through the ranks, I made a number of my poker connections that way. Not flattery, mind you. It does not help to be obsequious or to fawn over people. Most poker players, especially successful ones, find that kind of attention obnoxious. There is an art to complimenting. In the end, all poker players want to feel *respected* for their accomplishments. Most of what they are looking for is not money, but esteem. So give it to them. Find a way to make them feel like they're the kind of person they want to be.

Deep down, we're all more emotionally driven than you'd think—even poker players. If you can make someone feel good about themselves, if you are honest and forthcoming about what you want, and can humbly but genuinely communicate your respect for them, then there's a good chance they'll like you. With a little luck, they'll be willing to help you out.

Reach out and make connections. No matter how smart or capable or hard-working you are, you will never become a world-class player on your own.

Coaching and Mentorship

I remember one day, when I was an up-and-coming $10/$20 and $25/$50 regular, I tilted and played a long session against a very good nosebleeds player at $50/$100. He and I had never really talked before, but we knew of each other. In that session he decimated me. It felt like every hand he knew exactly what I had and rose above me again and again, making every right call and every right fold. My game felt maddeningly futile. Eventually I was down $150K, my worst losing day ever at the time, and I quit him.

But the story doesn't end there. I sat out, but I didn't leave. I decided to tell him how I felt during the match. I told him that he was the best player that I had ever played. I told him how much I admired his game. I told him that he had just given me the worst beating of my life—and I wanted desperately to know how he did it. I asked if he would teach me.

He did. He became one of my coaches, and eventually, one of my friends.

It doesn't matter how good you are. And it doesn't matter if, right now, things are going great or terrible—finding a coach or mentor is vital to your growth as a poker player.

In studies of mastery, mentorship has been demonstrated to be one of the best predictors of high-level success. This should come as no surprise. A mentor helps us to streamline the process of trial and error. They can nudge us in the right direction when we've reached an impasse, and can help position us toward better reaching our next breakthroughs. A mentor can see where you need to go next—and it is his job to guide you there.

In poker, there is only so much that you can achieve on your own through playing, reading, or watching videos. A good coach will shine light on parts of your game that you'd never otherwise be able to see. Coaching is now so ubiquitous in poker that extolling its virtues would be preaching to the choir—but if you don't have a coach by now, get one. See your coach once a week, or once every two weeks if it's all you can afford—but see someone. Always have that eye over your shoulder. No matter how good or bad things are going, you always want a second pair of hands guiding your development.

Be thoughtful with choosing a coach. Choose someone both who is a successful player and a good teacher (i.e., is intelligent, articulate, versed in theory). Bad players never make good coaches, but good players can sometimes be bad coaches. Look for people with communication skills and teaching experience. And, just as importantly, *choose a teacher whose style you like*. If they've ever made videos, written articles about poker, or have a blog, be sure to research them first and make sure you feel like a good fit. Don't be afraid to ask for a consultation beforehand, just to feel them out.

Once you're working with a coach, be sure to prepare before your sessions! When I was a strategy coach I taught over 100 students, and, consistently, the students who put spent time preparing learned much more in their sessions. Knowing exactly what you want to ask, which hands are giving you trouble, which aspects of poker theory you need help on, or pre-recording videos against the kind of villains who bother you—all that is great for maximizing your value as a student.

And, most importantly, grill your coach. He's there for *you*. If there's something you don't fully understand or agree with, don't be afraid to argue with him or call him out. It will not only train you to better engage in poker argument and navigate theory, but it will also keep him on point and prevent him from being sloppy. Remember, coaches make mistakes too. Keep your mind engaged, and your questions sharp.

Your relationship with coaching should not just end with hiring a coach. If you want to be a great player, I recommend that you yourself start teaching. It doesn't necessarily have to be professionally, or for money at all. But mentoring another poker player will teach a great deal about how to articulate theory, and how to understand and mold another player's mind. It also sheds light on how your own poker mind works. A student will see your ideas and your logic with beginner's eyes. He will often, merely in the process of trying to understand you, teach you something about yourself that you never knew. Teach and be taught. The two are instrumental in developing your poker mind and keeping it sharp.

Many of the greatest lessons and 'eureka!' moments that I had as a poker player came from teaching others. It forced me to refine my thinking, to explore and defend my thought processes in a way that I would never have had to do alone. I would say that teaching a challenging and incisive student is one of the best ways to deliberately practice your poker theory skills.

This is Water

As a poker player, the culture of poker is all around you. Its values, its ideals, its language, its attitudes, its history. You've been swimming in it since the moment you entered this game. Whether you want it or not, poker culture is your inheritance. This water will be your home. But it's up to you to take that inheritance, and to make it yours.

When I was playing, I was a very atypical poker player. I didn't really identify with poker culture. It teemed with values and attitudes that I didn't want to accept. So I didn't—and I encourage you to do the same.

Never accept any value that you do not yourself choose. If you don't want to be ruthlessly self-interested, don't be. If you don't want to be materialistic, don't be. If you don't want to be misogynistic, or to make light of degeneracy, or to be pessimistic about the goodness of people, then don't. You are free to choose.

Poker will change you, no doubt. It changes everyone who accepts it as a part of their life. But you must be conscious of what you won't let it change about you.

But the most valuable caution I could give an upcoming player is this: don't gamble. If you are a poker player, gambling will be all around you. Prop bets, sportsbetting, blackjack, roulette, craps. Even gambling within poker—taking enormous shots, buying pieces of someone that you can't afford, or entering a tournament with a quarter of your bankroll.

Poker players gambling in casino games has always baffled me. Casino games are, in a sense, the antithesis of poker. Poker is a game in which we repeatedly put down our money knowing that, even though this hand may be random, we will win out in the long run. Casino games are the opposite—every play whittles away at your EV. Playing a casino game contradicts what it means to be a poker player.

One could argue that prop bets and sportsbetting fall into different categories, being skill and knowledge-based, and hence winnable. While this is true, I recommend against them for an important reason. Once you start prop betting or sportsbetting, it is difficult not to let your gambling extend into other arenas. It sets a mental precedent for your brain that *some gambling* is okay. The brain already has enough trouble regulating itself when it wants to do something—it is an easy slide from gambling in sportsbets, to taking bad shots at high stakes, to Martingaling heads-up sit-and-gos.

I have seen numerous players who started with sportsbetting or prop betting, thinking they were being strategic, and who wound up having gambling take bitter root in their lives.

As poker players, we often think ourselves immune to such a thing as a gambling addiction—we're not addicted to gambling, we're running a business, we tell ourselves. This may be true for many of us. But it is unwise to tempt that boundary. We are all only human, and gambling is a quiet demon. It sneaks up on us, desensitizing us to it, and sinks deep into us, until it's just a part of our lives. It is easy to take it lightly, but our brains are wired to be bad gamblers. I implore you to treat gambling with healthy respect.

And yet, as we all know, there are many times when gambling is necessary. Sometimes the fish wants to gamble. Sometimes everyone at the table is partaking in sidebets, or straddling, or whatever. In this case gambling is fine—but only within the context of being *strategic within a poker game*. As long as you obey this rule, you can keep your relationship with gambling in check.

In many cases, however, we tend to think we need to gamble more than we actually do to appease the fish, the table, or the moment. In reality, you can elect out of a lot more than you think you can. So long as you are sociable and confident, you would be surprised how easily you can get away with a "no thanks, I don't gamble like that," or a "no thanks, I don't like to drink when I'm playing." If you turn things down with *confidence*, remain positive and friendly, people will respect you and want to play with you. Yes, gamble when you need to, take a drink when it's necessary, but don't surrender every decision.

You're a professional. Treat your life with dignity—let your body be a sanctuary to your mind. It is your only refuge. The better you treat it, the longer you will last in the poker world.

And on that note, in the next and final chapter, we are going to discuss the last, but most important part of the philosophy of poker—how to live.

10

THE LIFE OF A POKER PLAYER

Go and wake up your luck.

PERSIAN PROVERB

Nobody teaches us how to be poker players.

Poker culture teaches us how to slowplay, how to setmine, how to manage our bankroll. It teaches us how to think, how to talk, what is cool and what is not. We absorb these teachings eagerly. But when was it going to teach us how to *be* poker players?

If you know the lives of many professional poker players, you know this is a question that sorely needs answering.

Professional poker is a strange and isolating life. Nothing you have ever done before will prepare you for it. Over my career as a teacher of poker, I taught many things, but one thing I regret never emphasizing is the importance of *living well* as a poker player. This will be my attempt to rectify that, and recount everything that I think every poker player ought to live by—and what I wish I had heard when I began playing poker.

We will begin with practical things you can do to maximize your performance and structure your sessions. The recommendations I will offer are based on scientific research and on my experiences working with poker players.

Structuring your Poker Lifestyle

Freedom is a double-edged sword. Your freedom as a poker player means you can live almost any way you want. This lack of responsibilities disposes us toward unhealthy habits. As human beings, we tend to take the path of least resistance. And in the modern world, the path of least resistance is to live an unhealthy and unstructured life.

Structure is extremely important. As adept as you may think you are at playing poker at any time of day, structure and regularity are highly beneficial to learning and health. Remember, you alone are in charge of your poker playing. You must therefore regulate yourself in almost every way. It becomes much more difficult to control tilt, marathon sessions, or other forms of bad poker judgment without a defined structure to keep you in check.

Set a daily schedule for yourself. Decide when you're going to play poker, and for how long. I recommend not playing any sessions for longer than 3 hours, and taking a short break every 90 minutes. Studies show that there is a drop in performance and mental acuity around the 90 minute mark; taking a break and refreshing yourself, for just 5 minutes if you can, will make you much sharper throughout the entirety of your session.

If you want to play more than 3 hours a day, break it up into multiple sessions. Put enough time between them that you don't feel like the sessions bleed into each other. I.e., resist the urge to think "I have to get even from my first session." Your sessions should feel independent, and putting time between them will make that easier.

Always play at the same time every day. Plan these times out in advance. If it is difficult for you to keep to these times, try setting timers (kitchen timers are especially effective, due to their physicality). Try not to play extraneous sessions, especially not serious ones. Train your brain to think "this is when I play poker. Only at these times." Playing sessions at other times (such as late at night or on a plane) will circumvent much of the mental conditioning you've accrued during your normal sessions. You'll feel more like you can "bend your rules" when it doesn't feel like a "real session." Thus, when you break your structure, you will be much more susceptible to tilt and bad decision making. Don't take the psychological effects of your routines lightly! They will help you immensely in controlling tilt and maintaining your level of play.

Play tough matches sometimes, but not all the time. Whenever you are playing tough matches, do so consciously and intentionally. Focus on the game. Know what you're doing and what approach you're going to be taking, what you'll be experimenting with, what you're trying to exploit. Focus on learning and deliberate practice.

Always review sessions, ideally on a daily basis, with a thorough review at the end of each week. Go over hands in detail. Remind yourself what you did wrong and how to change it. Don't review your session immediately after you finish it, though—your memory is too fresh, and you'll be biased toward thinking that your reads were correct. Give some time in between; the next day is usually best.

Spread out onto as many sites as you practically can. Download every program that seems vaguely useful to you (Pokerstove? PokerEV? Tiltbuster?). Don't procrastinate on getting acquainted with any of them. Every day that you hold off on trying out a potentially helpful program, or moving onto another site, you are bleeding away money. Employ every possible tool. Search for every conceivable edge. As a professional poker player, you have no excuses.

Choose your rituals and stick to them. What do you do every morning when you wake up? Before you start your sessions? When you take breaks? Rituals allow us to divest much of our anxiety and negative emotions. Always engage in rituals of some kind before your sessions. And by ritual, it doesn't mean they have to be spiritual. They simply have to be consistent—choose a routine that prepares you to play, and then stick to it. These will go a long way toward mentally priming you, and warming you up for your sessions.

The Art of Quitting

A great player once told me that quitting is the most important skill in poker. The more I came to understand the poker life, the more I realized how right he was.

Almost all poker players quit too little when they're down and too much when they're up. It is imperative that you treat quitting as a skill, and practice it mindfully. Don't *ever* be afraid to quit when you're down.

Yes, sometimes you're ahead in EV, you believe you have an edge, you believe this player is worse than you. We've all heard those excuses a thousand times before, from others and from ourselves. They don't matter. The best players in the world are not afraid to quit players who they think are worse than them.

The skill of quitting, in fact, is *not* in quitting people who you think are better than you. We almost always quit once we *truly believe* that we are the worse player. The skill in quitting comes in quitting *before* you believe that you're worse. Because in every losing match you'll ever play, it will always take a certain amount of time before you reach that point of realization. Quit early. Never kick yourself for quitting (unless you're up).

It is even okay to quit fish sometimes. Some of the players I respect most have been known to quit fish. After all, 10% of the time, the people who you think are fish are not fish at all. And 1% of the time, even if they are fish, their strategies may be exploiting you, until you realize what part of your assumptions about them are mistaken. This scenario is not as uncommon as you think.

As poker players, we are constantly judging our opponents. It's in our blood; it's how we differentiate the skill levels of players and dissect their psychology. But this instinct works against us when it comes to quitting. When we see that the structure of someone's game is incongruous or shoddily put together, we are quick to lump them into the category of "fish." And, of course, once someone is a fish, we decide we cannot quit them no matter what.

One of the best pieces of advice I've ever received as a poker player was this: only play when you're having fun. Doesn't matter if he's a fish, doesn't matter if you're supposed to play a session today, or if you think you have to keep playing this guy—*if you're not having fun, quit.* No matter your session structure or how many hands you want to put in, never mentally penalize yourself for a good quit.

Poker should be played. *Play*ed! We use the word so easily that we sap it of its meaning. Poker should be fun! Not only because it makes it easier, but because it makes us perform better. Being at play, *enjoying* when you're playing not only maximizes your sensitivity to learning (as we'll discuss later), but also makes you more creative, free-flowing, and open to experiment.

Even if it is your passion, even if it is your livelihood, always remember that poker is a game. That is not to say that you shouldn't take it seriously—of course, you should. But if you are not enjoying it, then you should walk away until you can find a way to enjoy it again.

Outlasting the Mountain

Although poker can often feel like a race, it's not. It is, rather, a feat of endurance. It is more about lasting the longest than it is about being the swiftest. So make sure you last. Take your time.

Build up slowly, check your footing at every step, and treat the mountain with respect.

Be sure to take days off. Play almost every day, but not every day. Rest at least one day a week. It's important to have periods of rest and give your brain time to recuperate from the stress and mental taxation. Don't be afraid to take days off for important life events, or days when you're simply not up to it (and never play when you're feeling mentally unwell). This not only prevents burnout and keeps your brain healthy, it also allays some of the negative effects of stress, as well as consolidates learning. In any kind of training, you must engage in *cycles* of intense performance, followed by rest. Not giving your brain rest is just as bad as working out seven days a week. You must allow your body and mind some time to rest and recover.

Take longer breaks as needed. If things are going really poorly, you're very unmotivated about poker, or if you're going on a trip of some sort, don't be afraid to take a week or two off every once in a while. These sojourns can actually be very good for resetting your perspective as a poker player, and when you come back to the game, you will often have fresh eyes and an open mind. Breaks can also help to reintegrate your self-narrative after a painful downswing. Just be careful to always set a date when you start playing again, so that you don't stay away from the game too long, or start dreading your return.

However, if you are somebody who *continually* takes breaks (or has wider motivational problems), this is a more insidious problem to tackle. In that case, I would advise working with a mental coach or perhaps living with other poker players if you don't already—the grinding energy tends to be infectious.

Don't spend money. Don't withdraw. Play, play, play, and be as frugal as you can while you're building up your bankroll. In the early stages of your career, your money is not yours yet. It's your bankroll, not your money. Decide on a set amount that you'll cash out every month—more than the minimum you need to live reasonably, but not too much more—and don't cash out any more than that, even if you have a big day. Decide when you'll change these monthly cashout limits (perhaps once you reach 2/4, or 3/6, or whatever). This will keep you motivated, and keep your life connected to your success, but won't make you anxious about poker being able to sustain your lifestyle, or allow your lifestyle to drain your bankroll.

Right now, if you are growing as a player, it's all about building your bankroll. Poker is the egg you're nurturing. Take care of it, polish it, keep it warm, and it will grow into a big, healthy, egg-laying chicken. But for now it's still just an egg, so keep your dick in your pants and keep things simple.

Lastly, always have a poker goal, something guiding your development. Goals are invaluable motivation. They will stoke the fire in your belly and keep you climbing. Make sure your time-dependent goals are procedural rather than results-based. That is to say, don't make a goal like "I want to be at 2/4 in 2 months" or "I want to make $10,000 in the next week." Any goal connected to time should be about *procedure* such as "I want to play 7,000 hands this week," or "I want to obey a 3-buyin stop loss every day for the next 2 months."

It's okay (and thoroughly motivating) to have a results-based goal about eventually reaching certain stakes. But never tie that goal to a period of time. Let the goal come when it comes. And don't worry; there's nothing wrong with staring at 10/20 tables and daydreaming once in a while. That's part of being a poker player too.

Distress and Eustress

Poker will age you; make no mistake of that. Stress is ubiquitous in poker. But the degree of stress you will experience depends on how well you are able to manage that stress, and especially, how you manage your downswings.

We fear downswings because, obviously, they eat into our bankrolls and are painful experiences. But another reason why we should fear them is because they can contribute to **chronic stress**—long-term and consistent exposure to stressors. Evolutionarily, our stress responses were supposed to be short-lived and intermittent (usually related to food acquisition or combat). It should be no surprise then that the continual and complex stresses that poker places on us are unnatural, and we are not built to withstand it for long stretches of time.

You've probably heard about the various bad things that stress can do to your body and mind, so I'm not going to go into too much detail about the physiology of stress. But chronic stress inhibits neuronal growth, depresses energy levels and mental functioning, and weakens your immune system. On the whole, stress is very detrimental to health and mental fitness. Clearly, we want to avoid chronic stress.

But how can we? Downswings are inevitable, aren't they? Perhaps this is simply our Faustian bargain—that in exchange for the lucre of poker, we must cede our mental well-being.

It is true that with a game like poker, it is impossible to avoid stress completely. If you are being constantly challenged, you *will* undergo stress. But not all stress is created equal. There are different neurochemical pathways activated by the stress that results from *play*, and the stress that results from *work*. This former form of stress is sometimes termed **eustress** (as opposed to distress). It's analogous to the kind of stress your body undergoes during vigorous exercise, strength training, intellectual stimulation, or sexual activity—all of which are demonstrably *good* stressors for the body.

The idea, then, is that we must transform the stress of poker from distress into eustress. If we can manage this, we can subvert many of the negative effects of stress and maintain our mental well-being. The idea of *play*, as I stressed earlier, is paramount. When you play poker, you must be *playing*!

Make poker fun, engaging, interesting, and self-interested. Whenever it is not, step away from it. Don't be afraid to take breaks, and constantly search for ways to increase your enjoyment of the game. Poker should motivate you. You should inherently *want* to play and improve. Poker should not feel like a grind, but like an adventure.

How to be Happy for People

Every single day, some fish somewhere will win a tournament. This is a statistical certainty. Sitting in his mother's basement, clicking buttons and going all-in with his lucky cards, he binks more in one sitting than you make in an entire month—or an entire year.

How does that make you feel?

Perhaps this doesn't bother you. If you've played poker for a while, it probably shouldn't. So imagine instead one of the regulars at your stakes. Not the good one—no, he might almost deserve it. Think of the fishiest, scummiest, trash-talkiest nitreg you know. The guy you always want to pound on at the tables. And then imagine him binking a massive tournament for $400,000. You wake up one morning to find him at the top of the tournament leaderboards. He's donking around at $10/$20 PLO, laughing in chat and sending free money to the rail.

How about that? Steaming yet?

Or worse yet, imagine your poker rival. You know the one. Your closest poker friend, the one with whom you have competed side-by-side, the one who sets all of the milestones by which you measure your progress—what if it's *him* who binks that big tournament? What if he gets catapulted to high stakes, leaving you behind to grind out your .50/1 or 2/4 by yourself?

If there's one inevitability in poker, it's that things will be unfair. Great players will sometimes fail, and bad players will sometimes succeed. It has always been that way. But how can we *embrace* this fact? Intellectually, it becomes easy to accept after a while. But the challenge is in accepting it with grace—and eventually, with happiness for other people's fortune.

We naturally have two emotional responses to other people's success—envy and self-consciousness. Envy, because we want what they have. When they gain respect, fortune, or fame, we naturally resent them because we want those things for ourselves. But they also make us feel self-conscious, because their fortune separates them from us. Once your nemesis becomes rolled for high stakes, he is no longer a member of your caste. He has risen above you. It leaves you wondering—why not you? Were you not as good as him? Not as smart? Not as deserving? In the end, this reaction has more to do with negativity toward ourselves than toward others.

But the one thing we all have in common is our desire to be free from these emotions. No one *wants* to feel bad when others succeed. We want to be indifferent, or even happy for them. But how do we get there?

Survey yourself. When someone else succeeds and you feel negatively towards it, where does that negativity come from? Analyze your emotions as clearly as you can. You must then find and espouse a mental frame that diminishes that response.

For example, here is a very powerful mental frame: "I am climbing my own mountain of poker. My challenge is dealing with what happens to me; what happens to anyone else is irrelevant." If you'll remember, this is similar to the fog of variance frame discussed in Chapter 6. It reinforces the idea that other people's fortune is independent from your own. You must imagine your mountain is already set in stone, as are everyone else's—but that needn't bother you, any more than it should bother you that someone else at a table was dealt AA. People will get dealt AA. You know they will. But all you can do is focus on playing whatever you were dealt as well as you can.

Try being happy for people. Even people you don't like. It's not easy. We are inundated with stories of other people succeeding, while poker constantly nags at us: "why not you?" But you suspect—rightfully so—that your life as a poker player will be better when you can be genuinely happy for others.

This extends to bad beats, too. Stop telling bad beat stories. The desire to complain to others about your bad beats derives from a nearby artery—wanting affirmation that your failures are not your fault, and that you deserve more than what you have. Sharing bad beat stories also makes you pay inordinate attention to hands where you lose unjustly. Just by repeatedly re-living those spots, you reinforce negativity, and the belief that all of your losses are unjust.

Make a rule for yourself that you're no longer allowed to tell bad beat stories, but instead, are only allowed to show other people hands where *you* suck out. Remind yourself of how fortunate you are. Reinforce the belief—I am lucky to get the breaks I *do* get. Things could always be worse. This will not only make you a more positive and better poker player (and improve your well-being outside of poker), but focusing on your good fortune is bound to make you a better person on the whole.

Practice being happy for others. Tell a friend good job on his winning month. Write someone who won a tournament a private message applauding him. Maybe, if you want a challenge, write that regular you dislike, the one who outstripped you and is now a higher stakes player, and congratulate him on a success. Do little things. Make sure they hurt a little, kick up your bitterness, or make you a little sick to your stomach. Lean into your envy. This is the only way to extinguish it.

Eventually, it won't bother you anymore. You'll learn to be more relaxed about other people, and with yourself. You will find great relief in being happy for others.

Living Well

So far, we've primarily been discussing how to structure your poker life and career. But being a poker player is about more than merely playing poker—it is also in how you conduct your life around it.

It is no secret that poker is an unwieldy horse. It is stubborn, unpredictable, and will swiftly buck anyone who can't hold on. Most can't. You likely know someone who couldn't, and was trampled underneath the weight of poker.

I know many.

I want you to hold on. But it isn't easy. It requires attentiveness, hard work, and living well. You must honor your life and your health—which, in this line of work, is a struggle.

A Healthy Constitution

Poker drains us. It muddies our sleep, health, and diet. Many poker players have trouble balancing their lives; some never do. One of the greatest challenges to you as a poker player is to restore that balance. Not only for the sake of your game, but for the sake of your well-being.

The bedrock of your constitution comes from diet and nutrition. Even if the other pieces are missing—if you're sleeping poorly or not exercising—learning healthy eating habits is perhaps the most valuable thing you can do to immediately improve your health.

Stop eating processed foods. Try to throw them out completely. Cut out as much sugar as you can. Ideally, limit your diet to fruits, vegetables, nuts, meat, and unrefined grains (if you're ambitious, you can try cutting out grains entirely). Eat multiple meals a day—4 or 5 is ideal, but if you're not already, at least 3 meals a day is a good start. Eat to satiety, not fullness. When shopping, stay on the periphery of the supermarket—almost everything in the aisles is processed, or otherwise bad for you. Eat real food, as close to fresh and from the farm as you can. Take a multivitamin and fish oil to supplement any nutritional deficiencies.

Eat slowly. Savor your food. Be consistent in your meals. Cook if you can, or hire a personal chef if you can afford it. Pre-made healthy meals are also a reasonable option. Don't eat fast food, even when you're feeling lazy. Have your meals already planned out and accessible so you're never at a loss for what to eat. Be consistent, push through for a while, and soon you'll build up habits that will sustain you.

Cut out sodas and soft-drinks completely—they are essentially liquid candy. Energy drinks are especially sugary and come loaded with dangerous amounts of caffeine, so avoid them. Caffeine itself is a tolerable vice, so if you must have caffeine, ingest it from tea or coffee (look up "bulletproof coffee" for a healthy and delicious coffee recipe). Drink as little alcohol as possible (and always lock yourself out of your poker accounts when you plan to drink). If you must consume alcohol, give preference to wine (especially red), light beers, and wood-aged spirits (whiskey, brandy, scotch, cognac).

Eating multiple, smaller meals a day, consisting of foods that have lower glycemic loads (foods that don't have as much sugar and don't spike your insulin levels) will make your blood sugar more consistent throughout the day. More consistency means that you won't have the ups and downs of sluggishness and depression that often comes from a poor diet. You will feel more rounded and energetic throughout the day.

You don't have to follow all of these recommendations at once. If your diet is in an especially bad place, then I would encourage you to just take a few of these that seem doable, and implement them in your life. Work your way up toward getting healthier, and remember that your environment will always be more powerful than your self-will.

The Power of Exercise

In a lifestyle as sedentary and chaotic as poker, regular exercise can feel like it's difficult to maintain. But getting regular exercise is one of the most valuable investments you can make in your life.

Regular vigorous exercise triggers rushes of endorphins, which not only make us feel euphoric, but also increase our mental clarity and stimulate learning. It also helps to keep our energy levels stable throughout the day. It's been proven time and time again that exercise is the *most effective* treatment for depression (individually more effective than either antidepressants or therapy), and this has a dose response, meaning the more exercise you do, the more your overall affect will improve. This is not to mention that it dramatically increases your life span, your immune system, makes you look better, burns fat, and allows you to eat more (who doesn't love eating?). Exercise is as close to a panacea as it gets for human beings.

If you're not exercising at all, start. Find something easy and doable. It may be something like powerwalking, a basic regimen of pushups and situps, jogging, or some mild yoga. For poker players who travel often, it is important to remember that you can get in very intense body-weight workouts *anywhere*. There are no excuses. When I was traveling through Europe, I would often do my workouts in a hotel room, out in a park, or on a secluded street corner.

A word of advice: don't just get a gym membership and think you've got exercise taken care of. Statistically, the act of paying for a gym membership in and of itself doesn't make it very likely you'll actually go consistently, or get in good workouts. Instead, sign up for exercise classes, hire a personal trainer, or find a motivated workout buddy to train with you. The latter three, because they involve *structure* and *social pressure*, make it much more likely that you will end up exercising and being consistent with your workouts. They will also make your workout intensity much higher on average.

It may help to emphasize skill development rather than just "working out." Focus on building strength, or improving your flexibility, or developing skills like kickboxing or yoga. The more motivating and goal-oriented you are, the easier it will be to exercise continually. It goes back to as we discussed in an earlier chapter—co-opt your environment. Assume your unconscious self will generally take the path of least resistance, so stack the odds in favor of exercising. It will pay off in the end.

And lastly, don't fear overtraining. The odds of overtraining for someone who's just beginning or is at an intermediate workout regimen is so low as to be negligible. Workout as much and often as you possibly can—It will hurt at first, and be cumbersome. But eventually, you will mentally associate it with the feeling of efficacy and the proceeding endorphin rush that comes after a good workout. Eventually, you *will* start to enjoy it—I promise. It takes time to get over the initial hump, but the fruits of good exercise are invaluable for your body and mind.

Sleep and Sleep Cycles

Finally, we come to sleep. Sleep is one of the most notoriously chaotic elements in a poker player's life. The poker player who goes to bed at 6 A.M. and wakes up at 3 P.M. has become almost a cliché. But sleep is not only essential to physical recovery and health, it is *vital* to the consolidation of learning and memories. Sleep is when your brain is reorganizing itself, processing everything it's learned from the previous day, and replenishing its energy stores. Getting good and adequate sleep, therefore, is essential to learning poker.

Studies show that aligning with your natural Circadian rhythms (being awake during times of light and sleeping during dark) minimizes fatigue. Your body has been acclimated over hundreds of thousands of years to be awake during the day and asleep at night, so inverting that rhythm is suboptimal for your mental and physical functioning.

For some, inverted sleep may be unavoidable, especially those who play live poker. But for the rest of us who have more freedom over where and when we can play, we should try to adjust our sleep to be awake during the day and asleep at night. Being aligned with the cycle of sunlight will increase your energy levels, your overall health, and perhaps just as importantly, will keep you more connected to the rest of the waking world. Being a citizen of the night is profoundly isolating, and is probably one of the reasons why depression is so rampant among poker players. An inverted sleep cycle disconnects you from the rest of the world.

Be wary of your **sleep hygiene**. Sleep hygiene is the term psychologists use to describe healthy, consistent sleeping habits. The basis of good sleep hygiene is going to sleep at the same time every night, and making sure you get continuous 7-9 hours of sleep. In fact, studies show that the most important element of sleep hygiene is sleeping *at a consistent time*. Inconsistent sleep is far worse for your body and mental functioning than inverted sleep. So treat your sleep as sacred, and take extra lengths to try to sleep at the same time (or close to it) every day.

Other elements of sleep hygiene are simple recommendations: don't eat heavy meals before sleeping, avoid any stimulants such as caffeine or nicotine, and avoid alcohol. Don't do anything in your bed except sleep and have sex—no reading, laptop use, or TV watching. Associate your bed solely with sleep, and it will become easier for you to fall asleep.

A good way to structure good sleep habits is by having a pre-sleep ritual. Brushing your teeth, changing into pajamas, or reading before bed—having pre-established rituals that signal your body and mind to get ready for sleep will ease the nighttime transition, and relax your mind so that falling asleep becomes easier.

But as poker players, our sleep hygiene is constantly assailed by the vagaries of poker. Most commonly, sleep patterns tend to be disrupted by big losing days, or after marathon sessions. It's vital that you don't allow this to happen. Letting bad poker days affect your sleep will only magnify the loss' effects, and make it that much harder to mentally and emotionally recover the next day.

If it's time to sleep and you have just quit a losing session (or are still stewing over one), you must first find a way to relax yourself. If you're still stinging from the loss, practice some relaxation techniques, take a warm bath, call a friend, watch funny Youtube clips—whatever will calm you down so that you can sleep properly. Writing about the session immediately afterward may help to divest you of the feelings and thoughts you're experiencing, so you can leave them behind when you crawl into bed.

Remember, when you get up from a bad session, you have not absolved yourself of responsibility. A challenge still remains from the moment you leave the table—the challenge of resuming your normal day-to-day habits with minimal disruption. If you want to live well as a poker player, you must strive to live well *in spite* of poker. Being able to get a good night's sleep after a bad day, eat a good breakfast in the morning and have a vigorous workout is, in and of itself, a victory. Your normal routine will abate much of the negativity that usually settles after a bad losing day. Think of your lifestyle as your frame—the frame of "despite this, my life moves forward." Fight for that frame, and it will carry you forward.

If any of this needs fixing, start fixing it now. Move your sleep slowly toward nighttime. Start cutting out bad foods, little by little. Go for a jog, or sign up for a jiu jitsu class. Fortify yourself step-by-step, and always feel like you're moving forward. If you take the care to nourish your body and mind, I promise that they will excel and be of great use to you.

Need and Ego

It always struck me as odd that the vast majority of world-class poker players came from the same place—they are mostly young, college-educated Western males from comfortable middle-class backgrounds. Of course, you can attribute a lot of this to cultural factors. College is where middle-class, analytically-minded young men have a lot of free time (and poker is marketed primarily towards males), so that explains some of it. But it doesn't explain this: why don't more great players come out of poverty? Why aren't online poker sites inundated with grinders from China, or India, or other parts of the developing world where people could *truly use* the money? To be a bit cynical, it seems all of the money in poker mostly goes to the people who don't really need it.

What *are* these Western kids are playing for, then? It's hard to encapsulate it in a word. Perhaps ego. Competition. Validation. Fighting for a dream, or a fantasy. Although you might say that such motivations are less meaningful, it's hard to escape the conclusion that they are somehow more powerful motivations than need.

In fact, studies in behavioral economics have demonstrated the adverse effects of monetary need on creative performance. The more you have physically at stake, the further your creative performance plummets. But once you find intrinsic motivations—e.g., ego, competition, self-mastery—your performance at a creative task becomes more steady and robust.

Comparing poker to a video game is a common trope, but it may have a great deal of insight to it. Imagine if you had to play a

272

video game, but every time you lost a life, you lost actual money. Do you think you'd play better or worse? I'm guessing the pressure would likely not only make you play worse, but also stress you out and lessen your enjoyment of the game. Poker is very much the same way.

Those who feel that poker is a safe haven, a playground, an arcade game on their computer—they are most free to be creative, to explore, to *play*. They are able to learn and experiment uninhibitedly. And, as is common knowledge now in the world of business, intrinsic motivations tend to be stronger and more sustaining than extrinsic ones. It is more powerful to want to attain mastery at something, or to prove something to yourself, than to want to reach an arbitrary monetary amount or achieve some kind of external goalpost.

This, again, speaks to the importance of having the right kind of motivation. Embrace a goal of self-mastery, or becoming better than your competition. Don't play because you need to. Play because you *want* to.

The Obsession

Most poker player's relationship with poker begins out of obsession. If you have never spent hours tinkering with Excel sheets, PokerStove, your HEM stats, or railing the $25/$50 games immersed in a personal fantasy, then you will probably never be a great player. Every great player I have ever known has started with this obsession.

The obsession is not always a healthy one. It usually isn't. For many, it digs into them, and handful at a time, scoops out the pulp of their life. Before long, through fantasies, through poker books and forums, through breakfasts contemplating how to balance their turn overbetting ranges—poker possesses them. It enters them like a virus, a parasite. It rallies every resource they have toward fulfilling the dream of poker.

No one else will tell you this, but I will tell you the truth: if you do not have this—if you have never been taken over, if this mania has not hijacked your mind—then you should give up on poker. Walk away now. You will never be a great player. Chances are, you will only lose money and time. You are liable to only hurt yourself and those around you.

This is the truth. If you are not a little bit crazy, you will never reach the level of excellence and dedication required to master poker.

But let's say you are a little bit crazy. Let's say you wake up in the middle of the night from dreams of hands you've played the day before. Let's say you fantasize, calculate, strategize, obsess. Then perhaps poker is for you. Perhaps that fire will propel you. Dive further into its depths. Once you do, poker itself will be the easy part. Even when it's not easy, it will be easy.

That is where the real work begins—in taming the obsession. When you are developing as a player, poker is constantly pumping through your veins, like a drug. But after a while, perhaps years, or however long it takes you to reach a place of maturity, or security—after that, you must be ready to retake control of your life. For most poker players, it takes a long time to take back the reins. Some never do at all.

This retaking is essential. It is the basis upon which we as professional poker players can find peace, happiness, and flourishing. There comes a point for every burgeoning professional at which you must steal back your life and make it your own. Perhaps you are at that point now.

So far, I've given much advice on how to manage your career, your health, and your enjoyment of poker. But what I have not yet discussed are the spiritual and philosophical challenges of life as a poker player.

How should we live our lives *away* from poker? What relationship should we have with the game? How can we be happy, and still be poker players?

I cannot promise that what I have to say will fully answer these questions for you. Only time and repeated failures will provide you with those answers. But I can promise that what I have to say will stimulate your thoughts, and hopefully, spur you toward finding your own answers. Let us move forward then, from the health of the body to the health of the mind.

Spiritual Health

The basis of a good life is balance. Not just balance in physical health, but in mental and spiritual health as well.

Do not neglect your spiritual needs. And by spiritual needs, I don't mean religious needs—though if you are religious, then religion can be a powerful source of spiritual nourishment. But for those who are not religious, there are still many paths to spiritual health.

Meditation has been practiced in various forms for thousands of years. Studies show that regular meditation has transformative effects on the brain. It can increase pain tolerance, strengthen self-regulation, improve resilience to stressors, and is correlated with an increased sense of well-being. There are many different types of meditation that you can incorporate into your life—zazen, vipassana, qigong, mindfulness, to name only a few. If you've never meditated before, an easy place to start is at the UCLA Mindful Awareness Research Center (just Google it).

But, if you are a poker player, meditation alone is unlikely to sustain you. Meditation is largely about detachment. But as poker players, we are deeply engaged in the world, and so detachment alone cannot solve all of our problems. We must face the world and our desires head on. The greater part of our spiritual fulfillment must derive from our **self-actualization**. Self-actualization comes from aligning the *self-we-are* with the *self-we-want-to-be*.

The ancient Greek poet Pindar once wrote, "Be what you know you are." This is, to my mind, the best encapsulation of self-actualization. Decide what kind of person you want to be, and then move, thoughtfully and actively, toward that ideal self. When humans are aligned with this trajectory, they experience a deep sense of well-being.

Self-actualization makes you feel like you're on the right path. It becomes easy to love yourself, and to honor the process of your life. When humans are misaligned with this trajectory, they often feel lost, as though they are squandering their lives. As a poker player, you have the freedom to pursue self-actualization in a way that most human beings on this planet don't.

Think about the kind of person you want to be. Not just in poker, but in all things. Visualize that person. Fix it in your mind. Write it down. What is that person like? What do they do? How do they see themselves?

In whatever way you are unlike that person, in whatever way your ideal self outshines you, move toward it. If you are too pessimistic, try to be more optimistic. If your ideal self can do something you can't, start learning that skill. If your ideal self is in better shape, or is better-read, or knows another language—follow it. Inch toward who you really want to be, and don't let a week go by that you don't make progress. Learn new things. Become stronger, kinder, wiser. These are nourishment for the spirit. And it is your spirit, above all else, that will sustain you in poker.

The Journey of Poker

Although it's important to be positive, a poker player must also be a realist.

We've discussed with great optimism the importance of diligence, being healthy, and studying poker seriously. But it would be delusional to claim that following these precepts means you will necessarily succeed. While it is essential that any poker player become a rigorous student of the game, the fact remains that these things alone, no matter how thorough, are not a golden ticket.

Poker makes no promises.

Perhaps you will not be smart enough. Or mentally tough enough. Maybe you won't have enough time, or energy, or money to brave the torrents of variance that poker will unleash on you. Perhaps—dare I say it—you will simply get unlucky. Poker is ultimately a gamble from start to finish. We don't get to choose our success. We can supplicate, make libations, practice prudence, but in the end, it is the poker gods who choose whether we will prosper.

Part of the journey of poker is its uncertainty. We must live with that. But at the same time, we must take full responsibility for who we are and our success as poker players. There is no excuse not to take up every arm, not to scour for every shortcut, not to attempt every unexpected checkraise and slow-play that crosses our path. Though we are at the mercy of the poker gods, we must nevertheless struggle, push uphill, and keep our heads up. This uncertainty is also what it means to be a poker player. It is the journey we all have chosen.

The great imperative, as Nietzsche put it, is to love your fate—*amor fati*. Receive every moment that comes upon you as if you had invented it yourself. Embrace every failure, every success, every downswing and upswing, every hero call and failed read as your own. That's not to say that they are all your fault—but you must take them all as unquestionably yours. Don't seek justice. There is no such thing in poker. There is only fate—so seek your fate.

Accept everything that comes. This is the only philosophy that survives in poker. If you must suffer, suffer gladly. Love whatever happens, because it is yours.

I think Bruce Lee put it best: "Do not hope for an easy life. Rather, hope for the strength to endure a difficult one."

The Importance of Being Happy

In American culture, we are fond of telling people to "find happiness." The phraseology suggests that this is a relatively straightforward task. Supposedly, there exists a thing somewhere called happiness, and we just need to find it. It may take a lot of looking around, we may have to fulfill certain obligations first, collect a certain amount of money, or join a certain social class— but once we jump through those hoops, it will be there, waiting for us.

Unfortunately, happiness is not just hard to find. It is impossible to find. Happiness is not found, but rather *constituted*.

There is a well-known factoid that 90% of lottery jackpot winners lose their fortune within 5 years or less. Much of this can be attributed to the fact that lottery winners, like the rest of us, are stupid. But there is a less well-known factoid: in longitudinal studies of happiness, people who won the lottery had no sustained changes in their happiness level after one year, even if they were still rich. That is to say, their elevated levels of happiness and life satisfaction from winning the lottery very soon dropped completely back to normal.

Perhaps you find this surprising, perhaps you don't. But the opposite effect is even more surprising. Happiness studies of people who become significantly physically disabled, the same

278

effect can be found—happiness levels drop, but return to normal within about a year. People permanently confined to wheelchairs, after a year, are just about as happy as they were before being disabled—as happy as they'd be if they had won the lottery a year before.

This seems perverse to us. It seems to brush off some of the most basic human metanarratives we have—the idea that if we work hard, our lives will be better, and if our lives are better, we'll be happier.

Time and time again, the evidence insists: happiness cannot be found.

Much of these effects can be attributed to what psychologists call **habituation**. Habituation is the psychological process by which we adapt to a constant stimulus by filtering it out. An obvious example of habituation is wearing clothes—as soon as you put your pants on in the morning, you feel them on your body, how they fit, their texture and warmth. But right now, as you examine yourself, you likely have no awareness of your clothes at all. It's almost as though your body has incorporated your clothes as part of you, and stopped registering them as foreign. The stimuli are being filtered out.

Habituation is essential for any complex organism. If we did not habituate, then we would constantly be overloaded with sensory information, so much so that it would impair our ability to strategically direct our attention. From an evolutionary perspective, things that are important tend to move (people, predators, prey). Thus, we evolved to filter out things that are stable and unchanging.

Incidents like winning a large amount of money, or being permanently confined in a wheelchair—these are all situations that, once they occur, are unchanging. Once you have a lot of money, you just have a lot of money. Once you're in a wheelchair, you're just in a wheelchair. It becomes the normal, and your brain doesn't pay attention to the normal (it's too busy worrying if a saber-toothed tiger is going to jump out of that rustling bush).

Although it runs counter to many of the narratives we've been taught, neither having a lot of money nor becoming physically disabled seems to have a sustained effect on happiness. So what does? The most inclusive answer would be: your disposition.

This is what I mean when I say that happiness is constituted. We do not *find* happiness, but we create it out of the ingredients of our lives *as they are*. People who are happy tend to be happy because of their disposition to see the world and themselves that way. Likewise for people who are unhappy. Our happiness levels tend to be fairly resilient—they usually stay around the same level for most people's lives.

But there are a few things we *can* say about how to be happy. Happiness studies reveal a few unsurprising results—couples are happier than single people, religion makes people happier, and optimists are happier than pessimists. People of means tend to be happier than poor people, but studies show rather robustly that income above $75,000 has no effect on happiness levels. That is, income has a moderate correlation with happiness until 75K, at which point the money really stops making a difference (perhaps because past that point, anxiety about money becomes trivial).

Experiences tend to make us happier than material goods, and so you should aim to spend your money on experiences, rather than stuff. This is in no small part because it is very easy to habituate to material objects, but new experiences are, by their nature, impervious to habituation.

We can extend this insight to other aspects of our lives. How do we become happier? One answer is to try to resist habituating to the good parts of life. Find ways to continually remind yourself of how fortunate you are, or how good you have it, or how awesome it was that you accomplished a goal. Savor and mentally relive your good experiences. Some psychologists suggest that you write a gratitude journal every morning, naming 5 different things that you're grateful for. Another strategy is to go without something you like for a while, and then reintroduce it. To some extent, we *can* train ourselves to be more optimistic and appreciative of the world around us.

280

Studies also show that being happy bolsters our ability to perform. The science of learning demonstrates that people learn and retain new information best when they are feeling good, and creative performance significantly improves while experiencing positive affect (contradicting the idea of the "tortured artist"). It increases your life span, your resilience, it makes you more likeable. One is almost inclined to say that being happy will keep you happy.

And yet, the question of how to *become* happy still stumps us. Many cultures have offered their own answers to this question, and there is no answer that will fit everyone. But for my own part, on the question of happiness I look to the transcendentalists. To them, the question "how do I become happy?" was in itself the wrong one to ask. Rather, one should lead a good life, better oneself continually, and be good to others. Happiness, to my mind, not the *purpose* of a good life, but rather, one of its consequences.

In the words of Ralph Waldo Emerson: "The purpose of life is not to be happy. It is to be useful, to be honorable, to be compassionate, to have it make some difference that you have lived and lived well."

I try to live by those words. But if they do not suffice for you, don't worry; you are not alone. It simply means you must keep on searching.

Staring out the Window

In the end, if you are to be a professional poker player, then poker will be the chief focus of your waking life. Things will be that way for a while. But you must not derive your sense of self from poker. Remember that you are more than your poker-playing self.

I stress this, in no small part, because I failed at this when I was a poker player. And I believe now that this was largely what made me unhappy throughout my career. After enough time, I could not sever my larger identity from my identity as a poker player. I forgot who I was. I lost myself to the game.

Do not lose yourself. You are *you*. Explore every side of yourself. Even while you are studying poker and invested in this journey, you must not forget who you are, and what you are worth in the absence of poker.

Find balance. And when I say find balance, I mean integrate yourself in the world. Keep in touch with your friends outside of poker. Always be learning new skills, reading and learning about the world, making new friends and challenging your sense of reality. Think often of your family. We all start being consumed by poker, but you must not remain consumed by it.

None of us will play poker forever. So don't bury all of your seeds in this plot. Once you have a sizeable bankroll, I would advise you to cash out half of your bankroll and invest it, then treat it as off-limits. Have a backup plan in case things go wrong (either on your end, or by some catastrophic incident). Have some sense of what you are going to do after your poker career is over. Think about it seriously. It's an important question. Even if you love poker, to be a consummate professional, you must be thoughtful about all of the possibilities.

Please, don't be cynical about poker. It's easy to be. It's easy to say that poker is a useless game, to treat it with contempt, to see it as a mere money-making machine. Poker can be those things, of course. It can be whatever you want it to be.

But don't do yourself that injustice. It's a waste. Poker, if you treat it with respect, can be a rite of passage for the rest of your life. It can be an arena for practicing self-mastery. Poker can teach you patience, fortitude, thoughtfulness, strength. It doesn't have to be meaningless. It shouldn't be. Let poker challenge you, let it raise you up. Let it make of you a greater human being than you were when you came to it. It can do all of those things if you treat this game, and yourself, with dignity.

Be careful. Don't let poker make you jaded or negative. Don't let yourself lose connection with the rest of the world. Don't forget the poor, the unlucky, the self-sacrificing. Don't forget art. Don't forget books. Don't forget working with your hands. Don't forget helping people. Don't forget sunrises, or mountains, or taking walks on autumn mornings. Poker may be around for a long time, but you won't. Don't let your time slip away.

This, as best I know it, is the philosophy of poker. Of all the things I learned from my career as a poker player, these have been the most important lessons. I hope that they will serve you well as you work your way up your mountain.

One last thing.

If you ever find yourself staring out the window on a quiet Sunday afternoon... whatever you do, don't think about poker.

I wish you the best of luck. I mean it. I really do.

Haseeb

Wow, did you actually make it through to the end? That's crazy.

Thanks for reading my first book. I'm really proud of it. Six years ago, the idea of this book was just rattling around in my head, and now it's rattling around in your head! How awesome is that? Life is cool sometimes.

If you enjoyed it, please leave this book a review at your favorite online retailer. I mean it—it would be a huge help! You can connect with me and read more material at haseebq.com. But only if you really want to. I promise I won't get mad if you don't.

Haseeb

GLOSSARY OF POKER TERMS

$1/$2, $5/$10, $10/$20—A way of notating the size of the blinds in the stakes being played. $10/$20 means a $10 small blind, and a $20 big blind. In this book, it generally refers to no-limit stakes, so a normal buyin for a $10/$20 game is 100 big blinds, or $2000.

3-bet—To reraise; a raise over a raise. (The initial bet on any street is a 1-bet, the raise a 2-bet, but those terms are not used. Preflop, the big blind is considered the initial bet, so the first raise is a 2-bet.)

4-bet—To reraise a reraise; to raise a 3-bet.

Air—Cards that completely missed the board; a nothing hand.

Backdoor—To hit a hand using the turn and river cards, and only one or no flop cards. Generally considered to be a sneaky (or lucky) hand to hit. Synonymous with "runner runner."

Bad Beat—To initially have a stronger hand than your opponent, but have your opponent get lucky and improve his hand, causing you to lose.

Balance—Having different kinds of hands (such as strong and weak) in your range to "balance" it out.

Baller—Slang for someone with a lot of money, or someone very successful. Derives from footballer or basketballer.

Bankroll—The amount of money you have allocated for playing poker. Also known as your "roll."

Barrel—To bet continually postflop.

Bb (big blind)—The minimum possible bet in a no-limit or pot-limit game. Also refers to the player at the table who's in the position of having to pay the big blind preflop (considered the worst position at the table).

Betting Pattern—The sequence of bets that a player makes during a hand, or habits that a player has in how he bets certain hands. A player with a transparent betting pattern will implicitly reveal how strong he is during a hand.

Bink—To get lucky and hit something.

Blank—A card that doesn't change the board significantly. Usually a low card, but not always.

Bluffcatcher—A hand that is strong enough to beat a bluff, but is not itself a strong hand. If the preflop raiser bet every street on A♣K♦9♥ T♥ 2♠, and you called him down with K♦Q♥, that would be a bluffcatcher.

Board—The totality of the community cards. We say the board "changes" if the addition of a new community card dramatically affects hand values.

Board Texture—The way the arrangement of community cards interact with each other. A board like 9♣ 4♥ 2♠ would be a considered to have a "dry" texture, because the cards don't really interact with each other, and there are few draws or strong hands that connect with it. On the other hand, a board like J♠ 9♠ 8♥ would have a very "drawy" texture.

Bumhunter—Someone who only waits around for very fishy players, and refuses to play anyone else. Generally a pejorative in poker culture.

Button—The person with the dealer chip. This is the last player before the blinds, and the player with the best position.

Buyin—The amount of money one brings initially to the table. It's also used as a measure of big blinds—one buyin is considered 100 big blinds, since that's the standard buyin for a no-limit game. (You can technically buy in for many different amounts though. In most games, there is a cap on how much you can buy in for, which varies depending on the structure and size of the game.)

C-bet (continuation bet)—To follow up a preflop raise with a bet on the flop, regardless of how the board connects with one's hand. It's called a continuation bet because it's essentially a "continuation" of earlier aggression, exploiting the power of taking initiative.

Calling Station—Someone who calls a lot. Generally a pejorative.

Call Down—To keep calling someone's bets.

Call Time—In online poker, to go into one's time bank for extra time to think about a decision.

Check Back—To check after you've been checked to.

Check Down—To check all the way to showdown.

Checkraise—To first check, and then raise over a bet.

Cold 4-Bet—To make your first raise be a 4-bet over someone's 3-bet. Basically, if some other player raises, and someone else reraises him, and you reraise that person as your very first bet, that's called a cold 4-bet.

Connect—For a hand to interact positively with the board in some way. Your hand connects with the board usually if you've made a pair or a draw.

Deepstacked—Playing with generally 200 big blinds or more at a table.

Donk—Donk can be either a noun or a verb: as a noun, it's slang for a donkey, or a bad player. As a verb, to donk can mean to lead out into the preflop raiser before he gets a chance to bet, or in a phrase such as "donk around," it can mean to act stupidly.

Donkey—A bad or stupid player. Pejorative.

Downswing—An extended losing streak.

Draw—A draw (or drawing hand) is a hand that is not yet complete, and needs another card in order to become a strong hand. Four cards of one suit (drawing to a flush) and four consecutive cards (drawing to a straight) are the most common.

Drawy—A drawy board is one on which drawing hands are likely, or with which many good starting hands will connect with draws. J♠ 9♠ 8♥ is an example of a board with a very drawy texture.

Dry—A dry board is a disconnected, unsuited board, with which most starting hands won't connect or make draws. A board like 9♣ 4♥ 2♠ is an example of a dry board.

Early Street—The earlier betting rounds in a poker hand. This typically refers to preflop and the flop.

Equity—Your hand's percentage likelihood of winning the pot. For example, if you have AA against QQ all-in preflop, you have about 80% equity.

EV—Expected value; this refers to how much money you should win or lose *on average* for a given decision. EV is a statistical concept—in a sense, it's what you "should be making" for any given play.

Exploitation—Taking advantage of weaknesses in an opponent's game. For example, if someone is bluffing too much, you can exploit them by calling more bluffcatchers; if someone is bluffing too little, you can exploit them by never bluffcatching.

Flatcall—To call.

Flatting—Also means to call. Short for flatcalling.

Float—To call a bet with air, usually intending to take away the pot on a later street by betting or raising. Tricky players will float often.

Flop—The flop consists of the first three community cards. "The flop" can refer to either the community cards, or to the round of betting which occurs once the first three community cards are dealt.

Flopping a Hand—To immediately make a strong hand using the first three community cards—the flop.

Fold—To throw away your hand against a bet.

FPS—Fancy Play Syndrome. Poker slang for being too elaborate or fanciful in one's play, where a simpler decision would've been better.

Frontbet—To bet into the preflop raiser.

Game Flow—The pattern of decisions and emotions that occur over time between two people. Game flow is very intuitive and highly complex, and so can often not be communicated adequately unless one sees all of the hands that contribute to it.

Grinding—To play poker, usually in a slow and steady fashion.

Gutshot—A straight draw that can be completed with only one card. For example, having 9♣T♦ on 2♥6♠7♣, where only an 8 can make a straight.

Heads-up—One-on-one.

Hero—A term used for a protagonist in a poker hand, largely for the purpose of anonymity. Usually refers to the person recounting the hand. His chief opponent is usually termed the "villain."

Hero-call—To call with a bluffcatcher, usually for a lot of money.

High card—A high card generally refers to a T, J, Q, K, or A. "High card" is also the name for the weakest possible hand—for example, if you have K♣T♦ on J♥Q♣4♦5♠2♣, this hand would be called "high card king" or "king high."

Hitting a Hand—To make one's hand.

Hole Cards—The (two) cards you are dealt.

HUD—Heads Up Display. Refers to a program that displays stats or information real-time over your poker tables.

Implied odds—Your pot odds, but adjusted for expected future bets. To rely on implied odds generally means you're inferring that when you make a strong hand, you'll get paid off.

Kicker—Your side card; a kicker is not used to make your hand, but is used in tie-breakers between hands of the same type. For example, if you have A♣T♦ on A♥5♣4♦9♥2♥, you have a pair of aces with a ten kicker. If your opponent had A♠7♠, you would win the pot.

Lead—To bet out into the raiser (or previous aggressor).

Made Hand—A completed hand.

Martingaling—A strategy of continually doubling your bets every time you lose. For example, you might play a $20 match and lose, then play a $40 match and lose, then an $80 match and lose, until eventually you manage to get even. Most associated with tilting.

Metagame—The higher level of strategy in poker, which is played above the momentary strategy constrained by individual hands. Metagame is generally only meaningful if you are playing many hands with another person.

Minbet—To bet the minimum possible amount—in a no-limit Hold'em game, one big blind.

Minraise—To raise the minimum possible amount—in a no-limit Hold'em game, at least twice the initial bet.

Monster Hand—A very strong hand. Can refer to two pair or better.

Muck—To fold your hand and not show your cards.

Nitreg—A tight, boring regular.

Nitty—Tight and boring.

NL—Abbreviation for no-limit.

NLHE—Abbreviation for No Limit Hold'em.

No-limit— Means there is no maximum on the amount of money that can be bet on any street.

Nuts—The best possible hand on a given board.

o—Short for off-suit in hand notation, such as AKo referring to A♣K♥.

OESD—Open-Ended Straight Draw. Refers to a straight draw that can be completed with two cards. An example of an open-ended straight draw would be 9♣T♦ on 8♥7♣3♦, which can make a straight with either a J or a 6.

Offsuit—Cards of different suits.

Outs—Cards that will make a drawing hand into a made hand. If a card will "complete" a draw, then it's an out.

Overbet—To bet more than the size of the pot.

Overcard—A card that is higher than any card on the board.

Overpair—A pair that is higher than any card on the board. Having an overpair implies that you have been dealt a pocket pair preflop.

Playing Fast—To play a hand fast means to play it aggressively and straightforwardly, usually betting every street. It's the opposite of slowplaying.

PLO—Pot-Limit Omaha, a game like Hold'em except it is played with four hole cards instead of two.

Preflop—The first round of betting, which occurs before the flop is dealt.

Pocket [hand]—Having a pair dealt to you preflop. For example, 9♣9♦ would be known as "pocket nines."

Postflop—The rounds of betting that occur after the flop—that is, the turn and river, which are generally considered the most tricky streets.

Pot (verb)—To bet the size of the pot.

Pot-limit—A variant of poker in which you can only bet up to the size of the pot, and no bigger.

Pot odds—The ratio of the current size of the pot to the cost of calling a bet. By comparing your pot odds to the probability of winning the hand, you can calculate the EV of a call.

r—Stands for "rainbow" in poker notation, such as in J94r.

Rainbow—A board that has all different suits; implies that no flush draws are immediately possible. Called a rainbow because it contains every color.

Range—The set of all possible hands that someone can have in a situation. We might say someone has a "wide" range, meaning he likely will have lots of different kinds of hands there, or that he has a "narrow" or "tight" range, meaning he'll be playing very few hands in that way.

Regular—Someone who regularly plays certain stakes or in a certain game.

Rep—Slang for "represent."

Represent—To represent a hand is to bet in a way that is consistent with having that hand. Often implies that one does not actually possess the hand one is representing.

Reverse Implied Odds—A situation in which when you make a big hand, you are only likely to lose more money, because your opponent will already have a better one. The antithesis of implied odds.

River—The last community card. Also refers to the final round of betting, which occurs after the last community card is dealt.

Rivered—To "river" something means simply that a certain card was dealt or a hand was made on the river. You might river an ace, or river your straight. To "get rivered" generally means to get sucked out on the river by your opponent.

Roll—Slang for bankroll. Refers to the amount of money a player has allocated for poker.

Run-out—The run-out simply refers to how the board turned out. Often specifically means what cards were dealt after the money went all-in.

Runner Runner—When the turn card and river card both contribute to make a strong hand. For example, 9♣T♦ on K♥3♦7♣8♥6♣ would be a runner-runner straight (also known as a backdoor straight).

s—Short for "suited" in hand notation, such as 78s.

Second Nuts—The second best possible hand on a board.

Semibluff—To bluff with a hand that has some equity in the pot, with cards left to be dealt. Usually refers to betting aggressively while you have a draw.

Set—Being dealt a pocket pair and making three of a kind, using both of your hole cards. Considered an extremely strong hand.

Setmine—Setmining is the simple strategy of calling many pocket pairs preflop to raises, hoping to hit sets and get paid off. Setmining is generally considered a very tight and simplistic strategy.

Shove—To go all-in.

Show Down (verb)—To show the hands at the end of the final round of poker and award the pot to the winner.

Slowplay—To initially play a hand passively or slowly, hoping to deceive your opponent into thinking you're weak when in fact you are strong.

Snapcall—To call instantly.

Soulread—To predict someone's gameplay perfectly; to "read their soul."

Speed Read—A read on someone's tells with regards to how long they take with different kinds of hands.

Splash Around—To play liberally and make lots of risky or foolish plays.

Spot—A situation.

Street—A betting round.

Suckout—To initially have a worse hand than one's opponent, but then improve to be better than theirs.

Suited—Being of the same suit (diamonds, hearts, clubs, or spades).

Sweat—To watch someone else play poker, sometimes while advising them.

Tank—To think for a long time.

Tankfold—To think for a long time and then fold.

Tilt—To let your emotions affect your play or decision-making.

Tiltmonkey—Someone who tilts wildly or stupidly.

Top Pair—The highest possible pair that connects with the board.

Trips—Three of a kind. Generally refers only to when a pair is on the board and the third card is a hole card.

Turn—The fourth community card. Also refers to the round of betting that occurs after the fourth community card is dealt. A hand or card can be "turned," which simply means it appears or is made once the fourth community card is dealt.

Upswing—An uptick in one's money or buyins.

Value—Value generally refers to the betting strategy of betting to increase the pot size and entice others to call, because you have a strong hand. When you have a big hand, you need to "maximize value," which basically means making as much money as possible.

Value Hand—A hand that is strong enough to bet for value.

Valuebet—A bet for value. Usually means you have the best hand. The polar opposite of a bluff.

Variance—The natural fluctuations in winnings as a result of randomness and luck.

Villain—A term used for your opponent in a recounted hand. Its purpose is to anonymize the actual opponent.

Winrate—The rate at which one is winning.

Wired [hand]—Another word for a pocket pair. For example, 8♣ 8♥ would be wired eights.

ABOUT THE AUTHOR

Haseeb Qureshi started playing poker professionally when he was 16 years old. He soon became a world-class high-stakes professional online poker player, sponsored by Full Tilt Poker, known around the world as "DogIsHead." At age 21, he became entangled in the Girah Scandal, in which his protégé, Jose "Girah" Macedo, was caught cheating. Soon after the scandal, Haseeb retired from poker.

After extensive traveling, contemplating and writing about his past, Haseeb returned to Texas to be with his family and complete his education. He spent the next two years volunteering, meditating, and writing about poker and philosophy as he completed his B.A. at the University of Texas at Austin.

In December 2013, Haseeb decided to give away his poker earnings and start over from scratch. He donated $75,000 to charity and gave the remainder of his assets to his family. At the same time, he published his first book, *How to Be a Poker Player: The Philosophy of Poker.*

Haseeb resides in Austin, Texas, where he writes and continues to work with poker players as a mental coach. His coaching focuses on how to control emotions, manage one's mindset, and eliminate tilt to increase one's earnings. You can contact Haseeb and follow him at his website and blog, haseebq.com.

Made in the USA
Lexington, KY
20 January 2015